Art-Making as Problem-Solving

Melvin Chen

Art-Making as Problem-Solving

A Computational Philosophy of Art

palgrave
macmillan

Melvin Chen
Philosophy
Nanyang Technological University
Singapore, Singapore

ISBN 978-3-031-90638-1 ISBN 978-3-031-90639-8 (eBook)
https://doi.org/10.1007/978-3-031-90639-8

This Palgrave Macmillan imprint is published by the registered company Springer Nature Switzerland AG
The registered company address is: Gewerbestrasse 11, 6330 Cham, Switzerland

Declarations

Competing Interests The author has no competing interests to declare that are relevant to the content of this manuscript.

Contents

List of Figures

List of Tables

CHAPTER 1

Introduction

What is art-making? What is it in virtue of which an artifact counts as a work of art? In this book, it is contended that art-making is best understood in the context of problem-solving. Works of art are various ways in which artists solve problems and overcome obstacles, while typically exhibiting creative thinking. Our theoretical support will hail chiefly from the theory of problem-solving, its theoretical milieu, and various philosophical tools that will help us to build a robust, coherent, and consistent computationalist approach to art-making and the production of works of art.

What are the benefits of a computationalist approach to art-making? You might ask. Given its interdisciplinary nature, this approach will allow us to draw connections between art, philosophy, cognitive science, psychology, decision science, computer science, and other fields. True to the spirit of philosophy, our approach will likely confer a better understanding of how things in the broadest possible sense of the term hang together in the broadest possible sense of the term (Sellars, 1963). This understanding will be broad, systematic, and future-proof: as more machine-generated works will get produced in the future and at increasing levels of sophistication, they will be ripe for conceiving of in the computationalist terms of our approach. Our approach will provide theoretical support for the development and incorporation of computational models (for instance, artificial neural networks) into creative and art-making processes and even art education. It will challenge traditional theories of art and constitute a new perspective in the philosophy of art, all the while providing insights on

M. Chen, *Art-Making as Problem-Solving*,
https://doi.org/10.1007/978-3-031-90639-8_1

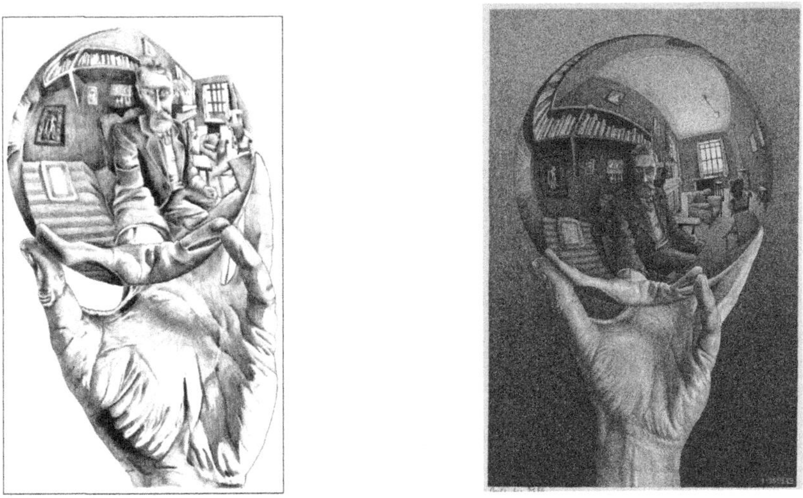

Fig. 1.1 From left to right: Melvin Chen's (2008) *Study of Escher's Hand with Reflecting Sphere (Self-Portrait in Spherical Mirror)*. Pen and India ink on paper. M. C. Escher's (1935) *Hand with Reflecting Sphere (Self-Portrait in Spherical Mirror)*. Lithograph.

how art-making and related creative processes can be modelled in computational terms. As a reflection of how the gap between the arts and sciences can be bridged, we need look no further than Escher's combination of a scientifically rigorous understanding of spherical geometry and the laws of optics with artistic mastery in his mathematically precise yet visually stunning depiction of a reflecting sphere (Fig. 1.1).

Just as an engine needs fuel in order to run, computation is driven by information. In Chap. 2, we will foreground the informational turn in philosophy and make sense of the term 'information', as it has been employed in both the information age and the informational turn in philosophy. In Chap. 3, we will distinguish between the philosophy of art and aesthetics and effect the informational turn in the philosophy of art. Three hypotheses will be identified as central to an information-theoretic philosophy of art: art-making is a goal-directed activity whose characteristic artifacts are works of art (H1); artifacts are communication channels through which art-makers (source) share semantic information with their intended audience (destination) (H2); and the generation of artifacts and their possible inclusion (as 'hits') in the artistic canon depend, in the final analysis, on answers to yes-no questions ('bits' or binary choices) (H3).

In Chap. 4, we will transition from the information-theoretic backdrop of an information-theoretic philosophy of art to a computationalist approach to art-making. The first key theoretical plank of our approach, the computational theory of mind, will be identified. In Chap. 5, the second key theoretical plank of our approach, the theory of problem-solving, will be introduced. The key concepts of the theory of problem-solving will be introduced: the goal to be accomplished, the problem space, the search for solutions in this space, heuristic search, search strategies, and an evaluation function. We shall first use the game of tic-tac-toe to illustrate these concepts, before applying our computationalist approach to Van Gogh's *Sunflower* series. In Chap. 6, we will identify 'What is art?' and 'What makes something beautiful or pleasing?' as the basic questions (respectively) of the philosophy of art and aesthetics. We will offer an account of the concept of art (as it is employed by philosophers of art) and trace its emergence in the eighteenth century from the concept of the fine arts. We will provide the case for theory construction as a key member of the methodological toolkit for philosophers of art.

In Chap. 7, we will engage with several theories of art that have been developed to address the basic question in the philosophy of art: what is art? These theories of art include mimeticism, representationalism, neo-representationalism, expressivism, formalism, neo-formalism, anti-essentialism, institutionalism, and historicism. We will attempt to infer the goals of art from these theories of what art is. In Chap. 8, the central artistic task will be characterized in terms of an art-specific challenge to be overcome or problem to be solved, the overcoming or solving of which is conditional on the available materials at the disposal of each art-maker. We will also express any problem (artistic or non-artistic) in the following manner: given a set P of elements, find a member of a subset S of P having certain properties. The examples of an n-position melody and an n-dot matrix picture will be used to illuminate how the subset S of P with which art-makers are concerned will have certain artistically valuable properties or relations. In Chap. 9, we will investigate how aesthetic criteria can be applied to mathematics, science, and other non-artistic domains and whether philosophers of art can draw any lessons from the possibility of aesthetic experience in mathematics. We will employ the Logic Theorist, an important proof of concept for the theory of problem-solving, as our case study. Since the Logic Theorist, cut from the same theoretical cloth as our computationalist approach, is capable of producing artifacts that are both (possibly) creative and the sources of aesthetic experiences, we will argue that this case study provides reasons for optimism.

In Chap. 10, we will investigate the understudied phenomenon of creativity. In particular, we will rely on Boden's computationalist account of creativity, which may be regarded as a natural extension of the theory of problem-solving. In Chap. 11, we will consider the ontological status of the work of art. We will distinguish between the physical object, imaginary entity, and abstract entity hypotheses and argue that it is the latter hypothesis that is the most compatible with our computationalist account of art. The abstract entity hypothesis, according to which works of art are abstract entities, entails a platonism about art. Common objections to artistic platonism will be fielded, including the Benacerraf–Field challenge. Our response to the Benacerraf–Field challenge will involve a conception of artistic knowledge or the store of artistic claims, accepted as true, as a map of the problem space of art, a map by which we steer.

In Chap. 12, continuities between the theory of problem-solving and the theory of computer science as empirical inquiry under the Newell-Simon research paradigm will be identified. The Newell-Simon research paradigm will be associated with the thinking rationally approach to AI research, logicism, and the two theoretical planks of the theory of computer science as empirical inquiry: the physical symbol system hypothesis and the heuristic search hypothesis. We will identify Goodman's philosophy as a possible locus of philosophical support, although we must be careful to distinguish between the parts we accept (cognitivism about art, the theory of symbol systems) and the parts we do not (nominalism, the calculus of individuals, irrealism).

In Chap. 13, the case in favour of machine art will be carefully laid out. Two objections to machine intelligence will first be considered: the mathematical objection and the Lovelace objection. We will argue in favour of the possibility of machines fashioning or constructing works of art, since they typically embody a lot of art-relevant knowledge, experience, understanding, and theory and may behave in ways that are both unintended and artistically valuable. Through the satisfaction of the epistemic-limitation condition, the case for machine intelligence and machine creativity will be strengthened. At the same time, this intelligence is insufficient for artisthood, since machines still lack the relevant intentionality, human perspective, and art-historical awareness. We will therefore refrain from describing machines as artists, notwithstanding their ability to fashion or construct works of art.

CHAPTER 2

The Informational Turn in Philosophy

2.1 Information Theory

The information age in which we live began at about roughly the same time as the computing age: their origins may be traced to Alan Turing's 1950 groundbreaking paper on computing machinery and intelligence (published in *Mind*). 1950 has been described as the beginning of the informational turn in philosophy, with information-theoretic concepts being applied to areas of philosophy such as philosophy of mind, philosophy of language, philosophy of science, computation theory, philosophy of science, decision theory, and even philosophy of music (Adams, 2003). This book constitutes an attempt to effect the informational turn in the philosophy of art, install a computationalist approach at the heart of an information-theoretic philosophy of art, and provide a twenty-first century update on philosophical discussions of the nature of art and art-making.

Before we do so, however, we must first understand the technical sense of the term 'information', as it has been employed in both the information age and the informational turn in philosophy. This technical sense hails from the mathematical theory of communication (Shannon & Weaver, 1949). The mathematical theory of communication (also known as information theory) is not the only available mathematical approach to the analysis of information: other mathematical approaches include algorithmic information theory (Solomonoff, 1964; Kolmogorov, 1965;

M. Chen, *Art-Making as Problem-Solving*,
https://doi.org/10.1007/978-3-031-90639-8_2

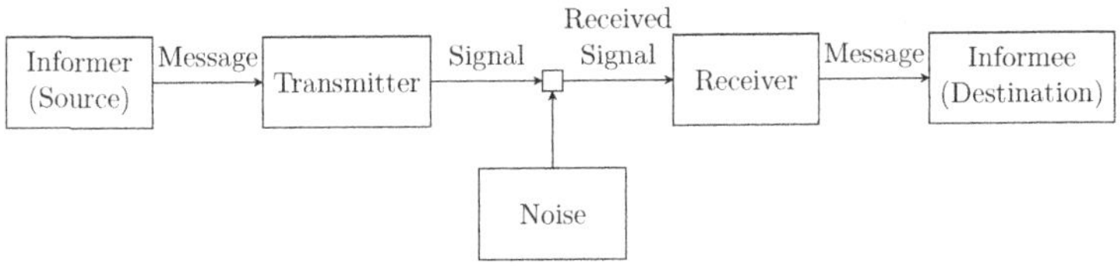

Fig. 2.1 Model of a communication system. (Adapted from Shannon and Weaver, 1949)

Chaitin, 1977) and Fisher information (Fisher, 1922; Frieden, 1998). However, the mathematical theory of communication is the most widely known and influential among philosophers and may be regarded as the official quantitative basis of the informational turn in philosophy.

A communication system consists of an informer, a transmitter, a communication channel, a receiver, an informee, and noise. An informer is an information source that selects a desired message out of a set of possible messages. A transmitter is an encoding procedure that changes the message into a signal that is sent over a communication channel. Communication channels include air (for oral speech) and space (for radio). A receiver is a decoding procedure that changes the transmitted signal back into a message. An informee is an information destination. Last but not least, noise refers to additions to the transmitted signal that were not intended by the informer. Figure 2.1 provides an diagrammatic illustration of the model of communication employed by the mathematical theory of communication.

Next, consider Edgar Allan Poe's raven from the poem 'The Raven' and George R. R. Martin's stable-boy character Hodor from the epic fantasy series *A Song of Ice & Fire*. Both Poe's raven and Martin's Hodor have only one response to any question: 'nevermore' in the case of the former and 'Hodor' in the case of the latter. They may be described as unary devices that serve as boring informers or information sources: they produce zero amount of information and we can never decrease our level of ignorance by communicating with these unary devices. If we think of the informer and the informee as communicating through a shared reliance on an alphabet (a finite and non-empty set of symbols), then unary devices rely essentially on a one-symbol alphabet. Neither Poe's raven nor Martin's Hodor produce any information, because the occurrence of a string of 'nevermore' or 'Hodor' is not informative (or, in Shannon's parlance, 'surprising').

Table 2.1 Communication devices & their information power (Floridi, 2009)

Device	*Alphabet*	*Bits of information per symbol*
Poe's raven, Martin's Hodor (unary)	1 symbol	log(1) = 0 (uninformative)
1 fair coin (binary)	2 equiprobable symbols	log(2) = 1
1 die (6-ary)	6 equiprobable symbols	log(6) ≈ 2.58

Binary devices, by contrast, can produce two symbols. A fair coin, for instance, has two equiprobable symbols: 'heads' or 'tails'. A die has six equiprobable symbols: '1', '2', '3', '4', '5', and '6'. The amount of information may be measured in terms of a logarithm (typically in base 2) of the number of available choices. The unit of information in a two-choice situation is known as a bit. The term 'bit' (first suggested by John W. Tukey), in turn, is a condensation of 'binary digit' (Shannon & Weaver, 1949). Given an alphabet of N equiprobable symbols, the average informativeness per symbol (or uncertainty) may be computed as $\log_2(N)$ bits of information per symbol. Table 2.1 provides information about various communication devices, the alphabet they employ, and their information power.

2.2 From Data to Information

Information refers to content that can be encoded, transmitted, and stored in physical implementations (natural objects, human brains, databases, encyclopaediae, websites, and so on), although it can exist independently of its encoding, transmission, and storage. Furthermore, philosophers typically distinguish between natural (environmental) information and non-natural (semantic) information (Grice, 1989; Scarantino & Piccinini, 2010; Søe, 2019). This distinction tracks a distinction between agent-independent physical occurrences in the world (states of affairs) and agent-dependent convention, intention, language, and communication (representation and interpretation). Examples of natural (environmental) information include concentric rings in the cross-section of a tree trunk (indicating the age of the tree), litmus paper turning red (indicating the presence of an acid) or blue (indicating the presence of an alkali), and tiny white spots inside the mouth (indicating measles). Three rings on the bell of a bus (indicating that the bus is full), by contrast, is an example of non-natural information (Grice, 1989, p. 214).

It is common to regard information as consisting of data. Data, in other words, is the stuff of which information (natural or non-natural) is made. The mathematical theory of communication addresses two fundamental problems: the problem of determining how small a message can be, given the same amount of information to be encoded (the ultimate level of data compression) and the problem of determining how fast data can be transmitted over a channel (the ultimate rate of data transmission). The fundamental problems of the mathematical theory of communication are technical or engineering-related, concerned with the speed, efficiency, and accuracy of transmitting sets of symbols or continuously varying signals from an informer to an informee. By contrast, the semantic problems are concerned with the identity or satisfactory approximation in the intended meaning of the informer and the interpretation of that meaning by the informee (Weaver, 1953).[1]

According to the standard definition of information, non-natural (semantic) information may be defined as data plus meaning (Davis & Olson, 1984; Silver & Silver, 1990; Checkland & Scholes, 1999). In situation logic, information is always taken to be information about some situation and it is built up from discrete items of information known as infons (Devlin, 1995; Israel & Perry, 2012). Situation logic provides us with the standard definition of information in terms of a tripartite definition. Where σ refers to infons, σ is an instance of information if and only if σ consists of n data (d) for $n \geq 1$; the data are well-formed (wfd); and the wfd are meaningful. Well-formed data (wfd) are data that are clustered together correctly, in accordance with the rules (syntax) governing the system, code, or language under consideration. Well-formed data are meaningful, just in case they comply with the meanings (semantics) of the system, code, or language under consideration.

Information depends on the occurrence of syntactically well-formed data. Data, in turn, depends on the occurrence of various physically implementable differences. These physically implementable differences

[1] There is some debate about whether the semantic problems are relevant to the technical or engineering-related problems. While Shannon holds that the semantic aspects are irrelevant to the engineering-related problems, Bar-Hillel (1955) believes otherwise. For a helpful overview, see Adams (2003).

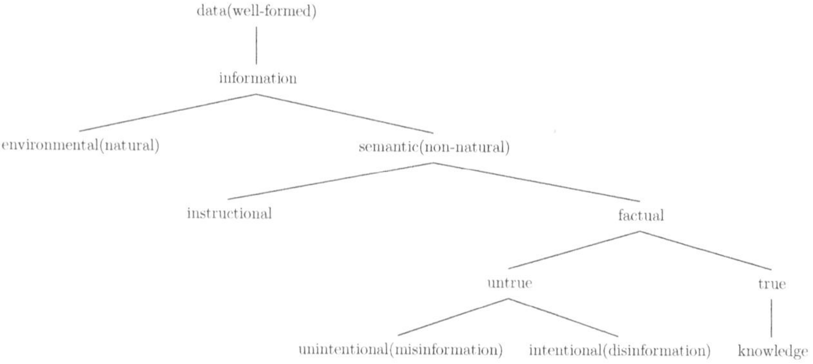

Fig. 2.2 An informational map (Floridi, 2009)

may consist of differences in two physical states (dots and dashes for Morse code, high and low voltages in transistors corresponding to 1s and 0s) or differences in two letters (the letters α and β of the Greek alphabet). In addition, information is often described as a difference that makes a difference: its quantum is a datum (a discrete state or 'difference') that is meaningful ('making a difference') (MacKay, 1969; Bateson, 2000).

The standard definition of information implies that there can be no such thing as dataless information: in the simplest case, information would still consist of a single datum. The standard definition of information equally implies alethic neutrality: there can be such a thing as false information. Misinformation (unintentionally misleading) and disinformation (intentionally misleading), though false, could still count as genuine semantic information rather than pseudo-information. In addition, 'It is true that *p*' would not count as a redundant expression. Not all philosophers, however, defend the alethic neutrality thesis with respect to information: at least some have argued that semantic information is well-formed, meaningful, and truthful data (Dretske, 1981; Grice, 1989; Floridi, 2007). Furthermore, semantic information may be factual (describing or representing a situation or a state of affairs) or instructional (intended to help bring about a situation or a state of affairs). Figure 2.2 provides an informational map in which the distinctions between data, information (natural and non-natural), and related concepts (misinformation, disinformation, and knowledge) can be represented.

2.3 The Ontological Implications of Information

Philosophy may be regarded as an investigation of the foundations of everything: the nature of reality (metaphysics), knowledge (epistemology), reasoning (logic), and value (axiology). Ontology is a branch of metaphysics that is concerned with the nature of being. Nihilism is the view that nothing exists at all (O'Leary-Hawthorne, 1995). Solipsism is the view that nothing exists beyond the self and its immediate experiences (Brunet, 1703). Materialism is the view that at least some things exist and everything that exists is made of matter (Gassendi, 1644/1964). Idealism is the view that at least some things exist and everything that exists is made of minds (Berkeley, 1710). Both materialism and idealism are forms of metaphysical monism, according to which there is exactly one fundamental substance or reality (matter or mind).[2] Metaphysical pluralism, by contrast, is the view that there are two or more fundamental substances or realities.

What are the ontological implications of an information-theoretic outlook?[3] We have already identified one possible ontological implication of the standard definition of information (information equals data plus meaning): there can be no such thing as dataless information (Sect. 2.2). Since there can be no information without physical implementation, physically disembodied information is impossible and we wind up with a materialistic interpretation of information. This materialist, information-theoretic outlook is supported by Landauer's principle ('information is physical), a principle in the physics of computation that relates information-processing to energy management. According to this principle, there is a minimum possible amount of energy (known as the Landauer bound) required to erase one bit of information (Landauer, 1991, 1996; Bennett & Landauer, 1985).

According to another anti-materialist, information-theoretic outlook, the material world has at bottom an immaterial source and explanation. This outlook is supported by the it-from-bit hypothesis (Wheeler, 1989/2002). The it-from-bit hypothesis, arising from an information-based interpretation of quantum physics, asserts that every 'it' (particle,

[2] Yet another example of metaphysical monism is neutral monism. According to this view, there is exactly one fundamental substance or reality and it is neither mental nor material but rather some stuff that is neutral between the two (Russell, 1921).

[3] For a more detailed discussion, see Floridi (2009).

field, the space-time continuum) derives its function, meaning, and existence from apparatus-elicited answers to yes-no questions ('bits' or binary choices, as we have described them in Sect. 2.1). That which we call 'reality' arises, in the final analysis, from the posing of yes-no questions and the registering of equipment-evoked responses. Physics is grounded in digital structures of bits and everything in the physical world around us is made of patterns of bits: tables, chairs, stars, planets, dogs, cats, electrons, and quarks. According to the it-from-bit hypothesis, substances are made of molecules, molecules are made of atoms, atoms are made of quarks, and quarks are made of bits. The information-theoretic outlook supported by the it-from-bit hypothesis is anti-materialist.

Last but not least, yet another information-theoretic outlook might recognize multiple fundamental substances or realities: matter, energy, and information (neither matter or energy) (Wiener, 1948; Doyle, 2016). Although information needs matter for its physical embodiment and energy for its communication, information is distinct from matter and energy. The materialist (information-is-physical) and anti-materialist (it-from-bit) outlooks are forms of metaphysical monism: reality is essentially either physical (it) or digital (bit) in nature. By contrast, the third information-theoretic outlook appears to advocate metaphysical pluralism. This metaphysical pluralism may be found in I-Phi (short for 'information philosophy'), the information-theoretic outlook of Doyle (2016).[4] According to I-Phi, the fundamental constituents of the known universe are matter, energy, and information. Matter and energy are conserved, whereas information is not. Three worlds may be identified: the material world, the biological world, and the ideal (mental) world. In the material world, information creation can be described as the order out of chaos when matter and radiation first emerged. Elementary particles later combined into nuclei and chemically emergent combinations of atoms (for instance, water from hydrogen and oxygen). In the biological world, biological parts (known as biomers) are communicating systems that share information with other parts of their wholes. DNA has been replicating its essential information for billions of years and biological systems are both information creators and information processors. In the ideal (mental) world, the brain, whose basic units are neurons, is a biological information

[4] I-Phi is a new philosophical method grounded in science, especially modern physics, biology, psychology, neuroscience, and the science of information.

processor and the mind is the software in the brain hardware. Furthermore, an important process of information creation is human creativity.

All three sets of ontological commitments (materialist, anti-materialist, and pluralist) are consistent with the standard definition of information (information equals data plus meaning). In this chapter, we have relied on information theory to define the technical sense of the term 'information' and characterize a communication system in terms of its constituents (Sect. 2.1). We have distinguished between natural (environmental) and non-natural (semantic) information and defined the latter in terms of data, meaning, and (possibly) truthfulness (Sect. 2.2). We have also identified the possible ontological commitments arising from an information-theoretic outlook (Sect. 2.3). In the next chapter, we shall apply this information-theoretic perspective to art and art-making and derive an information-theoretic philosophy of art.

CHAPTER 3

Towards an Information-theoretic Philosophy of Art

3.1 The Phenomenon of Art

Art is a relatively recent phenomenon. The ΛCDM (Lambda Cold Dark Matter) model, a standard cosmological model for describing the evolution of the universe, tells us that the age of the universe is approximately 13.8 billion years. Evidence of the first life on earth (in the form of single-celled organisms) may be traced to approximately 3.8 billion years ago. By contrast, the first modern humans or *Homo sapiens* evolved from their early hominid predecessors only around 300,000 to 200,000 years ago. The first agrarian civilizations developed in Mesopotamia around 5200 years ago and Western philosophy as we know it was born around 2600 years ago, with the emergence of the Presocratics. This implies that we have evidence for neither art-making nor artworks for more than 13 billion years, only the hum of physical, chemical, biological, and other related processes. Escher's rendering of a mathematically impossible object, the Möbius strip, exemplifies our unique human capacity for intelligence, abstract reasoning, symbolic manipulation, and recursive thought (Fig. 3.1). This wood engraving marks a striking departure from the natural processes that preceded us, giving concrete visual form to the complex cognitive

M. Chen, *Art-Making as Problem-Solving*,
https://doi.org/10.1007/978-3-031-90639-8_3

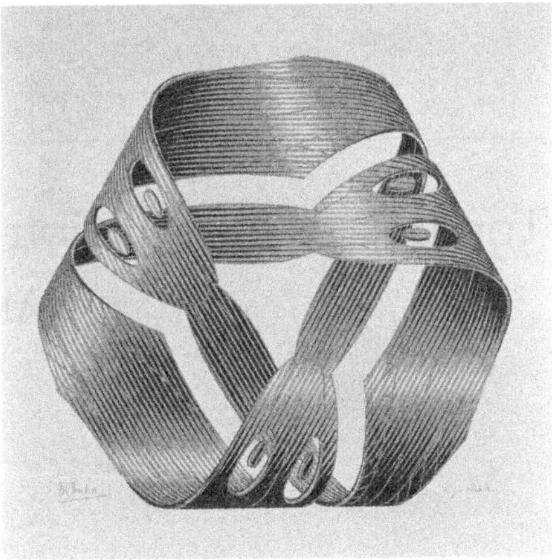

Fig. 3.1 M. C. Escher's (1961) *Mobius Strip I*. Wood engraving and woodcut in red, green, gold and black, printed from four blocks.

structures (including human brains) that emerged only relatively recently in cosmic time.[1]

In addition, art appears to be a peculiarly human phenomenon. Although one might, if one dug deep down enough, find a picture of a reindeer drawn by a man, one would have to dig much deeper to find a place where a reindeer had drawn a picture of a man (Chesterton, 1953, p. 35). At least one human cave-dweller, alive in c. 30,000 B.C.E., was responsible for the horse panel in the Chauvet-Pont-d'Arc Cave (Fig. 3.2).

The capacity to produce works of art is a trait that this cave-dweller has in common with Zhang Zeduan, Cimabue, Giotto, da Vinci, Michelangelo, Rembrandt, Goya, Van Gogh, Frida Kahlo, Ai Weiwei and a host of other less prominent human conspecifics. However, not the slightest trace of this capacity is observable in non-human animals. Furthermore, art appears to be a ubiquitous phenomenon. If we take the artistic capacity to mean the capacity to build temples and houses, make pictures and sculptures, weave patterns, and so on, then there is no human society or culture in the world without art (Gombrich, 1951, p. 19).

[1] Big history is the interdisciplinary study of the past, across the disciplines of physics, astronomy, geology, biology, and history, from the Big Bang to the present (Christian, 2004).

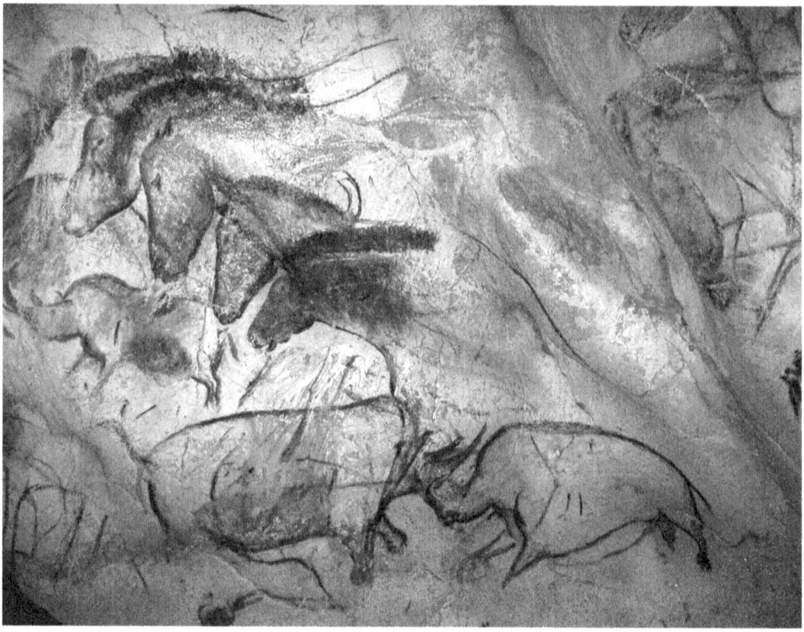

Fig. 3.2 Chauvet-Pont-d'Arc cave (Ardèche). Horse panel, Salle Hillaire. Charcoal on pre-smoothed surface. Detail of horses and rhinoceroses facing each other. © J. Clottes/Ministère de la Culture

3.2 The Philosophy of Art

Art is a relatively recent, peculiarly human, and ubiquitous phenomenon (Sect. 3.1). The philosophy of art may be construed as an investigation of the nature of this phenomenon (Nwodo, 1984). More precisely, the philosophy of art is concerned with the nature of art, various theories of art, and the relationship between the artist and the artwork. The philosophy of art should not be conflated with aesthetics. The term 'aesthetics' was first coined by Baumgarten (1750) to refer to the science of beauty, with 'beauty' in turn denoting perfection as perceived by our senses.[2] Aesthetics is concerned with our experiences or sensations of beauty,

[2] 'Aesthetics' hails from the Greek 'aisthēsis' for sense perception or aesthetic experience.

ugliness, disgust, aesthetic pleasure, the sublime, the mundane, or even the uncanny. Aesthetic experiences are not confined to works of art: we can experience everyday scenes (for instance, a courtyard or a piazza) as beautiful or pleasing (Nanay, 2018).

Likewise, not all experiences of works of art are aesthetic experiences: the aesthetic response is only one among several possible responses to art (Dickie, 1964; Goodman, 1968; Danto, 1981; Carroll, 2002). Therefore, we can have both aesthetic and non-aesthetic experiences of works of art. Example of works of art that offer non-aesthetic experiences include works associated with Dadaism, conceptual art, and political art.[3] We can equally have both aesthetic and non-aesthetic experiences outside the artistic realm. Examples of aesthetic experiences outside the artistic realm include our experiences of everyday scenes and our experiences of aesthetic qualities in mathematical proofs, scientific theories, and even chess games. A basic question in aesthetics is: what makes an experience beautiful, aesthetically pleasing, sublime, ugly, or disgusting? By contrast, a basic question in the philosophy of art is: what constitutes a work of art?[4]

3.3 The Informational Turn in the Philosophy of Art

In Chap. 2, we identified the informational turn in philosophy and characterized it in terms of an application of the information-theoretic outlook and its concepts to diverse areas of philosophy such as philosophy of mind, philosophy of language, philosophy of science, computation theory, philosophy of science, decision theory, and even philosophy of music. Dretske (1981) provides us with a famous example of the application of the information-theoretic outlook and its concepts to epistemological concerns. According to his information-theoretic analysis of knowledge,

[3] Conceptual art, in particular, is widely assumed to be anti-aesthetic. If, however, we follow Kant in conceiving works of art as expressions of aesthetic ideas that can stimulate our imagination to range freely and widely, then Kant's non-reductive theory of art as the expression of aesthetic ideas might compel us to recognize that even conceptual art has at least some aesthetic aspect (Costello, 2007). However, conceptual art may not involve the sort of sensory engagement typically emphasized by Kant. Furthermore, the focus that conceptual art places on ideas (aesthetic or otherwise) could fail to stimulate our imagination in the same way that more traditional, sensory-based works of art do.

[4] See Sect. 6.2 for a distinction between a grand basic question and a basic question.

a subject knows that an object or source of information s has property F if and only if she believes that s is F and this belief is caused or causally sustained by the information that s is F. In addition, a signal carries the information that s is F if and only if the conditional probability of s's being F is 1 (given the signal and the subject's background knowledge) and less than 1 (given only the subject's background knowledge).

Dretske's information-theoretic analysis of knowledge has important epistemological implications. Gettier cases refer to cases in which subjects can have a justified true belief concerning some claim, while still failing to know it because the reasons for their belief, though justified, turn out to be false (Gettier, 1963). Dretske's information-theoretic analysis avoids the Gettier problem, because the Gettier cases all appear to involve belief that is not information-based in the sense required by Dretske. This book will constitute an attempt to apply the information-theoretic outlook and its concepts to the philosophy of art, yielding an information-theoretic philosophy of art. An information-theoretic philosophy of art is distinct from an information-theoretic aesthetics, as we might expect to arise when the information-theoretic outlook and its concepts are applied to concerns in aesthetics rather than the philosophy of art.[5] As we shall see, certain hypotheses (H1-H3) lend themselves easily to an information-theoretic characterization:

(H1) Art-making is a goal-directed activity whose characteristic artifacts are works of art.

(H2) Artifacts are communication channels through which art-makers (source) share semantic information with their intended audience (destination).

(H3) The generation of artifacts and their possible inclusion (as 'hits') in the artistic canon depend, in the final analysis, on answers to yes-no questions ('bits' or binary choices).

Section 3.4 shall be devoted to an examination of H1, Sect. 3.5 to an examination of H2, and Sect. 3.6 to an examination of H3.

[5] Recall the distinction between aesthetics and the philosophy of art in Sect. 3.2. Information-theoretic aesthetics was developed in the 1960s in Europe by intellectuals seeking a mathematical basis for an objective aesthetic measure (Moles, 1966; Bense, 1969).

3.4 Art as Goal-directed Activity

At a first pass, art-making may be regarded as a goal-directed activity whose characteristic artifacts are works of art (H1). The idea of a connection between information-processing and goal-directed behaviour in general is not new (Rosenblueth et al., 1943; Mackay, 1951, 1956; Sommerhoff, 1974). Suppose that y denotes the current state (the actual state of some goal-directed system A plus its environment) and x denotes A's goal state (the desired state of A-plus-its-environment). When we say that A seeks the goal x, we mean that A seeks to minimize any discrepancy between x and y. In order for any sort of goal-directed activity to be possible, A must possess sensors (eyes, ears, and so on) that can help A to learn about its environment and detect changes in it, effectors (muscles) that can alter the state of A's environment, and controllers (brain) that can receive information from the sensors and control the activity of the effectors (Fig. 3.3). In addition, information about the magnitude of xy must be capable of being fed back to A's controllers.

In the case of art-making, A is the individual engaged in art-making and A's goal x (which we may term an artistic goal) includes at least one artifact, produced by A, that will be regarded or treated as a work of art. A few caveats with respect to H1 will be in order. In the first instance, art-making is not the only activity studied by philosophers of art: art criticism, art interpretation, and art appreciation are other activities typically associated with the peculiarly human and ubiquitous phenomenon known as art. Nonetheless, our primary philosophical concern shall be with the first-mentioned of these activities.

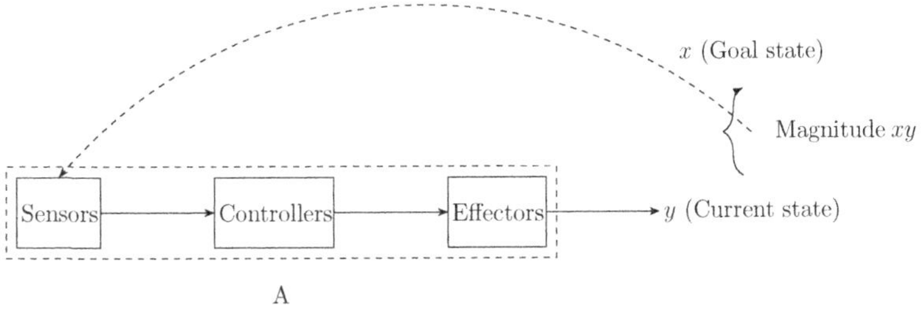

Fig. 3.3 Requirements for goal-directed activity. (Adapted from Mackay, 1951)

In the second instance, not all instances of art-making have been driven by artistic goals. Although Levinson (2006, 2007) has argued that works of art are artifacts that have been produced with the intention of being regarded or treated as works of art, this is not strictly true. To be precise, Levinson argues that something is a work of art because of the relation it bears to earlier artworks whose art status is unproblematic, which are in turn art because of the relation they bear to still earlier works, and so on. At some point along this relational chain, however, we shall arrive at the earliest artworks that can be seen as cases of first art. For Levinson's account of art to be sufficiently comprehensive, he needs to formulate a special account of what makes first art (as opposed to non-art).[6] A workaround may involve defining 'art' disjunctively: something is art if it either satisfies Levinson's basic definition (something's having been produced with the intention of being correctly regarded or treated as a work of art) or is an instance of first art. While the Chauvet cave paintings cited in Sect. 3.2 may be regarded as works of art, the cave-dweller responsible for these paintings (including the reindeer panel) probably had a different (non-artistic) goal state in mind. As the cave-dweller's intentions are art-unconscious, the classification of the Chauvet cave paintings as first art suggest that further theoretical provisions need to be made to ensure that someone who does not know the concept of an artwork can make an (art-unconscious) artwork.

In prehistoric and primitive cultures, art- or image-making was associated with magic, power, and religion: pictures and figurines were powerful tools that could be used to work magic. An interest in art for its own sake, quite apart from other non-artistic goals (religious, political, social, economic, and so on), is a relatively recent phenomenon. We shall discuss the possible goals of art in the context of theories of what art is in Chap. 7. For the moment, we will do well to recognize the historical contingency of the idea of an artistic goal.

[6] Demonstrating his acute awareness of the first art problem, Levinson (2011) points out that first art does not conform to his definition of the meaning of 'artwork', since there are neither earlier artworks nor correct regards prior to the first art.

3.5 Art as Communication

H1 asserts that art-making may be regarded as a goal-directed activity whose characteristic artifacts are works of art (Sect. 3.4). The following statement is a corollary of H1: the environment (source) conveys natural information to art-makers (destination). This natural information is detected, converted into electrical signals, and transmitted by the sensors and interpreted by the controllers. H2 is related to the corollary of H1: it tells us that art-makers (source) share semantic information with their intended audience (destination) through artifacts as their communication channels.

The idea of art as a form of communication is a much-peddled one. According to Cassirer (1953), art, religion, and science are among the symbolic forms through which human beings communicate and understand the world. In a related vein, Goodman (1968) identifies the philosophy of art as a branch of epistemology: paintings, sculptures, musical sonatas, and so on are all made of symbols and art is one symbolic activity among others in which we use symbols to discover or build the worlds in which we live. Dewey (1934) describes the relationship between the art-maker, the artifact, and the intended audience in terms of the communication of experiences. Furthermore, Carey (1985) distinguishes between two senses of the term 'communication'. According to the first sense (communication as transmission), the governing metaphor is one of geography or transportation: information is moved from one point to another, as goods or people might be. According to the second sense (communication as ritual), communication is not about the extension of messages in space. Rather, it is about the shared representation of beliefs and the construction and maintenance of an ordered and meaningful community.

While the first sense is present in philosophical conceptions of art as a form of communication, the second sense is both present and particularly acute. After all, art-makers and their intended audience have a shared background of cultural information: the ordered and meaningful human world, sustained by symbolic activities such as art-making. H2 involves a novel pairing of the idea of art as a form of communication (understood in terms of both information transmission and a shared ritual) with an information-theoretic outlook. Figure 2.1 had first been introduced in Sect. 2.1 to provide a general, information-theoretic model of communication. It may be adapted to illustrate how art as communication unfolds between the art-maker and her intended audience (Fig. 3.4).

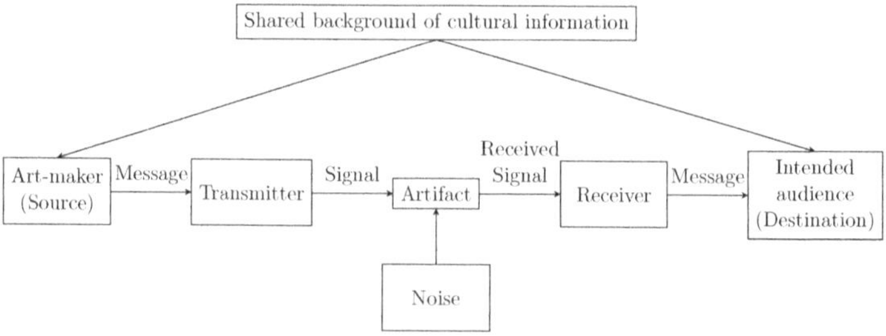

Fig. 3.4 Model of art as communication, adapted from Fig. 2.1

A few caveats with respect to H2 will be in order. In the first instance, not all artifacts are works of art: the earliest known artifacts are tools like Oldowan choppers (c. 2.6 million years ago) and Acheulean handaxes (c. 1.7 million years ago). However, Oldowan choppers, Acheulean handaxes, works of art, and other artifacts have in common the property of being intended output of human activities, produced with a certain purpose in mind (Baker, 2004; Hilpinen, 1992). This allows us to distinguish between artifacts (intentional and agent-dependent) and natural objects (non-intentional and agent-independent), just as we have already distinguished between environmental (non-intentional and agent-independent) and semantic (intentional and agent-dependent) information (Sect. 2.2).

In the second instance, artifacts constitute a special kind of communication channel. In the model of a communication system (Fig. 2.1), noiseless communication channels are an ideal: the transmitted message arrives at its destination exactly as it had been sent, without any distortion or interference. The signal-to-noise ratio of noiseless communication channels (computed as a ratio between the power of a signal and the power of background noise) will be infinite, maximizing the clarity and integrity of the transmitted message. By contrast, noiseless artifacts may not represent an ideal in the model of art as communication (Fig. 3.4). Indeed, artifacts are often valued as artworks precisely because of their ambiguity, lack of clarity, and (in certain instances) noisiness.[7] In the third instance, works of art could be conceptual (non-perceptual) or immaterial. A pluralist,

[7] In accordance with H2, we may regard artworks as artifacts that have been distinguished by their ability to reward effortful interpretation.

information-theoretic outlook typically maintains that the physical universe consists of matter, energy, and information and information needs matter for its physical embodiment and energy for its communication (Sect. 2.3). Such an outlook will therefore have to recognize that certain artifacts could be immaterial information (for instance, concepts, ideas, and musical works), first embodied in the brain of the art-maker (source) and then communicated to the other minds of her intended audience (destination).

3.6 The Hit-from-Bit Hypothesis

H1 (subjective) asserts that art-making is a goal-directed activity whose characteristic artifacts are works of art (Sect. 3.4). The art-maker is a goal-directed system, characterized in terms of sensors, effectors, controllers, and an artistic goal (the production of at least one artifact that will be regarded or treated as a work of art). H2 (intersubjective) asserts that artifacts are communication channels through which art-makers (source) share semantic information with their intended audience (destination) (Sect. 3.5). Beyond the mere transmission of information, communication is a shared ritual in which both art-makers and their intended audience share a background of cultural information. Last but not least, H3 (cultural) informs us that how artifacts are generated and whether or not they come to be regarded or treated as works of art ('hits') depend, in the final analysis, on answers to yes-no questions ('bits' or binary choices).

H3 is best described as the hit-from-bit hypothesis. Its physical counterpart, first encountered in Sect. 2.3, is the it-from-bit hypothesis. The it-from-bit hypothesis reveals the underlying digital nature of scientific activity. The scientific account of reality relies on the scientific method of observation, measurement, experimentation, and hypothesis-testing. Scientific activity, in turn, may be construed in terms of binary decisions (true/false, yes/no, on/off) that scientists make in the process of observing real-world entities (objects and events) (Wheeler, 1989/2002). In the final analysis, what scientists call reality arises from the posing of yes-no questions and the registering of equipment-evoked responses. Every 'it' or physical quantity derives its ultimate significance from 'bits' or binary yes/no decisions. The it-from-bit hypothesis implies both that all physical entities are information-theoretic in origin and that the universe is participatory in nature. The correspondence theory of truth asserts that beliefs are true, just in case they correspond to the facts or the way things are in the world (Russell, 1912; Moore, 1953). From an information-theoretic perspective, knowledge is semantic information that is factual (Fig. 2.2). It arises from an isomorphism (mapping or correspondence) between information structures and processes in the external world and their representations in minds. Scientists value truth (correspondence with facts) and knowledge (factual semantic information). The final binary decision in scientific activity is made by scientific peer reviewers: is there a correspondence with how things are in the world?

By analogy, the hit-from-bit hypothesis reveals the underlying digital nature of art-making activity. Human beings who engage in art-making activity are typically driven by the idea of an artistic goal. More specifically, they seek to produce artifacts that will be regarded or treated as works of art. Art-making activity may equally be construed in terms of binary decisions that human beings make in the process of producing artifacts that they hope will come to be regarded as artworks. Should the work convey a political message? Should the colour blue be added to this section of the painting? Should this caption be used for the work? H2 appeals to a shared background of cultural information between the art-maker (source) and her intended audience (destination) (Sect. 3.5). The final binary decision in art-making activity makes this shared background the foreground. The shared background of cultural information includes the cultural memory of works of high artistic value and significance ('hits'). This cultural memory is also known as an artistic canon. The final binary decision in art-making activity consists of a response to the following yes-no question: should the artifact be regarded as a work of art and (better yet) included in the artistic canon?

CHAPTER 4

Towards a Computationalist Approach to Art-making

4.1 From Information to Computation

In Chap. 3, we first distinguished between the philosophy of art (concerned with the nature of art, various theories of art, and the relationship between the artist and the artwork) and aesthetics (concerned with characteristics of beauty and the lack thereof). We then focused on a subset of concerns in the philosophy of art: the activity of art-making and artworks as its characteristic artifacts. We effected the informational turn in the philosophy of art and proceeded to characterize an information-theoretic philosophy of art in terms of a set of related hypotheses about art-making, artifacts, and works of art (H1–H3). In particular, H3 reveals the underlying digital nature of art-making activity: how artifacts are generated and whether or not they come to be regarded or treated as works of art ('hits') depend ultimately on answers to yes-no questions ('bits').

The common currency in scientific (it-from-bit) and art-making activity (hit-from-bit) is information. An information-theoretic outlook (broad) provides us with the tools for analyzing both the world and human activity (scientific or artistic) within it in terms of information content. A computationalist approach (narrow) provides us with a conceptual framework for understanding the processes and mechanisms by which information is processed by human minds. A black-box approach, by contrast, regards the human mind as a black box. It ignores the inner workings (processes

M. Chen, *Art-Making as Problem-Solving*,
https://doi.org/10.1007/978-3-031-90639-8_4

and mechanisms) of the mind, in favour of an analysis of the behaviour of organisms and their responses to stimuli.

A key plank of our computationalist approach is a theory in the philosophy of mind known as the computational theory of mind. According to this theory, the human mind is an information-processing system and cognition and consciousness are a form of computation (McCulloch & Pitts, 1943; Fodor, 1975, 1981, 2008). The classical version of the computational theory of mind maintains that the mind is a computational system and core mental processes (including problem-solving) are computations similar to computations that may be executed by a Turing machine.[1] A computationalist approach allows us to focus on systems (especially human minds and computers) that can perform computations according to well-defined rules and algorithms. If the hit-from-bit hypothesis (H3) is true, then the underlying nature of art-making activity is digital and a computationalist approach to art-making will function as a boon companion to an information-theoretic outlook on art.

4.2 The Human Mind

In the famous lead-up to the argument from design in favour of God's existence, Paley (1802) asks us to suppose that we find a watch on the ground. Unlike a natural object such as a stone, this watch, as described by Paley, has several parts that are framed and put together for a purpose. This watch is an artifact: it is a product of deliberate design by intelligent human agency. Therefore, we infer that this watch must have had a maker.[2] We can abstain from the theological aspects of Paley's argument, while agreeing with him that artifacts—whether they might be Oldowan choppers, Acheulean handaxes, works of art, or Paley's watch—are products of deliberate design by intelligent human agency.

We have already characterized art as a relatively recent, peculiarly human, and ubiquitous phenomenon (Sect. 3.1). We may now identify human-level

[1] A Turing machine is a simple and abstract computational device with unlimited time and storage capacity at its disposal (Turing, 1936).

[2] The rest of Paley's argument involves the following premises: like effects typically have like causes and certain entities in nature (for instance, the eye) are like the watch in certain relevant respects (for instance, having their parts organized for a purpose). Paley then infers that it is highly likely that these natural entities are also the product of deliberate design by intelligent and human-like agency (Ratzsch & Koperski, 2023).

intelligence as a necessary (though insufficient) condition for art-making and the production of works of art. The ability to understand and be guided by the idea of an artistic goal (H1), the ability to represent and share semantic information with other minded entities (H2), and the ability to understand and respond to yes-no questions and engage with cultural memory or the artistic canon (H3) all presuppose this human-level intelligence.

4.3 The Human Brain

The human brain is widely considered to be the physical substrate of this human-level intelligence. Human-level intelligence does not appear to be a function of absolute brain size: human brains (1.4 kg) weigh less on average than the brains of African elephants (5 kg), yet humans are more intelligent. Relative brain size (computed as a ratio between brain and body weights) does not seem to matter either: chimpanzees have smaller relative brain sizes than dolphins, yet are more intelligent. At the same time, human brains typically have a higher number of cortical neurons, higher neuron packing density, lower interneuronal distance, and higher axonal conduction velocity than non-human brains. It has been argued that this combination of brain traits best allows us to predict for degrees of intelligence (Dicke & Roth, 2016).

Neurons are the basic units of human brains: the average human brain has 86.1 ± 8.1 billion neuronal cells and 84.6 ± 9.8 billion non-neuronal cells (Azevedo et al., 2009). 15 billion of these neurons are cortical neurons. We have good reason to consider neurons, neuronal attributes, and the relationships between neurons as the correlates of human-level intelligence. Furthermore, we have good reason to consider neurons as information-processing units. After all, each neuron is an electrically excitable cell that takes up, processes, and transmits information through electrical and chemical signals. Individual neurons are capable of processing low-level information. For instance, V1 and V2 are two of the five areas into which the visual cortex is divided. V1 neurons process low-level features such as lines and edges. V2 neurons process features such as combinations of lines and edges, texture, and depth. V1 and V2 neurons interact with other information-processing mechanisms of the visual nervous system, resulting in progressively more complex and abstract representations of visual information and eventually yielding the perception of an entire visual scene.

When individual neurons combine to form neural networks, these neural networks are capable of performing more sophisticated computations and processing high-level information. This high-level information includes semantic information (for instance, concepts and the relationship between concepts). The ability to represent and share semantic information with other minded entities (H2) is essential to art-making and this ability has for its physical substrate neural networks. In summary, an information-theoretic outlook allows us to analyze both the world and art-making activity in terms of information content. Human-level intelligence may be regarded as a necessary (though insufficient) condition for art-making and the production of artworks. A computationalist approach allows us to make sense of the processes and mechanisms by which information is processed by human minds. These processes and mechanisms include the formation of neural networks, which facilitates the processing of high-level (semantic) information.

4.4 The Plurality Objection

The high-level semantic information of the artworld that human minds might process will encompass a pluralistic contemporary artworld, where artistic practices are often multidisciplinary. Indeed, the pluralistic nature of contemporary art presents a significant challenge for a computationalist approach, particularly in understanding the decision-making processes behind artistic creation. Contemporary artistic practices often blur the boundaries between art and non-art, as seen in works that incorporate activism, social participation, or conceptual provocation such as Rirkrit Tiravanija's communal cooking or The Yes Men's corporate parodies.

Tiravanija's intimate, participatory installations revolve around personal and shared communal traditions such as the cooking of Thai meals, while the Yes Men, a culture jamming activist duo, regularly pose as the top executives of corporations and lying to get into conferences and on news channels to parody corporate practices and neoliberal policies. A computational model that seeks to categorize art based on the production of artifacts that will be regarded or treated as works of art may struggle with cases where the intent is to resist, critique, or even reject traditional conceptions of art (for instance, as might be the case with anti-art movements).

Furthermore, since debates over what counts as art (as opposed to non-art) often centre precisely on these grey areas and edge cases, a computationalist approach must be able to engage in a more sustained manner with these grey areas and edge cases rather than bypassing them.

According to the plurality objection, engaging with and theorizing about these pluralistic forms of contemporary art may prove more challenging for the computationalist approach than non-contemporary art. H2 asserts that artifacts are communication channels through which art-makers share semantic information with their intended audience. According to the plurality objection, this may be questioned. After all, H2 may not be sensitive to the diverse nature of art practices (especially contemporary art practices) in the manner that much contemporary theorizing in philosophy of art and aesthetics is (and ought to be). Kieran (2004) argues, for instance, that the actions that we perform, through which we intend to express our feelings, thoughts, and attitudes, need not have any communicative intent or thought for how others may respond. Furthermore, at least some works of art should be understood as the embodiment of just this kind of action.

How might our computationalist approach accommodate the fluid and contested nature of contemporary artistic practices? In the first instance, artists who do not explicitly intend to communicate a message may still be engaged in implicit communication. Artifacts, by their very nature, embody decisions, styles, and contexts that contribute to meaning and significance, whether or not their artist might be consciously aiming for communication. In the second instance, the broader cultural, semiotic, and historical context and artistic canon within which artworks are situated serves as a reminder that each artist is preceded by a tradition. This tradition, in turn, serves as a communication network or a system of signs within which each work can be analyzed and understood. In the third instance, the cultural memory (artistic canon) is not fixed and immutable but rather dynamic and ever-evolving, shaped by social, institutional, and historical forces. Human minds that are adaptive and historically informed will be able to incorporate this cultural memory into their information base when making decisions in the art-making process. Through the use of fuzzy logic and probabilistic reasoning, binary classifications in favour of art versus non-art can be eschewed in favour of less rigid decision-making processes that are aligned with pluralistic, multidisciplinary, and conceptually fluid art practices.[3]

Contemporary artists are as implicated in the process of making binary decisions as traditional artists (Sect. 3.6). Tiravanija has to decide between physically cooking and serving Thai food in a gallery and refraining from doing so, whether to cook one Thai dish (tom kha gai soup) or another (pad thai), whether to use one recipe or set of instructions or another to cook the dish, whether to incorporate this recipe into one cooking method (the artist personally cooking for the audience) or another (sharing this recipe with the gallery staff and getting them to cook for the audience), and so on. Tiravanija's various participatory installations represent multiple solutions to the problem of how galleries can be transformed into spaces for shared experiences and communal activity through everyday objects, the universal language of cooking, and the culturally specific lens of Thai cuisine.

As contemporary works such as Tiravanija's installations and the activism of the Yes Men get canonized over time, the cultural memory (artistic canon) will get updated. This new high-level semantic information will in turn help human minds to better navigate the ever-changing boundaries between art and non-art in the future. Defenders of the plurality objection underestimate, at their own peril, the surprising degree to which human minds are able to cope, function as the loci of intentionality, and make art-making-relevant decisions in the face of fluidity, dynamism, complexity, volatility, uncertainty, grey areas, and edge cases in the artworld. In the next chapter, we shall develop our computationalist approach to art on the basis of a computationalist theory known as the theory of problem-solving.

[3] If contemporary artists at the vanguard cannot be completely certain whether their works incorporating activism, social participation, or conceptual provocation will finally be assigned the label of 'art' or 'non-art', then they could assign degrees of artistic status based on certain criteria (for instance, artistic intention, audience reception, institutional validation, and so on).

CHAPTER 5

The Computationalist Theory of Problem-solving

5.1 Problems during Art-making

In Chap. 3, art-making was described as an activity, governed by the idea of an artistic goal, whose characteristic artifacts are works of art (H1). Human beings engage in the activity of art-making with the intention of their output being regarded or treated as works of art. We further contend that art-making activity is a problem-solving activity: works of art represent various ways in which problems are solved and obstacles are overcome. For instance, Monet's (1890–1891) *Haystacks* series of 20–30 paintings can be interpreted as a bold, serial attempt to solve the problem of representing the same subject (stacks of harvested grain) under transient and varying conditions of light (sunrise, sunset), weath er (mist, frost, snow), and atmospheric effects across the different seasons of a year.

Examples of problems that may be encountered during art-making include the ideational (subjective) problem of conceiving the work, the technical (subjective) problem of executing this work, the intersubjective problem of communicating this work with an intended audience, and the cultural problem of securing the inclusion of this work in the cultural memory (artistic canon).[1] Furthermore, human beings who engage in

[1] The ideational and technical problems are associated with H1, the intersubjective problem is associated with H2, and the cultural problem is associated with H3 (Sect. 3.3).

M. Chen, *Art-Making as Problem-Solving*, https://doi.org/10.1007/978-3-031-90639-8_5

art-making typically exhibit creativity, a special class of problem-solving abilities. As we shall see, the theory of problem-solving, a highly influential theory in cognitive science and computer science, will help us to develop our computationalist approach to art-making.

5.2 Introspectionism about Problem-solving

Our view is that human-level intelligence may be regarded as a necessary (though insufficient) condition for art-making and the production of works of art (Chap. 4). Understanding how human minds work could therefore shed important light on art-making and the production of works of art. According to introspectionism, the best way to figure out how human minds work would be to gather introspective reports from world-leading thinkers across a variety of domains on how their own minds work. Both introspectionists and computationalists concur that the black-box approach is mistaken: human minds are not black boxes and their inner workings (processes and mechanisms) are ripe for analysis and understanding (Sect. 4.1).

In a letter to Jacques Hadamard, Albert Einstein shared that words did not play any role in the mechanism of his thought, only signs and images that could be reproduced and combined at will (Hadamard, 1954, pp. 142–143). In a letter to Anton Ridder van Rappard, Vincent van Gogh (1936) shared that it was possible for him to paint an expressive painting, because the picture had already taken form in his mind before he started on it. In an article on mathematical creation, Henri Poincaré (1910) shared how several of his best mathematical insights tended to arrive when he was on holiday by the seaside and not consciously working on mathematical problems. Einstein, Van Gogh, and Poincaré are examples of world-leading thinkers in the domains of physics, art, and mathematics, all of whom have provided introspective reports of their own mental processes.

The early 1950s were dominated by studious compilations of these introspective reports of mental processes (Hadamard, 1954; Ghiselin, 1952). We may therefore distinguish between non-aggregative and aggregative versions of introspectionism. The non-aggregative version of introspectionism is characterized by isolated epistolary exchanges. By contrast, its aggregative counterpart is characterized by magisterial compilations of introspective reports across multiple epistolary exchanges. In both these versions, the human genius (scientific or artistic) is typically privileged as an exemplum and a store of insights about the nature of the human mind at the highest echelons of human thought and activity.

5.3 Computationalism About Problem-solving

These introspective reports of mental processes (Sect. 5.2) curiously double up as testimonies of creative problem-solving. These processes have domain-specific problems (problems in physics, art, and mathematics) as their input and solutions (for instance, Einstein's (1905, 1915) special and general theories of relativity, Van Gogh's (1887–1889) *Sunflower* series, and Poincaré's (1892) qualitative theory of differential equations) as their output. Like Monet's (1890–1891) contemporaneous *Haystacks* series, Van Gogh's *Sunflower* series can be interpreted as a bold, serial attempt to solve a specific artistic problem. To be more precise, Van Gogh's process of art-making addresses the problem of producing a set of artifacts that will be regarded or treated as work of arts and (better yet) included in the artistic canon under the genre of floral still life.

Included in the cultural memory ('hits') are works of floral still life from Georges Jeannin (1841–1925) and Ernest Quost (1842–1931): Jeannin was known for featuring lush peonies and Quost for his use of hollyhocks. Part of the ideational (subjective) problem of conceiving the work would involve identifying a subject for a floral still life painting. Up till Van Gogh's *Sunflower* series, sunflowers had rarely featured in the floral still life genre due to their coarse and inelegant nature. As van Gogh (1889/2000, p. 128) declared in a letter to his brother Theo, if Jeannin had the peony and Quost the hollyhock, then the sunflower would be his subject.

Van Gogh's creativity in this art-making process involved binary decisions to feature both cut, dried, and withered sunflowers and sunflowers more traditionally arranged in a vase, experiment with colour, and rely on a variety of different brushstrokes. The artifacts associated with Van Gogh's art-making process are the *Sunflower* series, comprising the Paris series (executed in 1887) and the Arles series (executed between 1888–1889). These artifacts are now widely regarded as works of art, proudly displayed at art musea such as the National Gallery (London) and the Metropolitan Museum of Art (New York), and enshrined in the cultural memory. Van Gogh's *Sunflower* series therefore constitutes a solution to the problem of producing a set of artifacts that will be regarded as works of art and (better yet) included in the artistic canon.

If the computational theory of mind (Sect. 4.1) is correct, then the minds of Einstein, Van Gogh, and Poincaré are information-processing systems. Unlike the introspectionist, the computationalist is not an elitist: she includes ordinary human beings in her study of how human minds work, since ordinary human beings also use their minds to solve problems at their various capacities. As cognition and consciousness are essentially a form of computation, the computationalist also leaves open the possibility that processes in which problems get solved can be multiply realized in vivo (by human beings) or in silico (by information-processing computers).[2]

The theory of problem-solving is a computationalist approach to understanding the processes and mechanisms by which human minds process information.[3] This theory, invented by Allen Newell, Herbert Simon, and their collaborators at Carnegie Mellon University and the RAND Corporation in the late 1950s, receives its clearest articulation in Newell and Simon's 1972 *Human Problem Solving*. Furthermore, it should not surprise us that the mathematical theory of communication (Shannon & Weaver, 1949) provides the intellectual backdrop for this computationalist research paradigm (Sect. 2.1).

5.4 The Theory of Problem-solving

A central thesis of this theory of problem-solving is that human beings solve problems because they can choose tentatively among alternative actions (ϕ_i), anticipate the outcomes (s_i) of these actions, evaluate these outcomes, and back up and vary their approach when the evaluation is unfavourable.[4] This process is known as heuristic search. As we proceed over the course of this book, different aspects of the theory of problem-solving will be developed in more detail accordingly, especially as these aspects relate to our central concerns in the philosophy of art.

Suppose that a problem-solver begins at an initial state s_0. At this state, there are three possible courses of action: ϕ_1, ϕ_2, and ϕ_3. Each of these actions gives rise to a separate set of possible outcomes (s_i, where $i \in \mathbb{N}$ and

[2] According to the multiple realizability thesis, a single mental state type could be realized by many distinct physical state types (Putnam, 1967).

[3] This information includes the semantic information that is the centrepiece of an information-theoretic outlook on art (Chap. 3).

[4] For a useful review of the Newell-Simon research paradigm, see Ohlsson (2012).

$i \neq 0$) and may be evaluated in terms of an evaluation function f. Heuristic search takes place within a task environment or a problem space. The problem space is a generative representation of the set of possible solutions that a problem-solver might consider for a given problem. Problem-solvers mentally represent the problem, the goal to be accomplished, and the set of actions ϕ_i that may be considered in the course of solving the problem. When a particular search strategy is applied to a problem space, a solution path is generated. If the solution path ends with the goal, then it constitutes a solution to the problem. Otherwise, the path represents a failure to solve the problem.

The idea of encoding or uniquely identifying the alternative actions (ϕ_i) among which the problem-solver has to choose is related to the idea of binary choices or 'bits' (H3). Consider the instance in which six alternative courses of action ($\phi_1 - \phi_6$) are available. How many yes-no questions are required for us to distinguish between these six alternatives? The number of questions (n) required can be determined by the formula $2^n \geq k$, where k is the number of alternatives. For $k = 6$, we can solve for n in the following manner: $n = \log_2(6) \approx 2.58$. However, since n is a natural number, we can conclude that $n = 3$. At most three of the following five yes-no questions will be required:

(Q1) Is action in the first half of alternative actions (ϕ_1–ϕ_3)?
(Q2) Is action in the first third of ϕ_1–ϕ_3?
(Q3) Is action in the first third of ϕ_4–ϕ_6?
(Q4) Is the action ϕ_2?
(Q5) Is the action ϕ_5?

If the answer to Q1 is 'yes', then we go to Q2. If the answer to Q2 is 'yes', then we can conclude that the action is ϕ_1. Conversely, if the answer to Q2 is 'no', then we go to Q4. If the answer to Q4 is 'yes', then we can conclude that the action is ϕ_2. Otherwise, the action is ϕ_3. By contrast, if the answer to Q1 is 'no', then we go to Q3. If the answer to Q3 is 'yes', then we can conclude that the action is ϕ_4. Conversely, if the answer to Q3 is 'no', then we go to Q5. If the answer to Q5 is 'yes', then we can conclude that the action is ϕ_5. Otherwise, the action is ϕ_6. A maximum of three yes-no questions (Q1-Q2-Q4 or Q1-Q3-Q5) will allow us to uniquely identify each of the six alternative courses of action. This is equivalent to the claim that three bits will be sufficient for us to represent six alternative courses of action. With three bits, we can generate 2^3 (or 8) unique codes: 000,

001, 010, 011, 100, 101, 110, and 111. However, only six of these codes will be needed to encode ϕ_1–ϕ_6 and the remaining two codes may be left unused.

5.5 TIC-TAC-TOE

The theory of problem-solving is a computationalist approach to understanding how human minds work (Sect. 5.3). Certain games have a computationally tractable nature and may be studied as well-defined mathematical objects in a branch of mathematics known as game theory. The game of tic-tac-toe is widely played, straightforward to grasp, and computationally tractable. We will therefore use tic-tac-toe as our example to illustrate, to a first approximation, how the theory of problem-solving works.

Tic-tac-toe is a two-player game in which Player 1 (P1) and Player 2 (P2) take turns to mark the space in a three-by-three grid with either ◯ (a nought) or ✕ (a cross). The goal of tic-tac-toe is for each player to get three of their marks (◯ or ✕) in a horizontal, vertical, or diagonal row before their opponent. There are nine empty squares available to P1 (◯) on the first move, eight squares available to P2 (✕) on the second move, seven squares available to P1 (◯) on the third move, and so on. Therefore, a generous upper bound for the size of the complete game tree of tic-tac-toe may be computed as 9! ($9 \times 8 \times 7 \times \cdots \times 1$) or 362,880.[5] The problem space for tic-tac-toe may be associated with a complete game tree, starting with the game-initial position (an empty grid) as its root node and containing all possible moves from each position. The leaf nodes of a complete game tree of tic-tac-toe are the game-terminal positions: a win for P1, a win for P2, or a draw for both.

The initial state s_0 of the tic-tac-toe board is an empty one (Fig. 5.1). In this partial game tree, P1 has three possible actions to consider: ϕ_1 (placing a ◯ in a corner square), ϕ_2 (placing a ◯ in the centre square),

[5] However, this upper bound will contain many illegal games that continue even after P1 (◯) or P2 (✕) has won. A more careful count will yield an upper bound of 255,168 possible leaf nodes or game-terminal states for legal games. Furthermore, several board positions are essentially reflections or rotations of one another. If we retain only legal board configurations that are neither reflections nor rotations of one another, then we will be left with only 26,830 essentially different, possible, and legal leaf nodes. The game tree complexity of tic-tac-toe, computed as an upper bound and a log to base 10, will therefore be 5, since 26,830 is about 2.6×10^4.

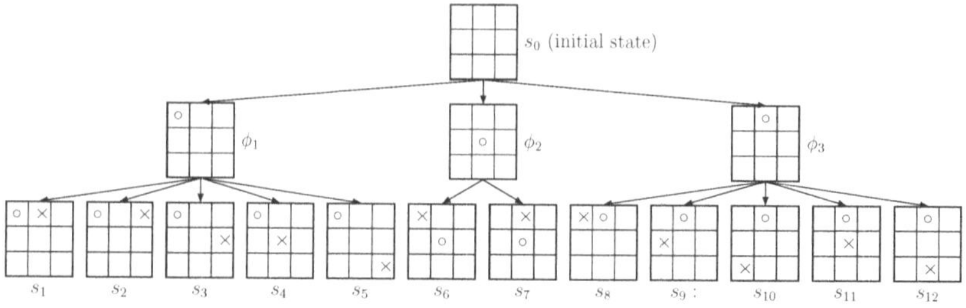

Fig. 5.1 Partial game tree for tic-tac-toe

and ϕ_3 (placing a ○ in an edge square).[6] The partial game tree in Fig. 5.1 represents five possible outcomes (s_1–s_5) after P2 responds to P1's ϕ_1, two possible outcomes (s_6–s_7) after P2 responds to P1's ϕ_2, and so on.

When searching for a solution in the problem space, P1 and P2 could try all possible lines of play in a complete game tree. This is known as brute-force search. Furthermore, the larger the game tree, the more computationally infeasible will this search process be. Alternatively, they could rely on heuristic search and focus on more promising lines of play, evaluated in accordance with a game evaluation function. A strategy is a collection of heuristics and the strategy of P1 or P2 could involve any of the following heuristics: complete three in a row (horizontal, vertical, or diagonal) on your move if you can do so (H_1); block your opponent if she has two of three in a non-blocked row already (H_2); play a fork or a scenario in which you have two non-blocked rows of two of three (H_3); mark the centre (H_4); and so on.

From the simple example of tic-tac-toe, we have managed to introduce several key concepts in the theory of problem-solving: the goal for each player, the problem space, the search for solutions in the problem space, heuristic search (H_1–H_4) and search strategies, and an evaluation function. Art is more complex than tic-tac-toe. At the same time, we have already identified the general problem confronting human beings who engage in art-making: the problem of producing artifacts that will be regarded

[6] There are nine possible moves that can be made by P1 on the first move, although the other six board configurations are reflections or rotations of the three board configurations that have been represented.

as works of art and (better yet) included in the artistic canon. This problem may be analyzed in terms of a set of smaller though connected problems: the ideational problem (conceiving the work), the technical problem (executing it), the intersubjective problem (communicating it with an intended audience) and the cultural problem (securing its inclusion in the cultural memory or artistic canon).

5.6 From Tic-tac-toe to Van Gogh

The general problem that human beings who engage in art-making set out to solve can be similarly represented by a problem space. As art-makers navigate the problem space, searching for solutions, alternative courses of action will present themselves. In the process of producing artifacts that they hope will come to be regarded as artworks, human beings will have to make binary decisions. We have already demonstrated how the alternative courses of action available to a problem-solver can be related to bits and the hit-from-bit hypothesis or H3 (Sect. 3.6).

It should be added that the process of backing up and varying an approach when the evaluation is unfavourable (heuristic search) can be related to the role of feedback and control when art is described as a goal-directed activity in H1 (Sect. 3.4). Furthermore, each time an artifact has been produced as a result of art-making activity, we may think of a solution path as having been generated through heuristic search.[7] If this artifact succeeds in conveying the requisite semantic information, then the associated solution path may be subsequently retraced by the art-maker's intended audience in reception. The discovery and retracing of solution paths can be related to the reception of the artifact by the intended audience in H2 (Sect. 3.5).

With respect to his *Sunflower* series (Sect. 5.3), Van Gogh had to make binary decisions about whether to select this or that flower species as his subject, this or that arrangement of flowers for pictorial representation, this or that colour for his palette, this or that brushstroke for a certain area of his canvas, and so on. In addition, Van Gogh relied on heuristic search over the course of his experimentation with colour: he backed up and renounced

[7] Currie (1989) proposes a similar view, according to which works of art are information structures (of sounds, colours, and so on), discovered through heuristic paths first used by artists and later retrodden by the audience in reception.

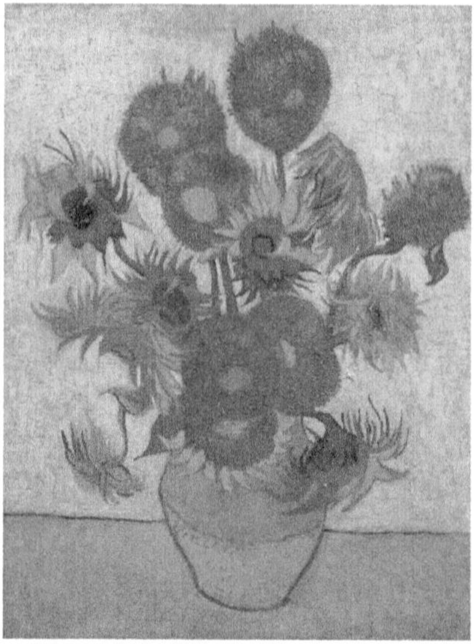

Fig. 5.2 Vincent van Gogh's (1888) *Sunflowers* from the Arles series. Oil on canvas. © Van Gogh Museum, Amsterdam (Vincent van Gogh Foundation)

his initial palette (yellow flowers on a blue background) in favour of a more original palette (yellow flowers on a yellow background) (Fig. 5.2).

The final artifact, the *Sunflower* series of paintings (1887–1889), represents a set of multiple solutions to the problem, with refinements gradually being made, sometimes through trial and error, as Van Gogh progressed from the Paris to the Arles series. Furthermore, Van Gogh intended two members of the *Sunflower* series to form, together with his 1889 portrait painting *Woman Rocking a Cradle*, a triptych. Augustine Roulin, the portrait's sitter, had been revered by Van Gogh as a model of love and family life. Van Gogh wanted the triptych (Roulin's portrait flanked by two sunflower paintings) to convey a sense of gratitude (semantic information) to his intended audience. The binary decisions made by Van Gogh for his *Sunflower* series mirror the binary decisions made by Tiravanija for his participatory installations (Sect. 4.4). Recall how Tiravanija, in an analogous fashion, has to decide between between physically cooking and serving Thai food in a gallery and refraining from doing so, which Thai dish to cook, which recipe to use, whether to cook the dish personally or share the recipe with the gallery staff and get them to cook instead, and so on. We now have a concrete example of how the theory of problem-solving can be applied to art, yielding a computationalist approach to art-making and the production of works of art (including modern works like Van Gogh's paintings and contemporary works like Tiravanija's installations).

CHAPTER 6

Theorizing about Art

6.1 The Basic Question

In order for something to count as a distinct field of inquiry, it seems that we must be able to locate its centre and boundaries. Grand basic questions help to organize a field, allowing us to locate its centre and boundaries. It has been argued that the question of how to live is the grand basic question of ethics (Gibbard, 2002, 2003). 'What do or can we know?' and 'What is there?' can similarly be regarded as grand basic questions, around which the fields of epistemology and metaphysics are respectively organized. An example of a grand basic question that could help us to organize the field of aesthetics is 'What is art?'.

Walton (2007) argues that 'What is art?' should not count as a grand basic question for aesthetics. Part of his argument involves pointing out how the contemporary aesthetic concerns (whether readers empathize with literary characters, the nature of realism in literature, painting, or film, whether fictional characters exist, and so on) have little if anything to do with the question 'What is art?'. Walton (2007) concludes that aesthetics does not have a grand basic question. However, it still counts as a distinct field, because we can mark its boundaries: the boundaries of aesthetics coincide with the boundaries of art and of beauty.

Following Nwodo (1984), we reject Walton's conflation of aesthetics with the philosophy of art. In the first instance, we should distinguish (as

M. Chen, *Art-Making as Problem-Solving*,
https://doi.org/10.1007/978-3-031-90639-8_6

Walton has signally failed to do) between the philosophy of art (whose boundaries are the boundaries of art) and aesthetics (whose boundaries are the boundaries of experience) (Sect. 3.2). Questions having to do with paintings, music, theatre, literature, film, and anything else that counts as art will be investigated in the philosophy of art, whereas philosophically interesting questions about anything that is beautiful, aesthetically pleasing, sublime, ugly, disgusting, and so on will be pursued in aesthetics. More broadly construed, aesthetic experience refers to any engagement with the environment or human culture (including artifacts such as works of art) that involves perception, sensation, or emotional responses. Aesthetic experience may therefore be positive (beautiful, aesthetically pleasing, or sublime), negative (ugly, uncomfortable, or disgusting), neutral (associated with mundance experiences or our engagement with everyday objects), and unusual (the uncanny). There can be no such unified field as aesthetics (broadly construed in Walton's sense), since not all works of art are aesthetic and not all aesthetic experiences are within the artistic realm (Sect. 3.2). There can however be two distinct though interrelated fields: the philosophy of art (involving works of art in some way) and aesthetics (having something to do with a broad range of experiences or sensations that are positive, negative, neutral, or even unusual).

Although Walton recognizes the similarities between the philosophy of science and the philosophy of art, he mistakenly claims that philosophers of science are not overly preoccupied with the question of how 'science' is to be defined. On the contrary, the demarcation problem is a central problem in the philosophy of science: it is concerned with whether and to what extent science may be distinguished from non-science (Laudan, 1983; Fuller, 2017). By analogy, we have good reason to expect philosophers of art to be concerned with where the cut-off is made between art and non-art (Chen, 2023). Grand basic questions help us to determine both the centre of a field and its boundaries. Basic questions, by contrast, help us to determine only the boundaries of a field. Although 'What is art?' might not count as a grand basic question in the philosophy of art, it will certainly count as a basic question. This question helps us to delineate the boundaries and scope of any inquiry in the philosophy of art. Likewise, 'What makes something beautiful or pleasing?' will be a basic question in aesthetics.

6.2 The Concept of Art

In Sect. 6.1 we identified 'What is art?' as a basic (though not grand) question in the philosophy of art. In this section, we shall focus on the concept of art, as construed by philosophers of art. According to McCarthy (2008), any philosophy of X, where X is a science, involves philosophers analyzing the concepts of X, sometimes commenting on what concepts are or are not likely to be coherent, and offering advice to practitioners of X about what they can and cannot do. If McCarthy's account of the philosophy of X can be extended to include the philosophy of art, then both the concept of art and the concepts employed in the artistic realm will be ripe for analysis.

We must first recognize that the concept of art, as employed by philosophers of art, refers not to a single art but rather a variety of them. Furthermore, we must recognize that this concept of art is a relatively modern one in the history of ideas. According to a particularly influential account, the origins of this concept (as understood by philosophers of art) may be traced to the eighteenth century as a result of the emergence of fine arts (Kristeller, 1951, 1952). This account has become an orthodoxy among historians of art, intellectual and cultural historians, and philosophers of art and even received a book-length treatment (Murdoch, 1977; Alperson & Carroll, 2008; Shiner, 2001). We could therefore do worse than rely on Kristeller's account of the etiology of this concept.

The Greek 'technê' and the Latin 'ars' did not refer to the fine arts in the modern sense. Instead, they were applied to all kinds of human activities, including crafts and sciences. The ancient sense of 'art' concerns that which may be taught and learnt. Martianus Capella, one of the earliest developers of the liberal arts system that structured early medieval education, identifies the seven liberal arts as grammar, rhetoric, dialectic, arithmetic, geometry, astronomy, and music. These seven liberal arts were subdivided into the trivium (grammar, rhetoric, and dialectic) and the quadrivium (arithmetic, geometry, astronomy, and music). Neither poetry nor the visual arts have a place in Capella's scheme, although poetry was closely linked with grammar and rhetoric. There was also no place for the visual arts in the domain of the muses: the nine muses of Greek mythology inspired history (Clio), astronomy (Urania), drama (Melpomene and Thalia), poetry (Calliope and Erato), music (Euterpe and Polyhymnia), and dance (Terpsichore). As a consequence, although poetry and music were among the subjects taught at schools and universities, the visual arts were confined to artisans' guilds.

The Renaissance was associated with the steady rise of painting and the other visual arts that began with Cimabue and Giotto in Italy, reaching a climax in the sixteenth century. This increase in prestige of the visual arts allowed them to be emancipated from the crafts. Another watershed was the Quarrel of the Ancients and the Moderns, a literary debate that took place in France during the late seventeenth and early eighteenth centuries. The Ancients maintained that the literature of Greek and Roman antiquity represented the pinnacle of literary achievement. The Moderns, however, believed that modern works could be as good as (or even better than) literary works from antiquity. The rise of modern science compelled Moderns to reason that, just as Galileo and Descartes had surpassed ancient science, it might be possible for ancient art to be surpassed. The Moderns, conscious of the achievements of science, were keen to shake off the weight of antiquity and think in terms of progress and innovation. The Quarrel of the Ancients and the Moderns prepared the ground for a clear distinction between art and science.

The concept of the fine arts, from which we have derived the modern concept of art, makes an appearance in Perrault (1690). Perrault first contrasts between the fine arts (*beaux arts*) and the liberal arts (*arts libéraux*), before rejecting the liberal arts and cataloguing the eight fine arts: eloquence, poetry, music, architecture, painting, sculpture, optics, and mechanics. The codification or systematization of the fine arts into their canonical form is attributed to Batteux (1746). The fine arts (with pleasure for their end) are distinguished from the mechanical arts (with utility for their end) and the five fine arts are music, poetry, painting, sculpture, and dance.[1] Batteux's programme was continued by Mendelssohn (1757) and Sulzer (1778), culminating in the modern concept of art that philosophers of art tend to take for granted. Indeed, philosophers of art typically have at least one of the fine arts (music, poetry, painting, sculpture, and dance) in mind when they speculate about the nature of art, the relationship between the artist and the artwork, and so on.

A few caveats about the concept of art are in order. The first caveat is that the concept of art is not static but rather fluid and mutable. Gardening, which may have been considered an art before the eighteenth century, has since lost its standing. By contrast, photography and film

[1] A third category, the mixed arts, have both pleasure and utility for their end: eloquence and architecture.

demonstrate how new technologies can give rise to new modes of artistic expression and boast a strong case for inclusion. The concept of art may therefore take the form of a prototype rather than the form of necessary and sufficient conditions, with music, poetry, painting, sculpture, and dance as its prototypical members.[2] The second caveat is that not everyone will agree with the grouping together of music, poetry, painting, sculpture, and dance, so different as they are in their modes of expression, under a single concept. This grouping, though useful to an amateur, may not be helpful at all to a practitioner of art. Goethe appears to have held such a view. The third caveat is that Kristeller's account of the etiology of this concept, though orthodox, is not without its detractors. Alternative historical narratives with respect to the concept of art may, for instance, be found in Porter (2009).

6.3 Theory Construction

Conceptual analysis, as might be inferred from McCarthy's 2008 account of the philosophy of X, is a key part of the philosophical methodology. Another key member of the methodological toolkit for philosophers is theory construction (Walton, 2007). Philosophers organize the data, develop conceptual frameworks, and construct theories to clarify and explain the data. Different theories may accommodate the same data (this is known as the underdetermination of theory by data in the philosophy of science) and each theory is subject to confirmation or disconfirmation by the data.

Not all philosophers of art agree that theory construction is a tool that should be used in the philosophy of art. In his presidential address to the American Society for Aesthetics on the occasion of its 50th anniversary, Kivy (1993) called for a moratorium on theorizing about art in the grand manner. Our obsessive concern with defining art and identifying what the fine arts (music, poetry, painting, sculpture, and dance) have in common should be replaced with a more modest (though no less philosophically respectable) concern with the individual arts, their individual problems, and what makes them individual. We should develop multiple philosophies of the individual arts, as opposed to a single philosophy of art. A key

[2] For research on concepts as prototypes, see Rosch and Mervis (1975), Laurence and Margolis (1999). For an application of the prototype theory of concepts to creative cognition research, see Chen (2018).

ingredient of Kivy's argument is absolute music. Absolute music is music without text, title, program, or other extra-musical accoutrement. In other words, it is a pure sonic structure that does not possess either semantic or representational properties. It is as problematic to force absolute music into the mold of the other fine arts as it is to force the other fine arts into the mold of absolute music, since absolute music is very different in crucial respects from the visual and literary arts.

In his own presidential address to the American Society for Aesthetics, Walton (2007) took issue with his predecessor in the office. According to Walton, the problem is with theories that focus on what it is to be art, not with grand theorizing as such.[3] Not all theories are theories of what it is to be art. Furthermore, good theories (including grand ones) can achieve illumination by bringing out differences no less than similarities. This implies that we do not necessarily have to choose between attending to the particulars or being sensitive to differences among the individual arts and developing grand theories. According to Walsh's (1990) theory of the nature of representation, all representations involve, in a certain way, an imaginative activity that he terms make-believe. All representations possess the function of serving as props in games of make-believe, establishing fictional worlds. Absolute music, given the richly imaginative nature of musical experiences, counts as representational under this theory. Therefore, Walton's theory allows us to recognize the similarities between absolute music and the other fine arts, even if certain differences might still remain.

We agree with Walton that theory construction remains a viable tool in the methodological toolkit for philosophers of art. Our computationalist approach to art-making and the production of works of art is a theory of art that relies on other theoretical precedents (the theory of problem-solving, information theory, and so on). We agree with Walton's blueprint for theory construction: start from the ground up, pay careful attention to works of art that interest us and to whatever else turns out to bear significant similarities to any of them, let our theories develop, and go for grandeur when we can. 'What is art?' might not be a grand basic question in the philosophy of art, but it is still a basic question. Our theory of art is

[3] For a survey of theories that focus on what it is to be art, see Chap. 7.

neither a grand theory nor a theory that focuses on what it is to be art, but it is still a theory of art. We hope that it is a sufficiently good theory, capable of achieving illumination. In the next chapter, we shall get acquainted with several theories that focus on what it is to be art and try to get a sense of the goals of art that might shape or direct art-making.

CHAPTER 7

The Goals of Art

7.1 Theories of Art

It is not easy to say what the goals of art are. In Sect. 6.3, we identified theory construction as a key member of the methodological toolkit for philosophers of art. At least some theories of art have been developed to address the basic question in the philosophy of art (Sect. 6.1): what is art? These theories of art, focusing on what it is to be art, have been criticized on a number of grounds. Each attempt to define art results in something that is not just different from previous definitions but seemingly unrelated to them (Walton, 2007). Furthermore, these theories fail to recognize crucial differences between the individual arts (Kivy, 1993).

Santayana (1904, p. 321) was definitely onto something when he observed how the group of activities we call 'aesthetic' (including art-related activities) is a motley one, created by certain historic and literary accidents.[1] Nonetheless, we should not throw the baby out with the bathwater: even that which is philosophically problematic can be instructive or valuable. If we take the basic question 'What is art?' to define a problem space, then the theory of problem-solving can be extended to capture the

[1] Among these accidents would be the accident of the modern concept of art (in the singular) emerging from the eighteenth-century concept of the fine arts (in the plural) (Sect. 6.2).

M. Chen, *Art-Making as Problem-Solving*,
https://doi.org/10.1007/978-3-031-90639-8_7

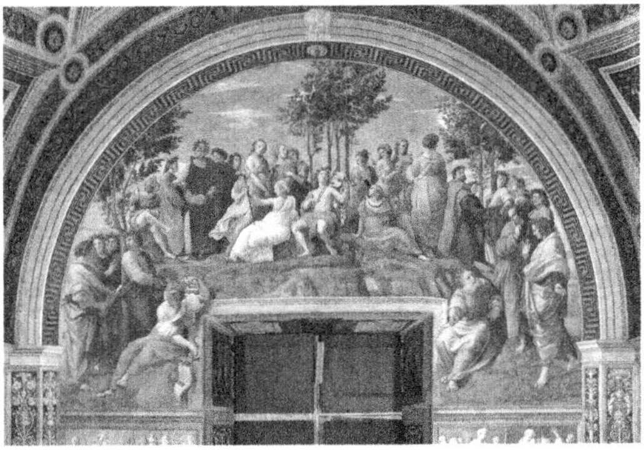

Fig. 7.1 Raphael's (1509–1511) *The Parnassus*. Fresco. Apollo is seated at the centre of the mythological Mount Parnassus, surrounded by the nine muses, nine poets from antiquity (including Homer, Virgil, and Dante), and nine contemporary poets. Photo copyright © Governorate of the Vatican City State-Directorate of the Vatican Museums

theorizing activity of philosophers of art. As philosophers of art navigate the problem space, they generate various theories of what art is. These theories may, in turn, be regarded as possible solution paths.[2]

Perhaps the demarcation problem (Sect. 6.1), though important, does not finally admit of a solution. Nonetheless, philosophical due diligence dictates that we at least retrace the different solution paths and acquire a sense of what philosophers of art believe the solution would have looked like. The theories of art that will be addressed in this chapter include mimeticism (Sect. 7.2), representationalism (Sect. 7.3), neo-representationalism (Sect. 7.4), expressivism (Sect. 7.5), formalism (Sect. 7.6), neo-formalism (Sect. 7.7), anti-essentialism (Sect. 7.8), and relationism (Sect. 7.9). Raphael's fresco, in which the poet-god Apollo sits atop Mount Parnassus, surrounded by muses and poets, offers a visual tableau of the diversity and plurality of the arts across time (Fig. 7.1). Just as no single figure in the fresco embodies poetry in its entirety, no single theory may suffice to resolve the demarcation problem.

[2] For a useful overview of these different solution paths to the demarcation problem in the philosophy of art, see Carroll (1999), Adajian (2022).

7.2 MIMETICISM

Mimeticism is the view that an artifact is an artwork only if it is an imitation (Carroll, 1999, p. 21). Being an imitation of a person, place, object, action, or event is a necessary condition of something's counting as a work of art. The goal of art in this instance would be to imitate people, places, objects, actions, or events. Whether or not an artifact is regarded as a work of art and (better yet) selected for inclusion in the artistic canon would then be a matter of the degree to which the artifact satisfies this mimetic ideal. Both Plato (360 B.C.E./1953), Aristotle (350 B.C.E.) believed that all the arts would have in common this feature of being involved in imitation. In his systematization of the fine arts into their canonical form, Batteux (1746) also expressed his belief that there is a single principle to which all the fine arts (music, poetry, painting, sculpture, and dance) can be reduced: the principle of imitation. Dramatic poetry imitates actions and events on stage, while painting imitates the appearances of people, places, and objects on a canvas.

A famous contest between two painters in ancient Greece suffices to illustrate the artistic goal, understood in terms of the ideal of mimeticism. Pliny (1938–1962, Book 35) chronicles the occasion when Zeuxis and Parrhasius decided to pit their artistic skill against each other. When Zeuxis unveiled his painting of grapes, the birds were deceived into pecking at the painted grapes. However, when Zeuxis requested for the curtain to be drawn to display Parrhasius's painting, he soon realized that the curtain itself was a mere painted illusion. As it takes greater skill to deceive a human artist than birds, it should not surprise us that Parrhasius was declared the winner of this contest. We should not forget that a painter's mimesis of reality already involves a certain degree of abstraction: Zeuxis's painting of grapes and Parrhasius's painting of curtains, however realistic, necessarily lack the three-dimensional quality of actual grapes and curtains (Fig. 7.2).[3]

Mimeticism, though credible until the nineteenth century, was eventually undermined and overtaken by developments in art from the late nineteenth century. As photography, a new mode of artistic expression, could copy how things look, the visual arts began to depart from the aim of imitating nature. Expressionists, Cubists, and minimalists generated

[3] It is only when the degree of abstraction is so great that it becomes no longer possible to recognize the shapes in a painting as the shapes of any identifiable objects that the painting is described as non-representational.

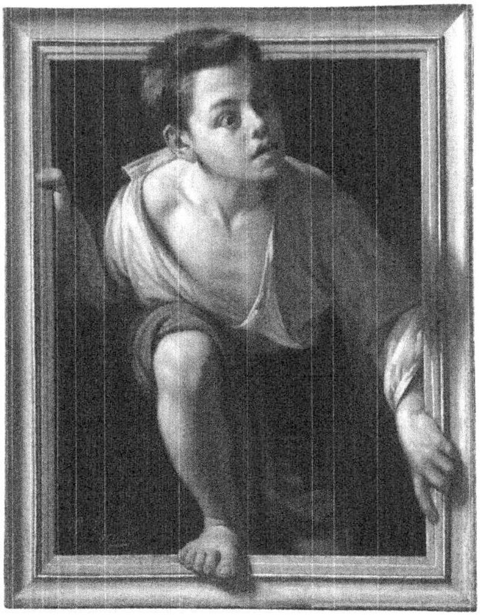

Fig. 7.2 Pere Borrell del Caso's (1874) *Escaping Criticism*. Oil on canvas. Colección Banco de España. Borrell's painting is a famous example of a *trompe-l'il* painting that tricks its viewers into perceiving painted objects or spaces as real, after the manner of the paintings of Zeuxis and Parrhasius

artifacts that were regarded as works of art, even though they were not imitative. Non-mimetic works of visual art have come to be regarded as important counterexamples to mimeticism. Furthermore, it is not clear how music (especially the absolute music first described in Sect. 6.3) or literature are imitative in the sense that drama and the visual arts might be.

7.3 Representationalism

Mimeticism (Sect. 7.2) may be interpreted as a version of representationalism: it tells us that an artifact is an artwork only if it is an imitative representation. Representationalism, more generally, is the view that an artwork is something that is intended to stand for something else and is recognized by the intended audience as such. Where y ranges over the domain of people, places, objects, actions, or events, x represents y if and only if the art-maker intends x to stand for y and intended audience realizes that x is intended to stand for y (Carroll, 1999, p. 25). For example, a portrait is intended to stand for whomever it is a portrait of, and its viewers recognize it as such.

The goal of art would then be to represent people, places, objects, actions, or events in a manner that the intended audience can recognize.

Whether or not an artifact is regarded as a work of art and (better yet) selected for inclusion in the artistic canon would then be a matter of the degree to which the artifact satisfies this representational ideal. Many works of architecture are not representations in the sense required by representationalism. St. Peter's Basilica (Vatican City) does not represent a house of God any more than the Capitol Building (Washington, D.C.) represents the legislature. Furthermore, abstract artworks and decorative art, though non-representational, may still be regarded as works of art. Neither mimeticism nor representationalism would appear to be sufficiently inclusive and general as theories of art to include all artworks and guide our understanding of the goals of art.

7.4 NEO-REPRESENTATIONALISM

Neo-representationalism makes a weaker claim than either mimeticism (Sect. 7.2) or representationalism (Sect. 7.3). According to this theory of art, an artifact is an artwork only if it is about something. More precisely, an artifact is an artwork only if it has a subject about which it makes some comment, says something, or expresses some observation (Carroll, 1999, p. 26). Neo-representationalism tells us that an artifact must have at least some semantic information in order to count as a work of art.

Neo-representationalism helps us to handle certain difficult cases in modern art. Take Marcel Duchamp's (1915) *In Advance of a Broken Arm* and (1917) *Fountain*: the former is an ordinary urinal and the latter is a regular snow shovel. These items are readymades or found objects because they came readymade off the factory assembly line. Although Duchamp's readymades are perceptually indistinguishable from their ordinary real-world counterparts, the former possess an aboutness that the latter do not. This explains why Duchamp's readymades count as art, whereas their ordinary real-world counterparts do not. To say that Duchamp's readymades possess aboutness is to imply that it makes sense to ask what they are about: Duchamp's readymades invite and warrant interpretation. An argument in favour of neo-representationalism may be constructed in the following manner (Carroll, 1999, p. 29):

P1: All artworks require interpretation.
P2: If anything requires interpretation, then it must be about something.
C: ∴ All artworks are about something.

This argument, though valid, could be unsound: the truth of P1 may be contested. Certain works of art (pure orchestral music or non-representational architecture), even though they might possess certain expressive properties, are not about those properties. If they do not require interpretation, then they become counterexamples to neo-representationalism. Yet other works of art (decorative art), though beautiful or aesthetically pleasing, are beneath interpretation and do not require interpretation. These works will equally constitute counterexamples to neo-representationalism.

7.5 Expressivism

For the expressivist, an artifact is a work of art if and only if it is an intended transmission to an audience of the self-same (type-identical) individualized feeling state (emotion) that the art-maker experienced and clarified by means of lines, shapes, colours, sounds, actions, words, and so on (Carroll, 1999, p. 65). The transmission version of expressivism requires that the clarified mood, emotion, or attitude is communicated to an audience. By contrast, the solo version of expressivism requires only the clarification of mood, emotion, or attitude by means of lines, shapes, colours, sounds, actions, words, and so on. Expressive artworks, it has been held, stand in relation to the artist's occurrent emotions as do tears to sadness (Davies, 1998).

At the same time, it may be objected that works of art are not immediate and transparent expressions of occurrent emotions. Besides emotion, attention to technique, detail, the nature of the medium, and overall structure would be required for the fashioning or construction of a work of art or music. According to Collingwood's (1958) expressivist ontology, the work of art is not a product hewn from the manipulation of a physical medium, but rather an imaginary entity existing in the minds of the artist and the audience. We shall have more to say about the imaginary entity hypothesis concerning works of art in Sect. 11.2. For the moment, it suffices to note how expressivists typically assert that art is imaginative expression: art helps to clarify emotion and works of art enable the communication of clarified emotion between artist and audience.[4]

[4] Collingwood's expressivism is similar to the expressivism of Croce (1909/1922). According to Croce, knowledge is either intuitive (based on the imagination and pertaining to

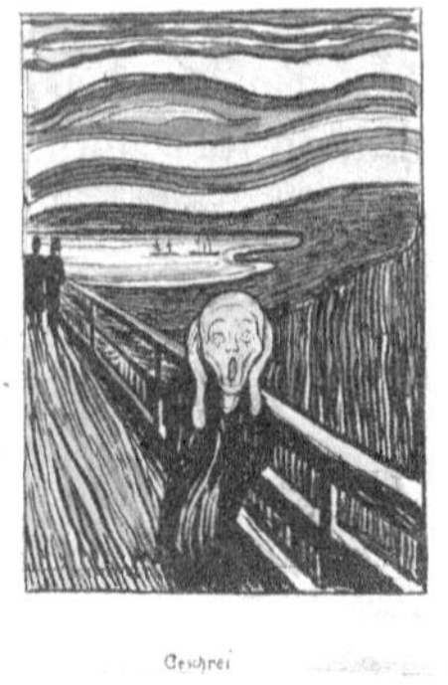

Fig. 7.3 Edvard Munch's (1895) *The Scream*. Hand-coloured lithograph. Photo by Munchmuseet/Ingrid Aas

Romanticism drew our attention to the fact that a work of art embodies the artist's attitudes, feelings, emotions, or point of view toward her subject. Expressivism is a highly suitable theory of art as far as Romantic art and its legacy are concerned. Furthermore, expressivism seems especially well-suited to handle music, unlike mimeticism (Sect. 7.2) and representationalism (Sect. 7.3). Last but not least, expressivism works perfectly as a theory of Expressionist art. Expressionism is a modernist movement whose primary concern is with presenting the world from a subjective perspective. Its key figure, the Norwegian painter Edvard Munch, has been described as a violent dreamer, filled with dramatic pathos and agitation, who paints life's nightmares and is possessed with its horror (Šalda, 1969). This description fits the expressivist account of art as an expression of internal emotion rather than an imitation or representation of an external reality. Munch's famous work, *The Scream*, is depicted in Fig. 7.3.

Objections to expressivism may be made. According to the solo version of expressivism, one can make a work of art for oneself. Is it however possible to make art without having in mind an intention to communicate to an audience? Language is in principle a public affair and we have

the individual) or logical (based on the intellect and pertaining to the universal) in nature. Art involves intuitive knowledge, obtained through the imagination and pertaining to the individual. Furthermore, each true intuition or representation is an expression, to be contrasted with the natural fact of sensation. Each of us has in herself something of the poet, since each of us expresses her intuitions. The artist merely possesses this faculty in a higher degree. This yields the famous Crocean doctrine that art is intuitive expression.

good reason to doubt that there can be a private language of words, images, sounds, shapes, and so on. According to the transmission version of expressivism, art-makers have to transmit the self-same mood, emotion, or attitude to their audience. In other words, the art-maker must experience a certain mood, emotion, or attitude and convey precisely that mood, emotion, or attitude to the audience. This cannot be right. At least some works of art can arouse emotions in their audience that their creators do not feel. While an actor playing a villain may inspire hatred for his character from the audience, he need not be feeling that exact hatred toward his own character in order to succeed dramatically. While at least some works of art (Romantic art, Expressionist art, certain works of music) do communicate individualized emotions, we must be careful not to overstate the case when developing a theory of art to cover all art.

7.6 Formalism

According to formalism, an artifact is an artwork if and only if it possesses significant form (Bell, 1914).[5] The possession of significant form is a necessary condition for an artifact to be regarded as a work of art: an artifact is an artwork only if it possesses significant form. The possession of significant form is also a sufficient condition: if an artifact possesses significant form, then it is an artwork.

The common denominator argument may be employed to support formalism (Carroll, 2000, p. 89):

P1: A necessary condition for an artifact to be regarded as a work of art is something all works of art share.
P2: The only alternatives to significant form are representation and expression.
P3: Not all artworks are representational and not all artworks involve expression.
C: ∴ The only necessary condition is significant form.

Form appears to be the property that all works of art share, whether their medium is any of the fine arts, drama, photography, film, literature, architecture, or whatever. However, since everything in some senses possesses

[5] For a detailed analysis of Bell's formalism, see Gould (1994).

form, it is only significant form that counts as a sufficient condition for art status. At the same time, entities such as effective political speeches and theorems in symbolic logic possess significant form, yet are not works of art. To establish significant form as a sufficient condition of artworks, formalism needs to add a hypothesis about the function of works of art. The primary function of a political speech is to convince an audience. The primary function of a logical theorem is to infer a conclusion. Unlike political speeches and logical theorems, works of art have for their primary function the display or exhibition of significant form.

The function argument is designed to ensure that the exhibition of significant form is a sufficient condition for an artifact to be regarded as an artwork (Carroll, 2000, p. 90):

P1: Only if *x* is a primary function that is unique to art can it be a sufficient condition for an artifact to be regarded as a work of art.
P2: The primary function unique to art is either representation, expression, or the exhibition of significant form.
P3: Neither representation nor expression are unique functions of works of art, since other entities also share these functions.
C1: ∴ The exhibition of significant form is a primary function unique to art.
C2: ∴ The exhibition of significant form is a sufficient condition for an artifact to be regarded as a work of art.

According to formalism, the artistically relevant properties of artifact are its formal properties (Bell, 1914; Fry, 1920; Beardsley, 1958; Greenberg, 1986). By formal properties, we mean the properties of a work of art that are accessible by direct sensation (typically sight or hearing). Formalists maintain that neither the intentions of the artist nor the audience's affective responses to a work of art are relevant to the evaluation of the work. The intentional fallacy is a misstep of reasoning that arises whenever we take the intentions of the artist to be relevant to the interpretation or evaluation of a work of art (Wimsatt & Beardsley, 1946). The affective fallacy is another misstep of reasoning that arises whenever we take the affective responses of the audience to be relevant to the interpretation or evaluation of a work of art (Wimsatt & Beardsley, 1949). If we want to discover what properties a work of art has, we need merely look at the work to grasp or apprehend its formal properties. An analysis of a painting is exhausted by a concern for colour, line, shape, texture, and other compositional elements, rather than representational content or socio-historical context.

Formalism is not without its problems. To begin with, what exactly is significant form and how do we distinguish (say) between significant form, form without significance, significance without form, and that which has neither form nor significance? Formalism offers us no way to make these distinctions. This makes formalism a useless theory of art, since its central concept (significant form) is vague or undefined. The common denominator argument, though valid, could be unsound. P1 could be false: perhaps there are no necessary conditions shared by all works of art (see anti-essentialism in Sect. 7.8). P2 could be false: there could be other alternatives to significant form besides representation and expression. In addition, the function argument, though valid, could also be unsound. P2 could be false in a number of ways: either other alternatives to the exhibition of significant form exist besides representation and expression or there may not be any primary function unique to art at all. Last but not least, formalism privileges the form of works of art at the expense of their content: the representational content of works of art is strictly irrelevant to their status as art.

7.7 Neo-formalism

Neo-formalism asserts that an artifact is an artwork if and only if it has content, it has form, and the form and the content are related to each other in a satisfyingly appropriate manner (Carroll, 1999, p. 125). The content of a work of art refers to its meaning, theme, or whatever it is about. Its form, by contrast, is the mode of presentation of its meaning or the way in which its meaning is embodied, presented, or articulated. Unlike formalism (Sect. 7.6), neo-formalism recognizes alongside neo-representationalism (Sect. 7.4) that content (aboutness) can be relevant to art status. Neo-formalism implies that whenever an artifact matches its meaning with a suitably satisfying form or mode of presentation, it will be regarded as art. Neo-formalism is also sensitive to the expressive dimensions of works of art in a way that mimeticism (Sect. 7.2), representationalism (Sect. 7.3), and formalism (Sect. 7.6) are not. Neo-formalism can count the expression of certain moods, emotions, or attitudes as the content or meaning of a work of art (what it is about) and then consider whether the formal means are suitable for articulating that expressive property. Furthermore, the neoformalist notion of the satisfying appropriateness of form to content seems less vague and more informative than the formalist notion of significant form.

At the same time, counterexamples to neo-formalism may be identified. Not all art has content: at least some works of art (pure orchestral music, pure dance) are below meaning, about nothing, and merely beautiful. Furthermore, some art is bad, precisely because it fails to find a satisfyingly appropriate form for its content. However, as bad art does not cease to be art, neo-formalism appears to track only good art as opposed to all art (good, middling, and bad). Therefore, the satisfying appropriateness of form to content cannot be a necessary condition of art.

7.8 Anti-Essentialism

According to simple functionalism, the possession of a single valuable property or function is what allows an artifact to be regarded as an artwork (Stecker, 2003). Mimeticism, representationalism, neo-representationalism, expressivism, formalism, and neo-formalism are simple functionalist theories. Simple functionalist accounts suggest that the goals of art may be variously interpreted in terms of imitation (mimeticism), representation (representationalism), the communication of semantic information (neo-representationalism), the communication of individualized and clarified emotions (expressivism), the exhibition of significant form (formalism), or the relation of form and content in a satisfyingly appropriate manner (neo-formalism). Since the 1950s, the trend has been to reject simple functionalism in all its forms (Stecker, 2003). There are clear-cut cases of tables, chairs, stars, planets, dogs, cats, electrons, quarks, and so on. However, it remains possible to dispute whether a particular painting is a work of art or not. Therefore, we might infer that there are and can be no clear-cut cases of works of art (Ziff, 1953). More generally, anti-essentialists regard the attempt by simple functionalists to define art as misguided, since it is doubtful whether any necessary and sufficient conditions are capable of supporting a definition of art (Ziff, 1953; Weitz, 1956; Kennick, 1958).[6]

[6] Although we have already identified it as a necessary condition for art-making and the production of works of art, human-level intelligence remains insufficient (Sect. 4.2).

Instead, anti-essentialists believe that the concept of art and related concepts are open rather than closed, since the conditions according to which we apply these concepts do not determine their application in every possible instance (Weitz, 1956). Consider the concept of a novel. Given the development of the novel from Richardson to Joyce, each time we consider whether a work (John Dos Passos's *U.S.A.* trilogy, Virginia Woolf's *To the Lighthouse*, or James Joyce's *Finnegans Wake*, for instance) may be regarded a novel, we are effectively making a decision about whether the work under consideration is sufficiently similar in certain respects to other works called novels to warrant the extension of the concept of the novel to cover the new case.

Anti-essentialists typically appeal to Wittgenstein's philosophy of language in general and the doctrine of family resemblances in particular to support their claim that it is doubtful that necessary and sufficient conditions for art exist. Think about the various uses of the term 'games' (for instance, card games, board games, ball games, and so on) (Wittgenstein, 1953/2009, §§ 66–67). It appears that we have a complicated network of similarities overlapping and criss-crossing, as opposed to an essential core in which the meaning of the term 'games' may be thought to reside. These similarities are akin to resemblances between members of a family (build, features, eye colour, gait, temperament, and so on), which overlap and criss-cross in the same way.

According to the doctrine of family resemblances, we should not suppose that all instances of entities to which we apply a common term (for instance, 'games' or 'family') in fact possess any one property in common. If the search for common characteristics among works of art is taken to imply the search for some common denominator, then we shall be led on a fool's errand. What could the common artistic denominator possibly be between Joseph Beuys's (1974) *I Like America and America Likes Me*, Grant Wood's (1930) *American Gothic* painting, and George Gershwin's (1928) symphonic or tone poem *An American in Paris*, setting aside the thematization of the United States and its citizens in their titles?[7] If, however, this search for common characteristics is taken to imply the search for similarities and resemblances in art in the Wittgensteinian sense

[7] Joseph Beuys's (1974) *I Like America and America Likes Me* involved a performance in which the artist spent eight hours a day for three consecutive days living with a live coyote.

of family resemblances, then the search may yet turn out to be a fruitful and enlightening exercise (Kennick, 1958).

Gaut's (2000; 2005) cluster concept approach to art may be regarded as an advanced or sophisticated form of anti-essentialism.[8] It asserts, as do other more traditional forms of anti-essentialism, that art lacks any necessary and sufficient conditions. However, whereas more traditional forms of anti-essentialism take this to imply that the search for definitions of art will therefore be futile (Weitz, 1956), the cluster concept approach suggests instead that a set of criteria can be used to characterize art, although none of them are strictly necessary. Instead, something qualifies as a work of art just in case it meets a sufficient number of these criteria. These criteria comprise something's (1) possessing positive aesthetic qualities such as beauty; (2) being expressive of emotion; (3) being intellectually challenging; (4) being formally complex and coherent; (5) having a capacity to convey complex meanings; (6) exhibiting an individual point of view; (7) being an exercise of creative imagination; (8) being an artifact or performance that is the product of a high degree of skill; (9) belonging to an established artistic form; and (10) being the product of an intention to make a work of art.

Several philosophers have pointed out that the cluster concept approach amounts to a disjunctive definition of art (Davies, 2004; Longworth & Scarantino, 2010). There is exactly $\binom{10}{10}$ or one way of being art when all ten criteria are satisfied. There are $\binom{10}{9}$ or 10 ways of being art when nine criteria are satisfied. There are $\binom{10}{8}$ or 45 ways of being art when eight criteria are satisfied. Therefore, there are 56 ways of being art if any work that counts as art must satisfy at least eight of Gaut's ten criteria. More generally, there are $\sum_{k=x}^{10} \binom{10}{k}$ ways of being art if at least x of Gaut's ten criteria must be satisfied.

One objection to the cluster concept approach is that it does not refute essentialism: instead, it offers a flexible yet structured framework in which essentialism can still be true. Another objection to the cluster concept approach is that it fails on its own terms: something might not count as a work of art even when all ten criteria are satisfied. Carroll (2012b) asks us to consider a cake made by a baker to commemorate the anniversary of

[8] The cluster concept approach represents the revival of a Wittgensteinian approach to art. We are grateful to two pre-publication reviewers for having encouraged us to engage with this recent variety of anti-essentialism.

his marriage to his wife under certain conditions. For instance, since the baker and his wife celebrated their marriage by taking a car trip and visiting several cities, the cake is made in the shape of their car. Furthermore, as the baker's wife is an amateur cryptographer, the baker notes each of the cities they visited in alternating colours, along with remarks about what they saw there in code on the side of the cake. This cake possesses positive aesthetic properties; expresses the emotion of love; is intellectually challenging with its use of non-obvious code; is formally complex and coherent; has the capacity to convey complex meanings about the history of the beginnings of the marriage; exhibits the point of view of the baker in love; evinces both the creative imagination and skill of the baker; belongs to the recognizable art form of sculpture; and is intended by the baker to be a work of art. The baker's cake satisfies all ten of Gaut's criteria: that, according to the cluster concept approach, will be sufficient for it to count as an artwork. However, few cognoscenti will accept it as such.

7.9 Relationism

What anti-essentialists fail to recognize is that the literal notion of family resemblances includes the fact of a genetic connection (a common denominator) no less than it includes phenotypical resemblances between family members (features, eye colour, and so on). There is a property held in common among individuals who share a family resemblance: they are related through a common ancestry. Common ancestry or history (the continuity between a work and existing traditions of art) appears to function as a necessary condition for something to count as a work of art, and all forms of anti-essentialism (including the cluster concept approach) appear to have overlooked this fact. Through this critique of anti-essentialism and its reliance on the doctrine of family resemblances, Mandelbaum (1965) invites us to invites us to consider what might fill the gap left by anti-essentialism, undergirded by the doctrine of family resemblances, and play the connecting role played by relation through a common ancestry in the context of literal family resemblances. According to relationism, the relationship that something enjoys with other entities in the world of art is what qualifies it as art. Relationism may be construed as a more sophisticated version of functionalism. Both simple functionalists and relationists believe, unlike the anti-essentialist, that it is meaningful to ask and respond to the basic question 'What is art?'. In addition, relationists believe that a response to this question will have to invoke a relation rather than a property.

According to institutionalism, art institutions in the artworld, including museums, galleries, and agents working within these institutions, have the power to determine what is art and what is not art (Dickie, 1974). The artworld, in turn, refers to the atmosphere of art theory and knowledge of the history of art (Danto, 1964). An artifact is a work of art if and only if it has been conferred an official status by individuals and institutions authorized to act on behalf of the artworld. In other words, works of art count as art because they occupy a place in a certain institution: the institution of art. Institutionalism implies that something counts as a work of art, not by virtue of any of its properties (representational, expressive, formal, and so on) but rather by virtue of a relation that it bears to a larger context that is known as the artworld. The artworld is what ensures that Andy Warhol's facsimiles of Brillo boxes, piled high in neat stacks and made of wood though painted to look like cardboard, count as works of art rather than mere plywood facsimiles of commercially available Brillo boxes.[9]

Historicism is another example of a relationist view. For historicists, the relation in question, held in common among works of art, is historical in nature. Historical narratives link later works of art to their predecessors, there could be a historical relation between an artist's intentions and earlier artworks, and we may think of this historical relation in terms of historically evolving styles and functions (Carroll, 1994; Levinson, 1979; Carney, 1991; Stecker, 1996). Historicism is influenced by Danto's (1981) view that both the work of art and its interpretation require an art-historical context (cited in Carroll, 2012a). Historicists typically maintain that an artifact is regarded as a work of art, not by virtue of definitions (institutional or otherwise) but rather by virtue of narratives.

Showing that *x* counts as a work of art typically involves telling a certain kind of story about *x*: a historical narrative about how *x* came to be produced as an intelligible response to an antecedent art-historical situation about which a consensus with respect to its art status already exists (Carroll, 1994). The artistic tradition consists of an artistic canon, whose

[9] As Danto has astutely pointed out, Warhol could have made his Brillo boxes out of cardboard without their ceasing to count as art, whereas the commercial suppliers of Brillo boxes could have made theirs out of plywood without these boxes thereby becoming works of art.

members are related as ancestors and descendants and whose new members are postulants (Sharpe, 1978). Recall how, in our characterization of the hit-from-bit hypothesis (H3), we have already defined the artistic canon as a cultural memory of works of high artistic value and significance ('hit') (Sect. 3.6). At least some works of art have a contested nature: perhaps we cannot decide whether they are a hit or a miss. Whenever this might be the case, it will help to situate them within a tradition where they become more and more intelligible. The historicist approach, relying as it does on the use of historical narratives, presupposes at least some knowledge about art and its practices.

In summary, the goals of art might involve imitation (mimeticism), representation (representationalism), the communication of semantic information (neo-representationalism), the communication of individualized and clarified moods, emotions, or attitudes (expressivism), the exhibition of significant form (formalism), the relation of form and content in a satisfyingly appropriate manner (neo-formalism), the demonstration of a case for the inclusion of the artifact under the open concept of art (anti-essentialism), the development of a relation between the artifact and the institution of art (institutionalism), or the situation of the artifact within a historical narrative (historicism) (Sects. 7.3–7.9). The different theories of art identify different valuable properties or relations that an artifact must either possess or enter into, in order to be regarded as an artwork. Although many art-makers have answered 'yes' to the yes-no question 'Does a work of art have to imitate or represent reality?', giving rise to mimeticism or representationalism, not all the arts are mimetic or representational. Furthermore, the arts that contain mimetic or representational works may equally contain non-mimetic or non-representational ones. Both neo-representationalism and expressivism recognize that artifacts function as communication channels. More precisely, artifacts are communication channels through which art-makers share semantic information with their intended audience (H2), and neo-formalism and neo-representationalism capture this aboutness of artifacts. The idea of an artistic canon as a cultural memory of 'hits', evoked in H3, fits neatly with institutionalism and historicism. The individuals and institutions authorized to act on behalf of the artworld police the frontline of the canon and play the role of gatekeepers: they select, curate, criticize, review, influence through funding and financial support, and make decisions about which artifacts to include or exclude from exhibitions. Historical narratives in which later works of art are linked to their predecessors presuppose some form of cultural memory.

Our computationalist approach to art-making and the production of works of art is a theory of art. Unlike mimeticism, representationalism, neo-representationalism, expressivism, neo-formalism, anti-essentialism, institutionalism, or historicism, however, it is not a theory of what art is. We are not interested in grand theorizing as such (Sect. 6.3). Perhaps the question 'What is art?', though basic in the philosophy of art and therefore important (non-trivial) to philosophers of art, does not have a correct answer. Perhaps the demarcation problem in the philosophy of art, concerning where the cut-off is made between art and non-art, cannot be solved. The idea of an artistic goal does not depend on there being a correct answer to the 'What is art?' question. The various theories of what art is (mimeticism, representationalism, neo-representationalism, expressivism, neo-formalism, anti-essentialism, institutionalism, and historicism) yield important clues as to how this idea of an artistic goal might be instantiated in an art-maker.

Depending on which theory of art is the most persuasive, human beings engaged in art-making will strive to ensure that their artifacts imitate or represent an external reality, communicate semantic information or emotions, exhibit significant form, relate form and content in a satisfyingly appropriate manner, satisfy the state-of-the-art conditions of application for the concept of art, get an honorific status conferred by the artworld on their work, or secure the requisite historical relations with earlier works of art. Art-making is a goal-directed activity (H1). Human beings who take the goals of art seriously will seek alignment with these goals, derive artistic purpose therefrom, and acquire reasons and motivations for their actions. This sense of artistic purpose can help to sustain art-makers as they navigate the problem space, develop and apply heuristic search strategies, and generate solution paths that (hopefully) will lead them toward their artistic goals.

CHAPTER 8

The Central Artistic Task

8.1 Anticipating the Objections

In Chap. 5, we identified the theory of problem-solving as a computationalist approach that explains human problem-solving behaviour in terms of a problem space, a search strategy, heuristics, evaluating and choosing among alternative actions, and a goal to be accomplished. In Chap. 7, we made sense of the possible goals of art in terms of various theories of what art is (mimeticism, representationalism, neo-representationalism, expressivism, neo-formalism, anti-essentialism, institutionalism, and historicism). That by virtue of which an artifact qualifies as art rather than non-art has been parsed in terms of imitation, representation, the communication of semantic information (aboutness), the communication of individualized and clarified emotions, the exhibition of significant form, the relation of form and content in a satisfyingly appropriate manner, the satisfaction of emendable conditions of application of art and related concepts, the situation of the artifact within the institution of art, or the situation of the artifact within a historical narrative. In this chapter, we will make sense of the central artistic task.

Parmigianino's self-portrait exemplifies an attempt to engage with a set of art-specific challenges: using oil paint to depict the optical distortions of a convex mirror, painting on a specially prepared convex panel that mimics the curvature of the mirror, evoking the sheen of an actual mirror, and so

M. Chen, *Art-Making as Problem-Solving*,
https://doi.org/10.1007/978-3-031-90639-8_8

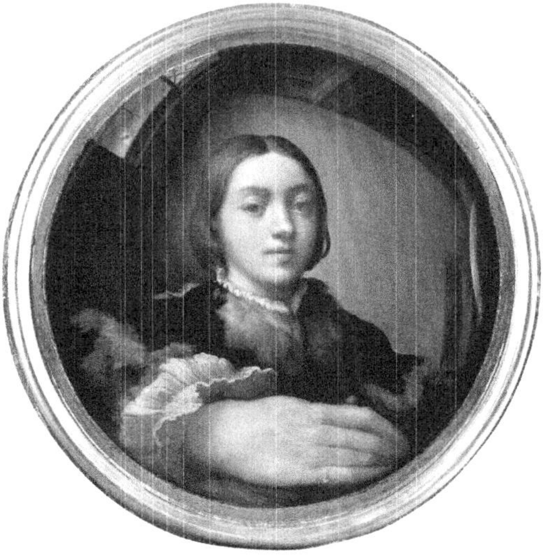

Fig. 8.1
Parmigianino's (c. 1524) *Self-portrait in a Convex Mirror*. Oil on convex panel. ©KHM-Museumsverband

on (Fig. 8.1). Here is our hypothesis concerning the central artistic task: there is an art-specific challenge to be overcome or problem to be solved, the overcoming or solving of which is conditional on the available materials at the disposal of each art-maker. Not all philosophers will agree: Beardsley (1965) denies that art-making is a problem-solving activity in the strict sense, since the art-maker's tasks are dependent not on some fixed goal but rather the state of the work at any given stage of its creation. This does not however constitute a knockdown argument, since we could permit the art-maker's goals to change over time, just as we have already recognized the possibility that the art-maker's goals may be subject to the emendable conditions of application of art and related concepts (as proposed by anti-essentialism in Sect. 7.8).

Furthermore, at least some philosophers have argued that neither alternative actions nor choices are explicit in aesthetic experience. According to Sheets-Johnstone (2011), the dynamic world that dancers explore is inseparable from the dynamic world that they are together creating. In this dynamic world, neither the dancers' possibilities at any moment in the ongoing present nor their choosing would be explicit. Again, this would not be a knockdown argument, since we could allow for both the alternative actions available to the art-maker and choices to be implicit rather than explicit.

Yet other philosophers might contend that the idea that making art involves solving a problem is reductive: it misses out all the complex drives, unconscious needs, responses to contingent events and occurrences, and processes of feedback between doing and thinking involving the manual manipulation of materials. The thesis of art-making as problem-solving, it may be objected, crudely reduces the process of making art to what will fit our argumentative purposes, much as Procrustes stretched or amputated people's limbs to make good his claim that he had a bed that would fit anyone. The Procrustean thesis of art as problem-solving will exclude much of art-making and, depending on its formulation, could even include output that we do not consider to be art.

Our counter is that there is something equally reductive about anthropocentric accounts of art that either exclude or fail to accommodate the possibility of machine art. Rather, our computationalist approach to art-making could be regarded as a theory of art that seeks to make the philosophy of art relevant and future-proof in the age of artificial intelligence.[1] If the philosophy of art is to be information-theoretic (Chap. 3), then our computationalist approach to art-making will function as its boon companion. In addition, our computationalist approach to art-making and the production of works of art allows us to develop continuities between art-making and other forms of creative and intelligent endeavour outside the artistic domain. Even if our theory of art is ultimately false, it could still provide us with a useful working model with which to reflect about art.

Finally, it may be contended that art-making is about exploring the vastness of the problem space and searching for and holding in view multiple possibilities rather than solving specific problems. According to neuroscientists, cognition tends to favour the adoption of metastable states in order to allow for an effortless transition to be made between many different states and alternatives in skilled intentional behaviour (Kelso, 2012; Bruineberg & Rietveld, 2014; Bruineberg et al., 2021). Nonetheless, both this view—art-making as problem-creating rather than problem-solving—

[1] For a similarly forward-looking account of art, see Helliwell (2023), who discusses the possibility of machine art and machine creativity, utilizing well-known theories of art, the work of Margaret Boden on creativity, and addressing the issue of autonomy. I am grateful to an anonymous reviewer for having pointed out this reference to me.

and ours have in common the senses of art-making as a response in an uncertain and unpredictable environment and art-making as involving the navigation of a problem space in which multiple possibilities exist.[2]

8.2 Art as Problem-solving

There is at least some philosophical precedent for the view that works of art may be construed as various ways of overcoming challenges and solving problems, conditional on the available materials at the disposal of each art-maker (Ecker, 1963; Chanan, 1972; Dutton, 1979; Baxandall, 1985; Eaton, 2012).[3] However, these philosophers typically make minimal reference to the theory of problem-solving: they rely on either isolated metaphors (such as art as an experiment) or the introspectionist approach (especially its aggregative version, with appeals being made to Ghiselin's *The Creative Process* in particular). Our approach is therefore a novel one. Its hypothesis is that the central artistic task involves overcoming a challenge or solving a problem relative to the artistic domain, conditional on the available materials at the disposal of each art-maker and its theoretical support hails from the theory of problem-solving.

We have already identified a number of possible goals for each art-maker in Chap. 7. The art-maker attempts to accomplish these goals with a variety of media: pencil, charcoal, ink, oil, acrylic, watercolour, gouache, etching, or woodcut (visual art); clay, wood, metal, or plaster (sculpture); collage and assemblage (mixed media); poetry, prose, and drama (literary art); human bodies (performing art); piano, violin, an orchestra of instruments, and electronic music (music); and film or animation (cinematic art). Each medium poses medium-specific challenges: visual artists often confront the challenge of creating the illusion of a three-dimensional space on a two-dimensional surface, musical composers often confront the challenge of

[2] I am grateful to an anonymous reviewer for having offered invaluable critical perspective here.

[3] Similar views have been defended by philosophers who regard works of art as experiences rather than artifacts. According to Dewey (1934), the art-maker does not shun moments of resistance and tension but instead cultivates them for their potentialities and not for their own sake. Nanay (2023) regards aesthetic experiences as forms of interaction in which we know neither how the object or person we are interacting with will react to what we do nor what kind of experience our aesthetic actions give rise to. I am grateful to an anonymous reviewer for having pointed this out to me.

using abstract sound to evoke certain feelings and communicate a narrative without visual aid, and filmmakers often confront the challenge of crafting a temporal structure that ensures that the audience will be sufficiently engaged over the course of the film narrative.

Besides having to choose among various media to accomplish certain aesthetic goals, artists also have to choose between various genres: realism, surrealism, pop art, impressionism, and cubism (visual art); classical, jazz, rock, hip hop, folk, and blues (music); fiction, non-fiction, poetry, and drama (literary art); and drama, comedy, action, documentary, horror, science fiction, and animation (cinematic art). Both the medium of choice and the genre of choice introduce certain constraints within which the artist has to work, even as she attempts to produce a work that will be favourably evaluated.[4] These choices may be included among the binary choices ('bits') that art-makers make in the process of generating artifacts that they hope will come to be regarded as artworks (H3).

8.3 Finding Members of Subset *S*, Given a Set *P*

Any problem (artistic or non-artistic) may be expressed in the following manner: given a set P of elements, find a member of a subset S of P having certain properties. For the art-maker, these properties will be the valuable properties that will qualify something as a work of art (Chap. 7). For the moment, however, let us rely on certain computationally tractable examples to illustrate what we mean by this.[5] Examples of problems to be solved include completing an English-language crossword puzzle, cracking the combination of a safe, and making moves in chess (Newell et al., 1959).

In a 50-square crossword puzzle, P consists of all the possible combinations of letters of the English alphabet that will fill the 50 empty squares of the puzzle. If each square can be filled by any of the 26 letters of the English alphabet, then we will have 26^{50} (or around 10^{70}) possible combinations for our set P. The subset S would comprise those combinations in which the linear (vertical, horizontal, or diagonal) sequences are well-formed English words that satisfy all the clues for that crossword puzzle. In a safe

[4] See however Sect. 10.3 for a computationalist account of how it may be precisely these constraints that undergo a transformation as a result of the creative artistic process.

[5] We will continue our tradition, first begun in Sect. 5.5, of selecting several examples from games.

whose lock has 10 independent dials, each with numbers running from 00 to 99 on its face, we will have 100^{10} (or 10^{20}) possible settings of our safe. The subset *S* is a singleton: it contains only one member, the unique setting that will unlock the safe. A would-be safe-cracker, turning these dials at random, will take an average of 50 billion (or $10^{20}/2$) trials to open the safe. If each trial takes a minute, this would-be safe-cracker would require an average of about 95 trillion years to open the safe.[6]

With respect to chess, there are about 30 legal moves you can make in any position (Shannon, 1950). This is known as the branching factor of chess. For a pair of moves (White followed by Black), we will therefore have 30×30 (or about 10^3) possible move sequences. As a typical chess game lasts for about 40 pairs of moves, we have $(10^3)^{40}$ possible move sequences or chess games. This yields 10^{120} and it is known as the Shannon number for chess.[7] The game tree complexity of chess, computed as an upper bound and a log to base 10, will therefore be 120. This entails that chess is a far more computationally complex game than tic-tac-toe relative to the measure of game tree complexity, since the game tree complexity of tic-tac-toe, you might recall, is 5 (Sect. 5.5). Out of these 10^{120} possible legal games of chess, chess players will only consider a subset *S* of move sequences that are both legal and good, as evaluated in terms of a chess evaluation function.[8]

We have already encountered the various heuristics (H_1–H_4) that may be employed to prune the game tree in tic-tac-toe (Sect. 5.5). Certain heuristics, principles, or rules of thumb may be similarly employed in chess (Chen, forthcoming). These heuristics can be analyzed in terms of

[6] $10^{20}/2$ (number of minutes) $\div$ 1440 (number of minutes per day) $\div$ 365 (number of days per year) $\approx 9.5 \times 10^{13}$ (number of years).

[7] Hardy (1999) has cited the second-order exponential $(10^{10})^{50}$ as an estimate of the number of possible legal move sequences, although neither working nor reasoning has been provided for this number. In any case, both the Shannon number (10^{120}) and Hardy's estimate ($(10^{10})^{50}$) easily dwarf the estimated number of atoms in the known universe: $[10^{78}–10^{82}]$.

[8] In addition, chess players typically consider only legal continuations five moves deep for each player at a given state of the chess board. This yields a set *P* with $(10^3)^5$ or 10^{15} possible legal move sequences, given the computational constraints of human chess players. See also de Groot (1978) for a detailed study of choice in chess by human players.

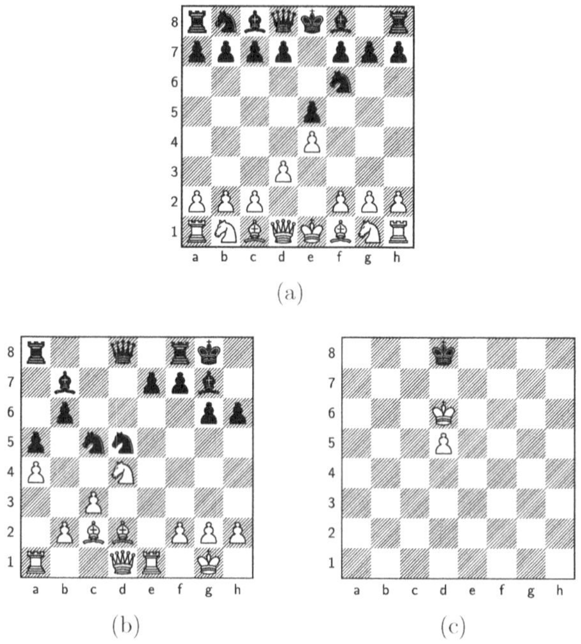

Fig. 8.2 Different phases of the game of chess. (a) Opening game. (b) Middle game. (c) Endgame

the three phases of a game of chess: the opening, the middle game, and the endgame (Fig. 8.2). During the opening, which generally lasts for about 10 moves until players have castled, development of the pieces to good positions is the main objective. Heuristics that apply to the opening include controlling the centre of the board, castling as soon as possible, developing your knights before your bishops, and developing your pieces in general (Fine, 1949). During the middle game, strategy and tactics will predominate. Heuristics that apply to the middle game include ensuring the safety of your king, gaining a material advantage in the game, and enhancing the mobility and activity of your pieces (Fine, 1952). During the endgame, the primary concern is with pawn promotion and converting strategic advantages gained during the middle game. Heuristics that apply

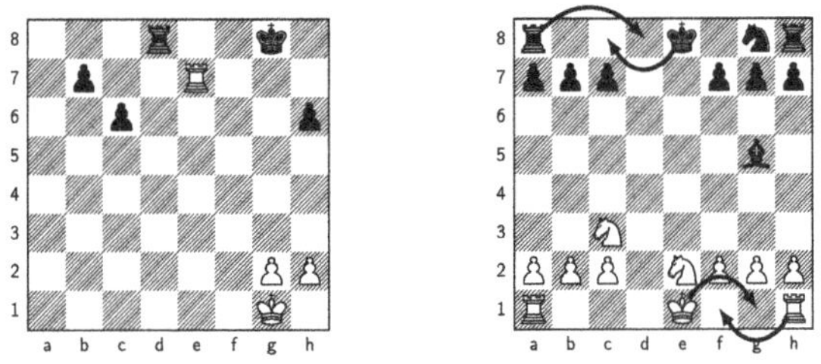

(a) (b)

Fig. 8.3 Possible features of a chess evaluation function. (**a**) White rook on the seventh rank threatening black pawn on b7 and trapping black king on the eighth rank. (**b**) Castling ability White king may castle to g1 (kingside) but not c1 (queenside) Black king may castle to c8 (queenside) but not g8 (kingside)

to the endgame include avoiding isolated, doubled, and blocked pawns, advancing passed pawns as quickly as possible, and advancing the rook to the seventh rank (Fine, 1941/1941).

A brute-force search of the complete game tree of chess will require combing through 10^{120} possible games of chess. By contrast, the knowledge-based approach of heuristic search, relying on the various heuristics that apply to the different phases of a game of chess, could focus on more promising lines of play, evaluating a select number of nodes in the game tree in accordance with a chess evaluation function. As these heuristics are phase-specific, the chess evaluation function ought to be sensitive to the different phases of each game. A function may be constructed such that it favours castling ability (Fig. 8.3b, an opening principle), more mobile pieces (a middle game principle), getting a rook on the seventh rank (Fig. 8.3a, an endgame principle), checks, and checkmate threats.[9] We expect heuristic search to help bring the game tree of chess down to more manageable proportions.

[9] A description of a standard chess evaluation function may be found in Turing (1953).

8.4 An n-Position Melody and an n-Dot Dot Matrix Picture

The activity of art-making may be construed along similar lines. Suppose we have n positions in our melody. Each position can be filled by either one of 12 pitch classes in the Western chromatic scale or a rest.[10] Our set P will therefore consist of 13^n possible combinations of pitch sequences and its complexity will be increased once we allow for further variation in rhythm, articulation, and so on. By contrast, suppose we have a Roy Lichtenstein-style dot matrix picture composed of n Ben Day dots. For its colour, each dot will be assigned a particular set of RGB (Red, Green, and Blue) values. 256 possible values may, in turn, be assigned to each colour channel. We will therefore have 256^3 possible colour combinations for each dot and 256^{3n} possible colour combinations for the n-dot Lichtenstein-style dot matrix picture. The complexity of this 256^{3n}-element P will be increased once we allow for further variation in texture, luminance or brightness, contrast, and so on.

The subset S of P with which musical composers and visual artists are concerned will have certain artistically valuable properties or relations. We can expect these valuable properties or relations to include verisimilitude (representationalism), semantic information (neo-representationalism), expressive potential (expressivism), a distribution of elements that promotes balance, contrast, and harmony (formalism), a certain degree of fit between form and content (neo-formalism), the satisfaction of medium- and genre-relevant constraints, coherence and intelligibility in an art-historical context (historicism), and whatever else the art-maker might take to be the goals of art. It may be helpful for philosophers of art to contemplate further about variables that contribute to the complexity of set P, and the valuable properties or relations that we expect members of subset S to have.

[10] The 12 pitch classes are: C, C♯ or D♭, D, D♯ or E♭, E, F, F♯ or G♭, G, G♯ or A♭, A, A♯ or B♭, and B. See our discussion of the chromatic scale in the context of Schoenberg's twelve-tone method in Sect. 10.3.

8.5 Works of Art as Permutations of Elements

We can afford to be more precise about what we mean by finding members of subset *S*, given a set *P*. Members of *P* are candidate works of art (artifacts), consisting of ordered arrangements of elements. Candidate works of art may be described mathematically as permutations of these elements. Schoenberg's twelve-tone method for dodecaphonic music, which we shall discuss in Sect. 10.3, is based on various permutations of the twelve tones of the chromatic scale. The sestina, a verse form whose invention is attributed to the troubadour Arnaut Daniel, involves a permutation of the line-ending words in six stanzas of six lines each. Lloyd Schwartz's (2003/2006) 'Six words' is an example of a sestina that employs only six words:

yes
no
maybe
sometimes
always
never

Never?
Yes.
Always?
No.
Sometimes?
Maybe —

maybe
never
sometimes.
Yes —
no
always:

always
maybe.
No —
never
yes.
Sometimes,

sometimes
(always)
yes.
Maybe
never …
No,

no —
sometimes.
Never.
Always?
Maybe.
Yes —

yes no
maybe sometimes
always never.

The cut-up technique of Dadaists, which involves cutting up a written text and rearranging it to form a new text, is another example of permutation in art. This cut-up technique is described in Tristan Tzara's (1920/2013) 'To make a Dadaist poem':

> Take a newspaper.
> Take some scissors.
> Choose from this paper an article the length you want to make your poem.
> Cut out the article.
> Next carefully cut out each of the words that make up this article and put them all in a bag.
> Shake gently.
> Next take out each cutting one after the other.
> Copy conscientiously in the order in which they left the bag.
> The poem will resemble you.
> And there you are — an infinitely original author of charming sensibility, even though unappreciated by the vulgar herd.

The combinatoric aspects of art have been addressed in several computationalist accounts (Terzidis, 2014; Barrière, 2017). In the spirit of these accounts, candidate works of art (artifacts) may be described in terms of a permutation of certain elements of composition. These elements of composition may, in turn, differ from one art to the next. The elements of composition in visual art have traditionally been identified as line, shape, colour, value, and texture (Ocvirk et al., 1968/2012).[11] The elements of composition in music, by contrast, have traditionally been identified as pitch, duration, intensity, and timbre (Ottman & Mainous, 1995).[12] Each work of visual art may be regarded as a specific permutation of line, shape, colour, value, and texture in a visual medium. In a related vein, each work of music may be regarded as a specific permutation of pitch, duration, intensity, and timbre in a sonic medium.

Set *P* will, in principle, contain all possible ordered arrangements of these elements of composition. Members of subset *S*, in turn, are ordered arrangements of elements that will be regarded as artistically valuable. A brute-force search will involve combing painstakingly through each and every single possible ordered arrangement to determine members of subset *S*. A heuristic or knowledge-based search, by contrast, may rely on certain heuristics, principles, or rules of thumb to identify more promising candidates for subset *S*. Members of subset *S* are permutations that will be regarded as works of art and (better yet) get selected for inclusion in the artistic canon.

[11] By value is meant the lightness or darkness of a colour (black, white, and all the shades of grey in between) used in a work. A nine-step value scale was developed by the American painter Denman Ross in 1907 to illustrate how values change between white (represented by 1) and black (represented by 9).

[12] By pitch is meant tone frequency. By intensity is meant the degree of loudness or softness of the sound. By timbre is meant a distinction in the tone colours of different musical instruments.

CHAPTER 9

The Analogy Between Logic and Art

9.1 Aesthetic Experience in Mathematics

We have already distinguished between the philosophy of art and aesthetics (Sect. 3.2). In addition, we have located our intellectual concerns primarily in the former rather than the latter. At the same time, we have conceded that the philosophy of art (involving works of art in some way) and aesthetics (having something to do with the beautiful or aesthetically pleasing) are distinct though interrelated in some way (Sect. 6.1). It is possible for aesthetic experiences to occur outside the artistic realm: certain mathematical proofs might for instance strike us as beautiful or elegant. How can aesthetic qualities (beauty, elegance, and so on) wander so far afield from the artistic realm and into the mathematical realm?[1] Can philosophers of art draw any lessons from the possibility of aesthetic experience in mathematics? We shall pursue these and other related philosophical concerns in this chapter, with a view to enhancing our computationalist approach to art-making and the production of works of art.

[1] For a philosophical treatment of the puzzle concerning whether or how aesthetic criteria can be applied to mathematics, science, and other non-artistic domains, see Osborne (1984) and Engler (1990).

M. Chen, *Art-Making as Problem-Solving*,
https://doi.org/10.1007/978-3-031-90639-8_9

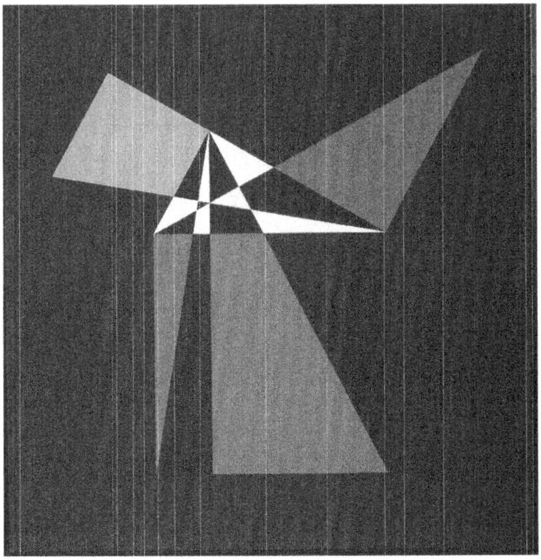

Fig. 9.1 Crockett Johnson's (1965) *Proof of the Pythagorean Theorem (Euclid)*. Oil on masonite and wood. Division of Medicine and Science, National Museum of American History, Smithsonian Institution

For the moment, let us consider three theorems, T1–T3:

(T1) It is impossible to tile an 8×8 grid (with the diagonally opposite corners removed) evenly with domino-shaped tiles, where each tile is the size of two squares.
(T2) $\sqrt{2}$ is not a fraction.
(T3) In any right-angled triangle, the square on the hypotenuse (the side opposite the right angle) is equal in area to the sum of the squares on the other two sides.

T1 is a theorem about tessellation or tiling. T2 is a theorem about the irrational nature of the square root of 2. T3 is a theorem in Euclidean geometry known as the Pythagorean theorem. A visual interpretation of one version of its proof can be found in Fig. 9.1 (more on which later). The proof of T1 could first invoke an empty 8×8 chess board (Fig. 9.2). Relative to this empty board, the diagonally opposite squares are either both light- or dark-coloured. Suppose we remove the pair of diagonally opposite dark-coloured squares. We will be left with a grid containing 32 light-coloured and 30 dark-coloured squares. Each domino-shaped tile will cover exactly one light-coloured square and one dark-coloured square. If 30 domino-shaped tiles are put down, we shall be left with two light-coloured squares that we will not be able to cover (QED).

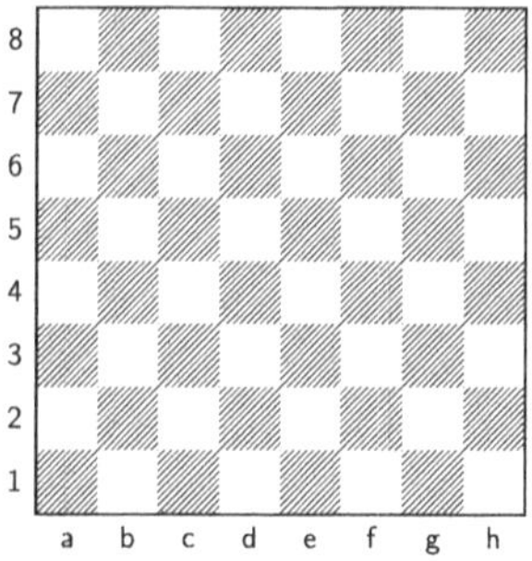

Fig. 9.2 An empty chess board

This proof of T1 does not strike us as being merely correct: it may also be described as elegant. In addition, this elegant is thought somehow to count in its favour. Relative to this elegant proof of T1, Gowers (2002, p. 52) has claimed that mathematical proofs can provide a similar pleasure to music with sudden relevations, unexpected yet natural ideas, and intriguing hints that there is more to be discovered.

At least two proofs exist for T2. For convenience, let us term these proofs Proof 1 and Proof 2. According to Proof 1 of T2:

1. Assume that $\sqrt{2} = p/q$, where p and q are integers. As p and q are in the lowest terms, they have no common factor
2. $\therefore 2 = p^2/q^2$
3. $\therefore p^2 = 2q^2$
4. $\therefore p^2$ is an even number.
5. $\therefore p$ is an even number.
6. $\therefore (2r)^2 = 2q^2$, where $p = 2r$
7. $\therefore 4r^2 = 2q^2$
8. $\therefore 2r^2 = q^2$
9. $\therefore q^2$ is an even number.
10. $\therefore q$ is an even number. However, 1 contradicts 5 and 10, since p and q will have a common factor (2) if they are both even
11. $\therefore$ It cannot be the case that $\sqrt{2} = p/q$ (QED)

Here is Proof 2 of T2:

1. Assume that $p^2 = 2q^2$
2. $\therefore$ As every integer can be factored into primes, there will be a certain number of primes doubled up in p^2, since $p^2 = p \times p$

3. ∴ There will be a certain number of primes doubled up in q^2, since $q^2 = q \times q$
4. However, there is no partner in $2q^2$ for 2 and 2 is a prime number
5. ∴ It cannot be the case that $\sqrt{2} = p/q$ (QED)

Proofs 1 and 2 of T2 illustrate how two proofs could be equally valid for a theorem, although one proof could be more elegant than the other. Most professional mathematicians will say that Proof 2 is more elegant than Proof 1. The application of aesthetic criteria in mathematics is justified, because the aesthetic quality of elegance is related to a purer vision: Proof 2 seems to reveal the heart of the matter, whereas Proof 1 conceals it, starting with a false hypothesis and ending with a contradiction (Davis et al. 2012, pp. 331–332).

As is the case with T2, at least two proofs exist for T3. Again and for convenience, let us term these proofs Proof 1 and Proof 2. Proof 1 of T3, known as Euclid's windmill proof, has been named after the shape of the diagram associated with Proof 1 (Fig. 9.3):

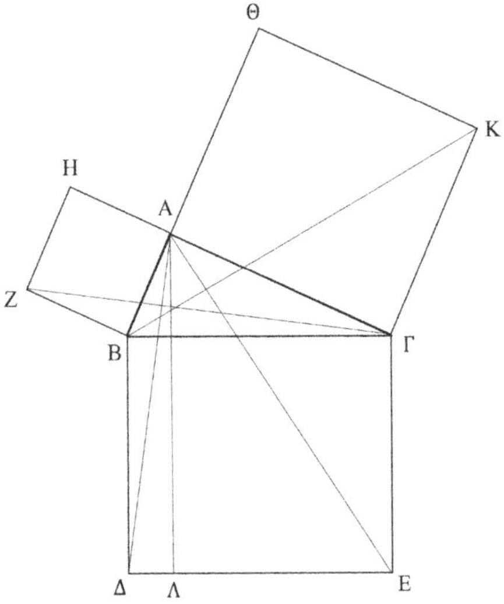

Fig. 9.3 Diagram for Proof 1 of T3 (Newman 1956, p. 191)

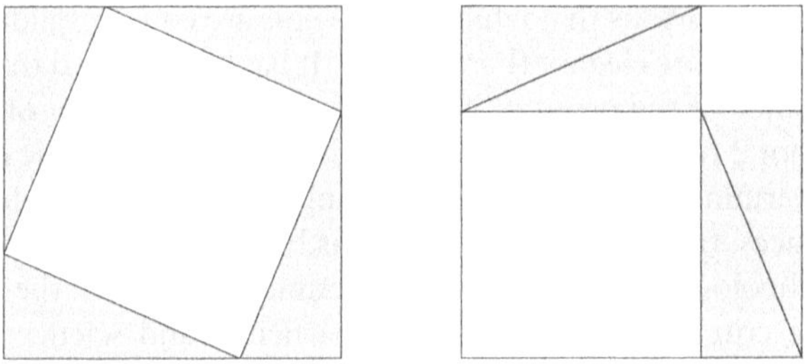

Fig. 9.4 Diagram for Proof 2 of T3 (Glynn 2013, p. 6)

A piece of artistic trivia is associated with the windmill proof: Fig. 9.3 has inspired Crockett Johnson's (1965) *Proof of the Pythagorean Theorem (Euclid)* painting (Fig. 9.1). Here is the rather elaborate Proof 1 in full:

1. Draw the squares on the sides of right $\triangle \mathrm{AB}\Gamma$.
2. $\angle \mathrm{BA}\Gamma = 90°$
3. $\therefore$ ΓA is in a straight line with AH and BA is in a straight line with AΘ.
4. $\angle \Delta \mathrm{B}\Gamma = \angle \mathrm{ZBA} = 90°$ (by construction)
5. $\therefore \angle \Delta \mathrm{BA} = \angle \mathrm{ZB}\Gamma$
6. $\Delta \mathrm{B} = \mathrm{B}\Gamma$ and $\mathrm{ZB} = \mathrm{BA}$
7. $\therefore \Delta \mathrm{B} = \mathrm{B}\Gamma$, $\mathrm{BA} = \mathrm{ZB}$, and $\angle \Delta \mathrm{BA} = \angle \mathrm{ZB}\Gamma$
8. $\therefore \mathrm{A}\Delta = \mathrm{Z}\Gamma$ and $\triangle \mathrm{AB}\Delta = \triangle \mathrm{ZB}\Gamma$
9. $\therefore$ Parallelogram BA is double the area of $\triangle \mathrm{AB}\Delta$
10. $\therefore$ $\square$ZBAH is double the area of $\triangle \mathrm{ZB}\Gamma$.
11. $\therefore$ Parallelogram BΛ and $\square$ZBAH are equal in area.
12. $\therefore$ Parallelogram $\Gamma\Lambda$ and $\square$ AΘKΓ are equal in area.
13. $\therefore \square \mathrm{B}\Delta\mathrm{E}\Gamma = \square \mathrm{ZBAH} + \square \mathrm{A}\Theta\mathrm{K}\Gamma$ (QED)

By contrast, Proof 2 of T3 is associated with the more straightforward Fig. 9.4. We first have four identical right-angled triangles with a frame around them on the left. The area enclosed by the frame is equal to the area of these four triangles plus the area of the central square, which is the square on the hypotenuse. When the triangles are rearranged within the same frame on the right, the area enclosed by the frame is now equal to the area of these four triangles plus the area of two squares, which are squares on the other two sides of the triangle (QED).

It should be obvious that while both proofs are equally valid, Proof 2 of T3 strikes us as more elegant than Proof 1. It has been argued that our sense of the elegance of the proof of T1 and the relative elegance of Proof 2 of T2 and Proof 2 of T3 involves epistemic feelings and aesthetic experiences that are determinate variations of the feeling of fittingness (Todd 2018). In these instances, the feeling of fittingness is both aesthetic and epistemic in nature. A theological justification is sometimes offered for the application of aesthetic criteria in mathematics in particular and science in general. Several scientists believe that God is a mathematician of the highest order who used mathematics to construct the universe (Dirac 1963). Leibniz's cosmic equation is an example of a formula for expressing the universal law of the general order of our world (Grene and Ravetz 1962).[2] The pre-established order in the universe, it is traditionally held, is best understood in terms of its mathematical foundations.[3] Indeed, God has been regarded as an arch-mathematician who, in choosing this world as the best of all possible worlds, chooses to actualize a superequation (the cosmic equation) in which each individual is a particular value.

9.2 Elegance and Mathematical Understanding

There is of course no need to postulate God in order to account for the mathematical nature and associated aesthetic structure of the universe. Aesthetic qualities such as beauty, harmony, order, precision, elegance, clarity, economy, significance, depth, simplicity, comprehensiveness or reach, and insight are the desiderata of mathematics. According to a particular view (known as mathematical platonism), mathematical reality lies outside us and it consists of a realm of abstract, mind-independent mathematical entities. We discover or observe this mathematical reality rather than create it and mathematical theorems are records of our observations. Furthermore, the most excellent or beautiful mathematical reality

[2] According to Grene and Ravetz (1962), a description of the abstract structure of our world can be given in terms of sets, elements, functions that describe relationships between entities, and matrices. An interpretation of the abstract structure of our world can be given in terms of complex variables and power series.

[3] In a related vein, Wiener (1948/2019, p. 12) considers Leibniz to be the patron saint of cybernetics, given his role in the historical development of contemporary mathematical notation and symbolic logic.

is thought to fit observed facts and will provide a map of the physical reality that is the subject matter of science (Osborne 1984). This is in line with the notion of fittingness, which has already been described in the context of the epistemic feelings and aesthetic experiences associated with the application of aesthetic criteria in mathematics.

We shall come to discuss mathematical platonism in Sect. 11.3.[4] Poincaré (1914) has described how new contributions to mathematical theory are guided less by purely intellectual considerations than by the feeling of mathematical beauty.[5] There is, however, an important difference between the function of elegance and related aesthetic qualities in art and their function in mathematics. Elegance may be a goal sufficient in itself in art. In mathematics and the other sciences, elegance is never a goal in itself but rather a signpost likely to lead to the goal of correct understanding (Osborne 1984).[6] Aesthetic criteria have both an aesthetic and an epistemic nature here. Our discussion of the various proofs of T1–T3 should suggest as much.

Given certain considerations about the mathematical nature and associated aesthetic structure of the universe, we may conclude that the aesthetic qualities (beauty, elegance, and so on) are equally at home and in their element in the artistic and mathematical realms. Furthermore, it is not merely plausible but rather desirable for aesthetic criteria to be applied in mathematics. An elegantly executed proof, such as LT's proof of T2.85 or Proof 2 of T1, may be compared to a poem in all but the form in which it has been written (Kline 1964, p. 470). A proof is elegant if it is short, does not contain any complicated steps, and makes use (when possible) of an unforeseen idea (Engler 1990). The hallmarks of mathematical understanding in particular and scientific understanding in general include coherence, harmony, and inevitability of fit (fittingness).

[4] To anticipate matters in Sect. 11.3, we will incur similar ontological commitments in the artistic domain when defending our computationalist approach to aesthetics. Our view may therefore be described as a platonist one.

[5] In theoretical physics, Einstein (1935/2011) uses the term 'simplicity' instead of 'beauty'. He believes that our search is for the simplest possible system of thought that will bind together the observed facts. By the simplest system is meant the system that contains the fewest possible mutually independent postulates or axioms necessary to support the structure of the theory.

[6] Philosophy is closer to science in this regard: while we may admire a philosophical system for the beauty of its coherence and compactness, what we demand from each system beyond these aesthetic qualities is the property of truth.

Therefore, aesthetic criteria can play an epistemic role as an indication of understanding (Kosso 2002).

9.3 Logic Theorist

We have already identified the central artistic task as consisting of an art-specific challenge to be overcome or problem to be solved, the overcoming or solving of which is conditional on the available materials at the disposal of each artist (Chap. 8). This account of the central artistic task fits neatly into the terms of the theory of problem-solving, which explains human problem-solving behaviour in terms of a problem space, a search strategy, heuristics, evaluating and choosing among alternative actions, and a goal to be accomplished (Chap. 5). Another important benefit arises from our reliance on the theory of problem-solving. More than a mere ivory-tower view about the nature of problem-solving behaviour, the theory of problem-solving has been followed through with the conscientious programming of computer systems capable of solving various problems.

One of the computer programs developed in accordance with the theory of problem-solving is the Logic Theorist (hereafter: LT). LT is an example of a computer program capable of mathematical problem-solving behaviour: it can construct proofs of theorems in elementary symbolic logic (Newell et al. 1957, 1958).[7] LT employs the sentential calculus found in Chapters 1 and 2 of the *Principia Mathematica* of Whitehead and Russell (1910, 1912, 1913/1956). Presented with the first 52 logical theorems in Chapter 2 of the *Principia*, LT managed to prove 38 (or 73.1%) of these 52 theorems. About half of the proofs were constructed in less than a minute each; most of the remainder took from one to five minutes; and a few theorems were proven in times ranging from 15 to 45 minutes.

Here is a set of theorems from the *Principia*:[8]

(T2.16) $\vdash: (p \to q) \to (\neg q \to \neg p)$
(T2.2) $\vdash: p \to (p \vee q)$
(T2.46) $\vdash: \neg(p \vee q) \to \neg p$

[7] Mathematicians typically distinguish between theorems, proofs, and conjectures. A theorem is a true statement that is deducible relative to a formal system L. A proof is an explanation of why a statement is true. By contrast, a conjecture is a statement we believe to be true, but for which no proof currently exists.

[8] I have retained the original enumeration for each theorem.

(T2.85) $\vdash$: $(p \vee q) \rightarrow (p \vee r) \rightarrow (p \vee (q \rightarrow r))$
(T2.31) $\vdash$: $(p \vee (q \vee r)) \rightarrow ((p \vee q) \vee r)$

LT was able to furnish proofs for T.216, T2.2, T2.46, T2.85, and 34 other theorems. Conversely, T2.31 was among the 14 theorems that it was unable to prove. After 23 minutes, LT reported that it had exhausted its resources and was still unable to prove T2.31. Recall our characterization of a problem (artistic or non-artistic) in terms of finding a member of a subset *S* of *P* having certain properties, given a set *P* of elements (Sect. 8.3). If no limits are imposed on the properties on proofs (length, rules of formation, and so on), then set *P* will contain an infinite number of possible sequences of expressions in symbolic logic.

Suppose that we restrict *P* to proofs consisting of sequences of not more than 20 expressions in symbolic logic, with each expression consisting of no more than 23 symbols in length and involving only the propositional variables p, q, r, s, and t and the logical connectives $\vee$ (or) and $\rightarrow$ (if $\cdots$ then). In this instance, the number of possible proofs in *S* has been estimated at 10^{235} (Newell et al. 1959). 10^{235} is a large and arbitrary number, especially compared with the game tree complexities of tic-tac-toe (10^5; see Sect. 5.5) and chess (10^{120}; see Sect. 8.3), and it will simply not do to run a brute-force search or test through trial and error each of the 10^{235} possible proofs in order to determine the desired proof of a particular theorem. We need to bring this task down to manageable proportions.

A British Museum algorithm can help us to generate members of *P* in a more constrained fashion.[9] Relative to this algorithm, we consider only sequences of expressions in symbolic logic that are valid proofs and proceed by first generating proofs that consist of a single expression (the axioms), before generating proofs two expressions long, and so on. A set *P* that has been generated in accordance with the British Museum algorithm will contain an estimated 10^8 or a hundred million possible sequences of expressions in symbolic logic, which is an advance on 10^{235}, although even more effective methods will be needed if problems in symbolic logic are to be solved within a reasonable amount of time.[10] If we take an average of

[9] The British Museum algorithm is a general approach to finding a solution that involves checking all possibilities one by one, beginning with the smallest (in this case: an axiom or a proof that is a single expression in length).

[10] It has been estimated that these 10^8 sequences of expressions will allow us to obtain all the theorems in Chapter 2 of the *Principia* (Newell et al. 1959).

two minutes to write down each sequence of expressions in symbolic logic, then we would need about 380 years to write down all the 10^8 possible sequences of expressions.[11]

9.4 LT's Methods

LT has four rules of inference: substitution, replacement, detachment, and syllogism (Newell et al. 1958). In a substitution, by uniformly substituting (say) $p \vee q$ for p in a true expression $(p \vee p) \rightarrow p$, we can derive another true expression $((p \vee q) \vee (p \vee q)) \rightarrow (p \vee q)$. In a replacement, $(p \rightarrow q)$ is defined as $(\neg p \vee q)$ and the two can be used interchangeably. In a detachment, if p is a true expression and $p \rightarrow q$ is a true expression, then q may be written down as a true expression. In a syllogism (chaining), if $p \rightarrow q$ is a true expression and $q \rightarrow r$ is a true expression, then $p \rightarrow r$ is also a true expression.

The methods of LT are based on these four rules of inference: substitution, detachment, forward chaining, and backward chaining. In forward chaining, if $p \rightarrow r$ is desired and $p \rightarrow q$ is already known, then it is sufficient to prove that $q \rightarrow r$. In backward chaining, if $p \rightarrow r$ is desired and $q \rightarrow r$ is already known, then it is sufficient to prove that $p \rightarrow q$. Previous experience in theorem-proving also matters, methodologically speaking. If LT has proven a theorem, then this theorem is stored in its memory and remains available as raw material for the proof of subsequent theorems. Furthermore, if the same subproblem has been obtained twice in the course of an attempt at a proof, LT will remember and refrain from trying to solve the subproblem a second time if it has already failed to do so once.

9.5 LT's Elegant Proof

LT is a useful case study for a number of reasons. Firstly, LT is a concrete example of the explanation afforded by the theory of problem-solving. Secondly, it is a successful example: it can furnish proofs of logical theorems in Chapter 2 of the *Principia* about three times out of four (Sect. 9.3). Thirdly, it is an art-relevant example: LT is capable of producing artifacts

[11] 2×10^8 (number of minutes) $\div$ 1440 (number of minutes per day) $\div$ 365 (number of days per year) $\approx$ 380 (number of years).

that possess the aesthetic quality of elegance. To be precise, LT discovered a proof for one theorem that is shorter, more elegant, and possibly more publication-worthy than the one published in Whitehead and Russell (1910, 1912, 1913/1956) (Newell et al. 1959).[12] All this should excite us: both LT and our computationalist approach to art-making are supported by the same theory of problem-solving. Our concern is with art-making or the process in which art-makers produce artifacts that they hope will be regarded as works of art. LT instantiates the process in which certain artifacts (proofs of logical theorems) are produced. While none of these artifacts (though mathematically respectable) are regarded as works of art, at least some of these artifacts possess aesthetic qualities (elegance).

Recall how T2.85 was among the 38 theorems that LT could prove (Sect. 9.3):

(T2.85) $\vdash$: $(p \vee q) \rightarrow (p \vee r) \rightarrow (p \vee (q \rightarrow r))$

Here is the correct version of LT's proof of T2.85 (Drucker 2009, p. 52):[13]

1. $(p \rightarrow q) \rightarrow ((q \rightarrow r) \rightarrow (p \rightarrow r))$ — T2.06 (Syllogism)
2. $(q \rightarrow (p \vee q)) \rightarrow ((p \vee q) \rightarrow (p \vee r)) \rightarrow (q \rightarrow (p \vee r))$ — Apply R1 to 1
3. $q \rightarrow (p \vee q)$ — T1.3 (Addition)

[12] At the same time, the *Journal of Symbolic Logic* declined to published an article, co-authored by LT, detailing this more elegant proof. The editors objected that the same theorem could be proven using certain metatheorems that were available to neither Whitehead and Russell nor LT.

[13] The first step of the proof of T2.85 relies on T2.06 or the principle of the syllogism (whose proof is already known). The second step applies substitution and uniformly substitutes q for p, $p \vee q$ for q, and $p \vee r$ for r throughout line 1 of the proof. The third step of the proof invokes T1.3 or the addition rule (whose proof is already known). The fourth step applies the *modus ponens* rule of inference (R3) to lines 2 and 3 of the proof. A definition $((p \rightarrow q) \leftrightarrow (\neg p \vee q))$ and its replacement permit us to derive line 5 from line 4 of the proof: we replace the logical connective $(q \rightarrow (p \vee r))$ by its definition $(\neg q \vee (p \vee r))$. The sixth step appeals to T1.5 or the associative principle (whose proof is already known). The seventh step applies substitution to 6 and uniformly substitutes $\neg q$ for p and p for q. The eighth step chains lines 5 and 7. Last but not least, the ninth step applies definition $((p \rightarrow q) \leftrightarrow (\neg p \vee q))$ and its replacement, allowing us to derive line 9 from line 8 by replacing $(\neg q \vee r)$ with $(q \rightarrow r)$. This completes the proof of T2.85.

4. $(p \vee q) \rightarrow (p \vee r) \rightarrow (q \rightarrow (p \vee r))$ — Apply R3 (*modus ponens*) to 2 & 3
5. $(p \vee q) \rightarrow (p \vee r) \rightarrow (\neg q \vee (p \vee r))$ — Apply D2 & R2 to 4
6. $(p \vee (q \vee r)) \rightarrow (q \vee (p \vee r))$ — T1.5 (Association)
7. $(\neg q \vee (p \vee r)) \rightarrow (p \vee (\neg q \vee r))$ — Apply R1 to 6
8. $(p \vee q) \rightarrow (p \vee r) \rightarrow (p \vee (\neg q \vee r))$ — Chain with 5 & 7
9. $(p \vee q) \rightarrow (p \vee r) \rightarrow (p \vee (q \rightarrow r))$ — Apply D2 & R2 to 8 (QED)

LT's proof of T2.85, constructed without human aid, is shorter than the original proof of Whitehead and Russell (1910, 1912, 1913/1956) and does not contain any complicated steps, so it has a claim to being more elegant.[14] In an epistolary exchange in 1956 between Herbert Simon and Bertrand Russell about LT's proof of T2.85, Simon conveyed LT's proof of T2.85, asserted that this proof was both straightforward and unobvious, and conceded that the AI researchers responsible for LT were struck by the virtuosity of their own theorem-proving program. In his response to Simon, Russell shared his delight in learning that the *Principia* could be mechanized and expressed his willingness to believe that everything in deductive logic could be done by machinery.

9.6 Machine Creativity

The ability of LT to show virtuosity in its proof of T2.85 prompts the question: can machines create? One might respond with the claim that machines can create and human beings are examples of such machines. We might accept the view that humans are machines, while clarifying that our concern is specifically about whether silicon- rather than carbon-based machines can create. A proper response to this question, however, may involve an analysis of creativity. Rhodes (1961) distinguishes the 4 Ps of creativity: person, process, press, and products. The term 'person' includes information about personality, intellect, temperament, traits, habits, attitudes, self-concept, value systems, and so on. The term 'process' refers to motivation, perception, learning, thinking, and communication. The term 'press' refers to the relationship between persons and their environment.

[14] Compare with Proof 2 of T2 (more elegant than Proof 1 of the same theorem) and Proof 2 of T3 (more elegant than Proof 1 of the same theorem) (Sect. 9.1).

Last but not least, the term 'product' refers to the embodiment of an idea in tangible form (for instance, words, paint, clay, metal, and so on).[15]

An approach to machine creativity could focus on the product or artifact: this approach is associated with the Turing test for creativity.[16] A machine passes the Turing test, just in case it can produce a work that is indistinguishable from one produced by a human being in a creative domain and it is seen as having as much value as the one produced by the human being (Boden 2010). However, it seems that we could still ask whether the machine is really creative even after it has passed such a Turing test. Researchers on machine creativity may therefore focus on the process and the capacities required for creativity (for instance, imagination or the ability to understand, evaluate, and appreciate the nature of art in the case of artistic creativity).

Considerations about fairness and equality of opportunity may persuade us against excluding machines *a priori* and preventing them from competing with human beings on an equal footing, with respect to the challenge of fashioning or constructing an artifact (a logical proof, a work of art, and so on) that qualifies as a creative work. In addition, empirical trends concerning technological progress suggest that machines will only get better at passing the Turing test for creativity, making it harder for us to shut the door outright on machines as technology pushes itself in. If the fear is about the competitive angle between humans and machines, then human-machine co-creation and collaboration could help to ease these fears, while still ensuring that machine creativity remains a live option.[17]

If we adopt a liberal approach and leave the door open for machine creativity, then LT may be identified as an instance of machine creativity. Are there any test criteria for machine creativity? It is typically held that one test criterion would involve machines surprising us. The appeal to surprise as a test criterion, without further clarification, is unsatisfactory. To help us distinguish between the relevant and irrelevant senses of surprise in

[15] We may think of products as artifacts of thoughts.

[16] See also the Turing test or acting humanly approach to AI research in Sect. 12.1.

[17] Similar ideas and arguments may be traced to Coeckelbergh (2016). Coeckelbergh displays a natural sympathy toward a computationalist account of creativity, although his philosophical outlook does not have the support from the theory of problem-solving that ours enjoys. We are anticipating matters that shall be discussed in greater detail in Sect. 10.3.

the context of machine creativity, consider the following expression in the context of first-order logic:

$\forall x(Px \rightarrow Q(Px))$

Px (the antecedent in the universally quantified expression) is a first-order predicate. In first-order logic, predicates such as P and Q can only take individual terms (such as x) as arguments.[18] $Q(Px)$ (the consequent) is a predicate that takes another first-order predicate Px as its argument. This entails that $\forall x(Px \rightarrow Q(Px))$ is nonsensical in first-order logic. Suppose we feed a theorem-prover an input file containing this nonsensical expression in first-order logic, the fact that Pa, and an assumption that $\neg Q(Pa)$. We may get this proof from the output file of our theorem-prover (Bringsjord et al. 2001, p. 220):[19]

```
------- PROOF -------
1 [] P(x)|Q(P(x)).
2 [] -Q(P(a)).
3 [] P(a).
4 [hyper,3,1] Q(P(a)).
5 [binary,4.1,2.1] $F.
------- end of proof -------
```

The semantic bug involves the theorem-prover reinterpreting parts of its code in such a way that Pa is at once a first-order predicate (line 3) and a second-order predicate (line 4). We are not interested in the sort of surprise that arises with semantic bugs when relying on surprise as a test criterion for machine creativity. Rather, we are interested in surprise in the epistemic sense, and it is this sense of surprise that Bringsjord et al. (2001) incorporate into their version of the Turing test for creativity, termed the

[18] By contrast, predicates can take both individual terms and other predicates as arguments in second-order logic.

[19] Line 1 of the proof accepts as true the universal implication $\forall x(Px \rightarrow Q(Px))$. Line 2 of the proof accepts as true $\neg Q(Pa)$. Line 3 accepts as true the fact that Pa. Through hyper-resolution in line 4, we resolve lines 1 ($\forall x(Px \rightarrow Q(Px))$) and 3 ($Pa$) to derive $Q(Pa)$. Through binary resolution of $\neg Q(Pa)$ and $Q(Pa)$ (lines 2 and 4), we derive the contradiction $Q(Pa) \wedge \neg Q(Pa)$, which is a falsehood F. Instead of receiving an error message (which we should expect, since $\forall x(Px \rightarrow Q(Px))$ is nonsensical in first-order logic), we get a proof that $Q(Pa)$.

Lovelace test.[20] According to the Lovelace test, a machine *M*, designed by its human architect *H*, passes the Lovelace test, just in case *M* outputs some work *w* (say, a logical proof or a work of art), *M*'s outputting of *w* is the result not of a fluke hardware error but rather processes that *M* can repeat, and *H* (or someone who knows what *H* knows and has *H*'s resources) cannot explain how *M* produced *w* by appealing to *M*'s architecture, knowledge base, and core functions.

LT is a candidate for a machine that has successfully passed the Lovelace test: it has generated 38 proofs for logical theorems in Chapter 2 of the *Principia* as a result of a specific method.[21] These proofs are not the result of a fluke hardware error or a semantic bug. In the case of LT's proof of T2.85, we have good reason to believe that LT's human architects were taken by surprise (in the epistemic sense) by LT's discovery of a more elegant proof. As Simon's epistolary exchange in 1956 with Russell indicates, even the programmers may be surprised (in the epistemic sense) at the output of their own machine (Sect. 9.5). All other things being equal, LT has a good claim to having passed the Lovelace test.

More generally, LT demonstrates how conscientious programming based on the theory of problem-solving can give rise to programs capable of producing artifacts that are both (possibly) creative and the sources of aesthetic experiences. To be certain, these aesthetic experiences occur outside the artistic realm. Nonetheless, our hope that a computationalist approach to art-making and the production of works of art will succeed in the context of the philosophy of art should be strengthened by the empirical case study of LT. After all, both LT and our computationalist approach are cut from the same theoretical cloth: the theory of problem-solving. We shall have more to say about the creative aspect of art-making in the next chapter.

[20] The Lovelace test has been named in honour of Lady Lovelace, who believed that only when computers originate things can they be believed to have minds. We will discuss the Lovelace objection to machine creativity in Sect. 13.2.

[21] As discussed, this method consists of certain rules of inference (substitution, detachment, forward chaining, and backward chaining) and memory of previous experience.

CHAPTER 10

The Creative Aspect of Art-Making

10.1 Creativity as an Understudied Phenomenon

We have already described the central artistic task in terms of a challenge to be overcome or a problem to be solved, conditional on the available materials at the disposal of each artist (Chap. 8). We should not forget that this task also characteristically involves the exhibition of creative thinking. In Chap. 9, we identified an analysis of creativity in terms of the 4 Ps: person, process, press, and products (Sect. 9.6). Creativity, whether in terms of person, process, press, or product, remains a relatively understudied phenomenon in the philosophy of art, much to the detriment of our understanding of art. For instance, Picasso's radical departure from classical representation in *Les Demoiselles d'Avignon* exemplifies the creative dimensions of the central artistic task: confronting and resolving artistic and conceptual problems within the constraints of available materials and cultural context (Fig. 10.1). The fragmented female figures, multiple perspectives, non-Western influences, and bold departure from tradition reflect not only the creative person and process, but also the press of social and artistic pressures at the time. This audacious painting paved the way for Cubism, transformed the landscape of modern art, and represents creativity of the highest order.

M. Chen, *Art-Making as Problem-Solving*,
https://doi.org/10.1007/978-3-031-90639-8_10

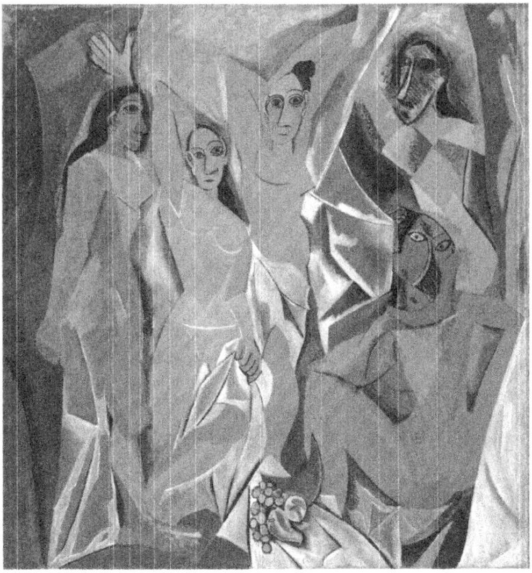

Fig. 10.1 Pablo Picasso's (1907) *Les Demoiselles d'Avignon*. Oil on canvas. Acquired through the Lillie P. Bliss Bequest. Acc. no.: 333.1939. Digital image, The Museum of Modern Art, New York/Scala, Florence

In a related vein, Paul and Kaufman (2014) take issue with the philosophical tendency to ignore the scientific literature on creativity. Last but not least, where philosophical research has been conducted, it may lack the requisite intellectual rigour. Stokes (2014) laments how few philosophers devote proper attention to the conceptual distinction between creativity and imagination. It may be observed that the philosophy of creativity is referred to far less often than other branches of philosophy (logic, aesthetics, metaphysics, epistemology, and so on) relative to the Google text corpus in English (Fig. 10.2).[1]

Until 1950, creativity remained similarly understudied by psychologists. In his presidential address to the American Psychological Association, Guilford (1950) identified the significance of creativity across a range of

[1] At the same time, it should be noted that the Google Ngram Viewer diagram in Fig. 10.2 only goes up to 2019, the most recent year covered in its dataset. There has been a lot of effort in recent years to address the relative philosophical neglect of creativity and related notions such as the imagination, as exemplified by Gaut and Kieran's (2018) *Creativity & Philosophy* and Kind and Langkau's (forthcoming) *Oxford Handbook of Philosophy of Imagination & Creativity*. We are grateful to a pre-publication reviewer for having prompted us to add nuance to our original claim.

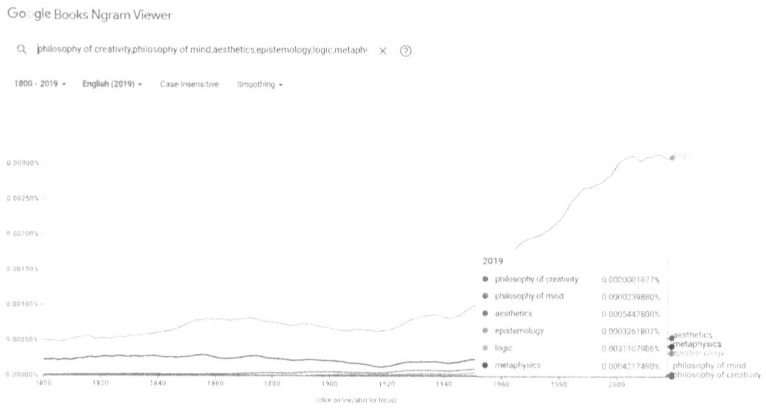

Fig. 10.2 Google Ngram Viewer diagram of the frequencies of 'philosophy of creativity', 'philosophy of mind', 'aesthetics', 'epistemology', 'metaphysics', and 'logic' relative to the Google text corpus in English. Retrieved on 13 Jan 2024

domains (industry, science, arts, education, and so on) and lamented the relative absence of research on the nature of creativity. One statistic stood out as particularly damning: only 186 out of about 121,000 entries listed in the index of the *Psychological Abstracts* between 1927 and 1950 were about creativity, imagination, and related notions. Since then, we have witnessed a comparatively greater volume of creative cognition research (Csikszentmihalyi 1997; Kaufman and Sternberg 2010; Koestler 1964; Weisberg 2006). At the same time, the psychological study of creativity continues to pale in comparison with other phenomena such as concepts, imagination, folk mind-reading abilities, and so on.

According to our computationalist approach to art-making, the central artistic task consists of challenges being overcome and problems being solved, conditional on the artist's material constraints, and the exhibition of creative thinking. Given the understudied nature of creativity in both psychology and the philosophy of art, we might have good reason to expect a theoretical lacuna as far as creativity is concerned. The surprisingly good news, however, is that the theory of problem-solving possesses a theoretical plank that allows it to specifically address creative thinking. We shall rely on this theoretical plank in the extension of our computationalist approach to cover concerns about creativity.

10.2 Creative Thinking

We have already characterized the theory of problem-solving as a computationalist approach to problem-solving that may trace its intellectual origins to the research paradigm of Allen Newell, Herbert Simon, and their collaborators at Carnegie Mellon University and the RAND Corporation in the late 1950s (Sect. 5.3). In addition, we have learnt how this theory of problem-solving describes problem-solving behaviour in terms of a task environment, a problem space, a search strategy, heuristics, evaluating and choosing among alternative actions, and a goal to be accomplished (Sect. 5.4). We shall now find out how a theoretical plank exists within this theory of problem-solving, according to which creative thinking refers to a special class of activities characterized by novelty, unconventionality, persistence, and a difficulty in problem formulation (Newell et al. 1959).

Einstein's discovery of the special theory of relativity, Woolf's crafting of her modernist novel *To the Lighthouse*, Picasso's painting of the *Guernica* mural, and Beethoven's composition of Symphony No. 7 in A major constitute famous examples of creative problem-solving in the domains of physics, literature, art, and music. The products of creative thinking have novelty and value, creative thinking is unconventional and typically requires the modification or rejection of previously-accepted ideas, creative thinking requires persistence either over a considerable span of time or at a high intensity, and part of the creative task may involve formulating a less vague and ill-defined version of the original problem. The good news is that everything we have learnt about problem-solving remains applicable to the creative aspect of the central artistic task, since creative thinking is a special class of problem-solving activities.

10.3 Computationalism About Creativity

The good news does not end there. Recall our discussion of the computational theory of mind, according to which the human mind is an information-processing system whose computations are similar to computations that may be executed by a Turing machine (Sect. 5.3). Notwithstanding the relatively understudied nature of creativity in psychology and the philosophy of art (Sect. 10.1), a computationalist account of creativity exists that equally takes it for granted that the human mind is an information-processing system. Furthermore, this computationalist account of creativity may be regarded as a natural extension of the theory of problem-solving.

Various definitions of computationalism about creativity exist (Cardoso and Wiggins 2007; Colton and Wiggins 2012):

> Computationalism about creativity $\stackrel{\text{def}_1}{=}$ The study and simulation, by computers, of behaviour (natural or artificial) that would, if observed in humans, be deemed creative;
>
> Computationalism about creativity $\stackrel{\text{def}_2}{=}$ The philosophy, science, and engineering of computational systems that exhibit behaviours that unbiased observers would deem to be creative.

Our aim here is not to settle the issue concerning how best computationalism about creativity might be defined or understood but rather to introduce a particular computationalist account of creativity that may be considered as a natural extension of the theory of problem-solving: Margaret Boden's account.

According to this account of creativity, we must first understand the distinction between improbabilist and impossibilist creativity (Boden 2004, 1994). Improbabilist creativity refers to novel combinations of familiar ideas that are positively valued, whereas impossibilist creativity refers to novel ideas that have never appeared before. The ideas generated under impossibilist creativity that could never have been generated before arise through the mapping, exploration, and transformation of the conceptual space (METCS). Combinatorial creativity involves novel combinations of familiar ideas and it is associated with metaphorical or analogical thinking. Exploratory creativity involves exploring novel possibilities within a conceptual space. Transformational creativity involves a radical and significant transformation of an existing conceptual space, going beyond the mere recombination of familiar ideas or the exploration of a conceptual space to the limits of its boundaries.

Since the problem space is the space within which possible solutions to problems are conceptualized, we may take the concept space to be broadly equivalent to the problem space. In addition, recall our discussion of genre- and medium-relevant constraints (Sect. 8.2). While these constraints are constraints within which the artist has to work, the transformation of conceptual space under Boden's (2004, 1994) computationalist approach to creativity implies that it is precisely these constraints that may undergo transformation as a result of the creative artistic process. Given their shared commitment to computationalism and similar approaches to understanding problem-solving and creativity in terms of the navigation of a space (problem or conceptual), the theory of problem-solving and Boden's (2004, 1994) computationalist account of creativity may be regarded as boon companions. Further gloss is added to our account by a careful consideration of Stokes's (2006) account of creativity in terms of constraints that are precluded and promoted in relation to particular arts.[2] The problem space, in which a problem is represented, has an initial state, a goal state, a set of operations that allow us to move from the initial state toward the goal state, and a set of constraints that help us to structure the solution path by precluding (limiting) and promoting (directing) search in the problem space.

Cubism is an example of a transformational moment in the history of art and music: it involves a departure from the traditional approach to perspective (one- or two-point).[3] For instance, Leonardo da Vinci's (c. 1495–1498) *The Last Supper* relies on one-point perspective: lines converge to a single vanishing point at the centre of the work, where Jesus Christ sits. By contrast, Masaccio's (c. 1426–1428) *The Holy Trinity* relies on two-point perspective. The first vanishing point may be located at eye level at the base of the cross and the second vanishing point, it has been argued, is located roughly at the height indicated by the Madonna's extended right hand (Bryson 1983, p. 108). Da Vinci's *The Last Supper* and Masaccio's *The Holy Trinity* are examples of works of art that heed the traditional approach to perspective. Their goal constraint, shared with representational paintings at large, remains to paint what you see (Stokes 2006).

The initial state of Cubism is the goal constraint for representational painting: painting what you see. The constraints precluded by Cubism include one-point perspective, local colour, and illusion of depth, while the constraints promoted by Cubism include multiple-point perspective, a

[2] We must extend our gratitude to a pre-publication reviewer for having alerted us to the intellectual kinship or affinity between the ideas of Patricia D. Stokes and ours and suggested how her ideas could be fruitfully recruited in support of our computationalist account of art-making as problem-solving.

[3] It should be added that this traditional approach to perspective creates the illusion of depth and three-dimensional space on a two-dimensional surface. With respect to a one-point perspective, all the lines converge toward a single vanishing point on the horizon. With respect to a two-point perspective, there are two vanishing points on the horizon, and lines converge toward them.

monochromatic palette, and a flat, patterned picture plane. This eventually yields the goal state of Cubism (which also happens to be the goal constraint of Cubism): painting what you know (Stokes 2006). Pablo Picasso's (1907) *Les Demoiselles d'Avignon*, an example of a Cubist work of art, relies on multiple-point perspective: the faces and bodies exhibit multiple perspectives simultaneously. Cubism, dropping the constraint of linear perspective, combines multiple perspectives into a single picture plane, shattering the illusion of depth and three-dimensional space.

Capablanca chess is an example of a transformational moment in the history of chess. With the proliferation of chess theory, book moves, and retrograde analysis, at least some parts of the chess world have been bedevilled by the fear that the game of chess may be played out, leading to the death of chess (Gligoric 2003). In *The Adventure of Chess*, Emanuel Lasker (1950) describes Capablanca chess, a variant of chess invented by the eponymous José Raúl Capablanca in the 1920s to address these worries and concerns. Capablanca chess includes two fairy chess pieces that are not used in standard chess: the archbishop (♘) and the chancellor (♞). The archbishop is placed between the queen's knight and the queen's bishop, while the chancellor is placed between the king's knight and the king's bishop (Gollon 1974). Each player starts with ten pawns, a king, a queen, two bishops, an archbishop, a chancellor, two knights, and two rooks. Figure 10.3 shows the game-initial position in Capablanca chess. In effect, Capablanca chess represents a transformation of the problem space of chess from an 8 × 8 board to a 10 × 8 board, with the inclusion of two new fairy pieces.

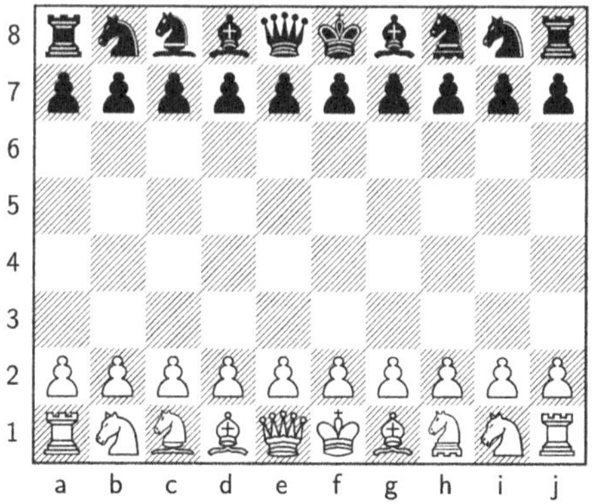

Fig. 10.3 Game-initial position in Capablanca chess on a 10 × 8 board, with the archbishops and chancellors on the c- and h-files respectively

Table 10.1 The C major scale

Note	*C (key)*		*D*		*E*		*F*		*G*		*A*		*B*		*C′*
Interval		1		1		1/2		1		1		1		1/2	

Table 10.2 The D major scale

Note	*D (key)*		*E*		*F♯*		*G*		*A*		*B*		*C♯*		*D′*
Interval		1		1		1/2		1		1		1		1/2	

The atonal music of Arnold Schoenberg represents another transformational moment in the history of art and music: it involves a departure from traditional harmonic structures and a dropping of the tonal constraint. To understand the revolutionary nature of Schoenberg's musical compositions, we must first understand how keys, scales, and tonality work. A key is the lowest or base tone of a group of pitches or notes. A scale refers to the internal structure of intervals within a group of pitches or notes. Where 1 denotes a whole tone and 1/2 denotes a half tone, any scale consisting of the sequence of whole and half tones 1 1 1/2 1 1 1 1/2 is a major scale. Here is the representation of the C major scale, where C′ denotes the note one octave above C (Table 10.1).

The C major scale does not have any flat (♭) or sharp (♯) notes. The D major scale follows the same 1 1 1/2 1 1 1 1/2 sequence as the C major scale, although it has two sharp notes (F♯ and C♯) (Table 10.2).

Whereas major scales follow the 1 1 1/2 1 1 1 1/2 sequence, minor scales follow the 1 1/2 1 1 1/2 1 1/2 sequence. An example of a minor scale would be the C minor scale (Table 10.3). The major and minor scales were used almost exclusively in Western music from about 1600 to the beginning of the twentieth century. Another scale, the pentatonic scale, follows the 1 1½ 1 1 1½ sequence: it is used in much Asian and African music. The major and minor scales may be contrasted with the chromatic scale (Table 10.4).

Schoenberg's twelve-tone method, inaugurated in his *Five Piano Pieces*, op. 23 and *Serenade*, op. 24 in 1923, is a method of composing with the twelve tones of the chromatic scale.[4] These notes can be arranged

[4] Schoenberg's music is also known as dodecaphonic music.

Table 10.3 The C minor scale

Note	*C (key)*		*D*		*E♭*		*F*		*G*		*A♭*		*B*		*C′*
Interval		1		1/2		1		1		1/2		1		1/2	

in any order whatsoever, but each note must appear exactly once before a sequence (known as a tone row) is completed. Gone are the tonal hierarchies of the major and minor scales, where the other notes revolve around the key (tonic or home note). In Schoenberg's revolutionary system, there is complete democracy in each tone row. Only the position of each note relative to its immediate predecessors would matter (Maor 2018).

If each of the twelve notes appears exactly once in a tone row and we ignore shifts by octaves, then a composer can choose from 12! (or 479,001,600) possible tone rows or sequences. With this twelve-tone method, Schoenberg effectively abandoned tonality, as none of the notes in tone rows are bound to home keys. Adorno (2006), who considered the possibilities of tonality to have already been thoroughly explored, famously contrasted the twelve-tone method of Schoenberg (representing progress and emancipation) with the neoclassical tendencies of Stravinsky (representing barbarism and regression). We can apply Stokes's (2006) framework of creativity in terms of constraints (goal constraints, precluded constraints, and promoted constraints) to an analysis of atonal music: the initial state or goal constraint for traditional tonal music is the establishment of a home key or point of reference around which the harmony and melodies are organized; the precluded constraints include the major and minor scales, the tonal centres, and the conventional chord progressions; the promoted constraints include twelve-tone tone rows, democracy in each tone row, and an emphasis on pitch-class relations; and the goal state (or goal constraint of atonal music) is the avoidance of tonal hierarchy and the equal treatment of all pitches.

10.4 Demystification

Besides their shared commitment to computationalism and similar approaches to understanding problem-solving and creativity in terms of the navigation of a space (Sect. 10.3), both the theory of problem-solving

Table 10.4 The chromatic scale

Note	C		C♯		D		D♯		E		F		F♯		G		G♯		A		A♯		B		C′
Interval		1/2		1/2		1/2		1/2		1/2		1/2		1/2		1/2		1/2		1/2		1/2		1/2	

and the computationalist account of creativity embody a thorough-going commitment to demystify reality through explanation. Intelligence, problem-solving, art, and creativity, often clouded in mystery, are regarded by computationalists as various puzzles to be solved by science. We have already learnt about the application of aesthetic criteria in science and discovered how scientific considerations may be guided by aesthetic qualities such as beauty, elegance, and simplicity (Sect. 9.1). Scientists aspire toward simplicity and elegance in their explanations and computationalists about art and creativity ought to be no different in this regard.

A possible concern may however arise, having to do with the draining of wonder from our experience of the world, once it has been rendered in simple and cut-and-dried terms. Simon and Newell (1971) compare the activity of problem-solving to the activity of a magician pulling a rabbit from the hat and suggest that the audience can respond with either mystification or curiosity. Curiosity is the scientist's natural attitude toward a mystery and computationalists like Newell and Simon are committed to explaining the phenomenon of human beings solving unfamiliar problems. Even if there is a relative simplicity to the phenomenon, once explained in terms of information processes and schemes of heuristic search, there should not be dismay or disappointment but rather an appreciation of the simplicity underlying the superficial complexity.

In Keats's poem *Lamia*, it is lamented that cold philosophy can '[u]nweave a rainbow' and destroy the beauty of the natural world.[5] Dawkins's (2000) *Unweaving the Rainbow* points out that natural science reveals rather than destroys the beauty of the natural world. Both the theory of problem-solving and the computationalist account of creativity concur with Dawkins (as do we). In a remarkably similar passage, Boden (2004) draws attention to our wonder at the ability of the hoverly to fly to its mate hovering nearby so as to mate in midair. However, the flight path of the hoverfly is determined by a simple and inflexible rule, hardwired into its brain. In accordance with this rule, a certain visual signal is transformed into a specific muscular response. Just as the theory of problem-solving is designed to increase our wonder at the simplicity of information processes underlying problem-solving behaviour, the computationalist account of

[5] The tongue-in-cheek accusation here is that Isaac Newton destroyed the poetry of the rainbow by reducing it to its prismatic colours.

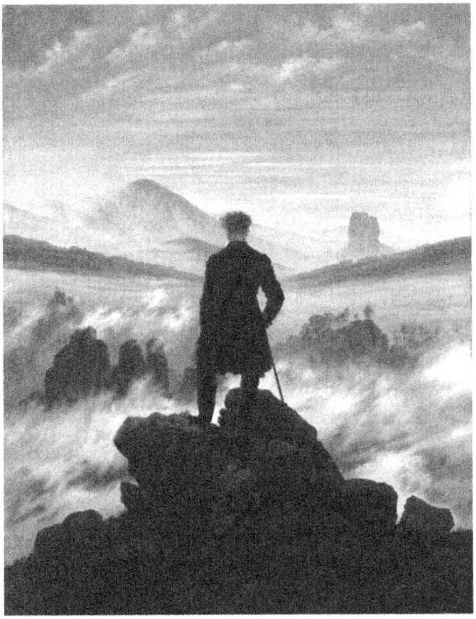

Fig. 10.4 Caspar David Friedrich's (c. 1818) *Wanderer above the Sea of Fog*. Oil on canvas. © bpk / Hamburger Kunsthalle, SHK / Elke Walford

creativity is designed to increase our wonder at the richness and discipline of the processes underlying the generation of creative ideas.

The demystification-through-explanation approach, evident in the theory of problem-solving and the computationalist account of creativity, may be contrasted with the myth-building approach of Romanticism, whose accounts of art typically appeal to the creativity of an artistic genius. Kant's (1790/2000) account of art, it is traditionally held, appeals to the creative activity of the artistic genius to explain fine art and works in the opposite direction: building myths about the artistic genius instead of demystifying reality through careful explanation.[6] Figure 10.4 offers an iconic representation of the Romantic ideals of the sublime, individual insight, and the solitary genius confronting the unknown, all themes closely connected to Kant's account of art.

[6] For the opposing view that there is nothing mysterious or problematic about the possibility of the production of art in Kant's account of art and artistic genius, see Murray (2007).

According to at least some philosophers, the concept of genius, which may be traced from its roots in antiquity to the form it takes in modern European and Anglo-American thought, has developed historically to exclude women artists (Battersby 1989). To make matters more insidious, certain traits traditionally associated with femininity (for instance, the capacity to give birth, nurture, be receptive, and so on) began to be transferred to male artists during the eighteenth century. We therefore have feminist grounds to resist the mystification of artistic phenomena through an appeal to the concept of artistic genius, alongside the healthy scientific grounds already provided by the computationalists (Newell, Simon, and Boden).

CHAPTER 11

The Ontological Status of Works of Art

11.1 The Ontology of Art

One of Magritte's most famous paintings places the caption "This is not a pipe" (translated from French) beneath the image of a pipe (Fig. 11.1). What then is the ontological status of this painting: is it an object, a representation, a symbol, or a mere idea? In this chapter, we shall address questions about the ontological status of a work of art. Metaphysics is a branch of philosophy that is concerned with the fundamental nature of reality (mind, being, existence, space, time, cause and effect, and so on). Ontology, in turn, is a branch of metaphysics that is concerned with the study of what there is. What are the different views that may be held with respect to the ontological status of works of art? Furthermore, do any of these views sit more easily with our computationalist approach to art-making than others?

A full-fledged ontology of a work of art will have to specify the sorts of entities (objects, events, and so on) that count as works of art, the existence conditions under which works of art come into existence, survive, or even cease to exist, the identity conditions that allow us to identify a work of art with itself and distinguish between numerically distinct works of art, and the relations of works of art to human intentions, physical objects, and processes (Thomasson 2005). One distinction that may help us on our way is the distinction between concrete and abstract entities. Concrete entities

M. Chen, *Art-Making as Problem-Solving*,
https://doi.org/10.1007/978-3-031-90639-8_11

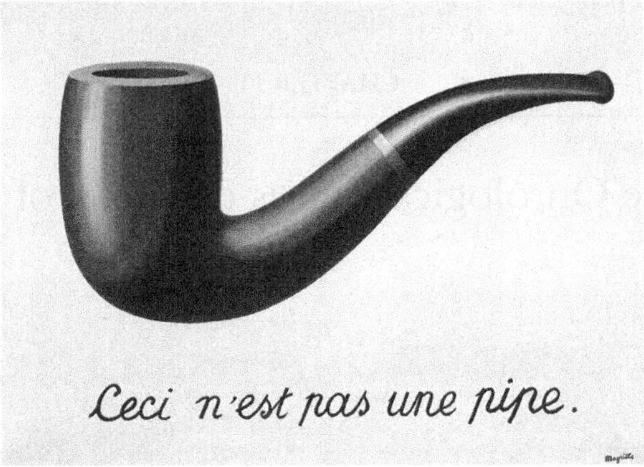

Fig. 11.1 René Magritte's (1929) *The Treachery of Images*. Oil on canvas. Photo © Museum Associates / LACMA

include trees, dogs, tables, the Earth, our Solar System, and so on. Abstract entities may include numbers, sets, proofs, theorems, propositions, postulated entities or theoretical constructs (strings and branes in theoretical physics, for instance), relations, values, possible worlds, and so on.

Abstract entities are often held to be non-spatiotemporal and causally inert: they exist neither in space nor time, are unable to make anything happen, cannot be affected by anything, and are incapable of change (Swoyer 2008; Rosen 2012). It seems intuitively straightforward for us to think of works of art as concrete entities. After all, must candidate works of art (artifacts) not be produced, conditional on the available materials at the art-maker's disposal? Does the latter condition not foreground the material aspect and means of production of the art-maker, which we can clearly locate in space and time?

11.2 Three Hypotheses

According to a hypothesis known as the physical object hypothesis, works of art are simply physical objects and concrete particulars (Rohrbaugh 2013). The Venus de Milo is nothing over and above a lump of marble, Georgette Chen's (c. 1960s) *Still Life with Durians, Mangosteens and Rambutans* is a pigment-covered canvas, Beethoven's *Symphony No. 7 in A major*, op. 92 is a sequence of sound waves, and the complete works of

Shakespeare are sequences of linguistic marks on pages. A problem with the physical object hypothesis is that it may be sufficient for a work of art to be an imaginary entity. After all, a composer may create a work of music merely in her head by imagining the relevant tune. This composer need not have written the score or played the notes. Furthermore, works of art and the physical matter that constitutes them have different identity or persistence conditions. Works of ancient Greek and Roman sculpture can survive the loss of polychrome and even the loss of arms and remain identical with themselves. At the same time, the physical matter constituting these works cannot survive these changes.

Works of visual art (painting, sculpture, photography, and so on) lend themselves easily to being regarded as concrete entities, especially given the physical and sensuous nature of their medium. Things may not be as easy for works of non-visual art: it is as absurd to say that the Old English epic poem *Beowulf* is in the British Library (where the only known medieval manuscript of *Beowulf* is housed) as it is to say that several tunes by the American singer-songwriter Woody Guthrie are in the Library of Congress (Thomasson 2006). Furthermore, a famous refutation of the physical object hypothesis occurred in 1928. The United States Customs Court had to decide whether a polished bronze sculpture by Constantin Brâncuşi was an ordinary metal object or a work of art (Rhodes 1961; Fincham 2015).[1] The object, entitled *Bird in Space*, had been imported into the United States for an exhibition, although customs officials had initially classified it as a piece of metal rather than a work of art, resulting in a 40% duty.[2] The court eventually reached the verdict that objects representing abstract ideas (in this instance, flight in its essential form) may be classified as art.

If works qualify as art in virtue of the idea or the concept instantiated in them, even in the case of works of visual art, then this observation lends credence to an alternative hypothesis known as the imaginary entity hypothesis (Collingwood 1958; Sartre 1966). Recall Collingwood's (1958) expressivist ontology, according to which the work of art is not a product hewn from the manipulation of a physical medium, but rather

[1] Brâncuşi v. United States, 1928 Cust. Ct. LEXIS 3.

[2] Here is the full description of the object by the customs officials: a production in bronze about 41/2 feet high supported by a cylindrical base about 6 inches in diameter and 6 inches high. If the physical object hypothesis is correct, then Brâncuşi's *Bird in Space* ought to have been nothing more than this object.

an imaginary entity existing in the minds of the artist and the audience (Sect. 7.5). According to the imaginary entity hypothesis, works of are just imaginary entities, created and sustained by human consciousness.

How, it may be objected, can one and the same work of art be experienced and evaluated as the same thing by many different people? Will each of these individuals not appear to have engaged in her own imaginative activities? Furthermore, if works of art exist only in the minds of artists and their audience, then works of art cannot truly be destroyed. Why then are we worried about works of art such as Caravaggio's (c. 1597) *Portrait of a Courtesan* and Dürer's (1507–1511) *Heller Altar* being destroyed respectively by the Flakturm Friedrichshain fire in 1945 and the fire in the residence of Duke Maximilian of Bavaria in Munich in 1729? Last but not least, has an artist really created a work of art of the relevant sort if she has created something merely in her head? If so, then would this not result in an overly bloated ontology?

Objections to the physical object and imaginary entity hypotheses lend credence to a third alternative view: the abstract entity hypothesis (Currie 1989; Wollheim 1968; Wolterstorff 1980). Moderate and strong versions of the abstract entity hypothesis are available. According to the moderate version of the hypothesis, at least some works of art (painting and sculpture, for instance) may be associated with physical and concrete entities. Some other works of art (literature and music, for instance) are however not physical objects and should instead be regarded as abstract entities (Wollheim 1968; Wolterstorff 1980). The moderate version of the abstract entity hypothesis, in other words, denies a theoretical unity across the various arts (painting, music, sculpture, drama, literature, and so on) concerning the sorts of entities that works of art are. According to the strong version of the abstract entity hypothesis, all works of art are abstract entities (Currie 1989). Accepting either the moderate or the strong version of the abstract entity hypothesis will entail a certain platonism about abstract entities.

11.3 Artistic Platonism

What is artistic platonism and how might it figure in our philosophical considerations? Platonists asserts that at least some abstract entities exist, whereas nominalists flat out deny the existence of abstract entities across the board. An agnostic is neither a platonist nor a nominalist: she neither asserts nor denies the existence of abstract entities. We have already encountered mathematical platonism (Sect. 9.2), the view that abstract mathematical entities exist in a manner that is independent of human thought, language, and practices (Linnebo 2023).

Artistic platonism is the view that at least some works of art may be identified as abstract entities that exist in a non-spatiotemporal, causally inert, and mind-independent manner. Several philosophers are drawn to artistic platonism because of the non-physical arts (music, literature, and so on): there is no concrete particular or physical object that we can plausibly take to be the work of art itself. They have therefore hypothesized that works of art exist as abstract entities of some sort (Margolis 1965; Wollheim 1968).

A common objection, raised against artistic platonism, relies on the following line of reasoning: if works of art are abstract entities (certain patterns or structures of sound, line, colour, and so on), then they must exist independently of the art-maker. To be precise, these abstract entities exist eternally and predate the art-maker in existence. Therefore, instead of creating a work of art, the art-maker is merely selecting a particular pattern or structure of sound, line, colour, and so on.[3] This line of reasoning may be sharpened into an argument known as the argument from creatability against artistic platonism (adapted from Dodd (2000)):

P1: If artistic platonism is true, then works of art are patterns or structures of sound, line, colour, and so on.
P2: If works of art are patterns or structures of sound, line, colour, and so on, then they could not have been created or brought into being by art-makers.
P3: Works of art have been created or brought into being by art-makers.
C1: ∴ Works of art are not patterns or structures of sound, line, colour, and so on.
C2: ∴ Artistic platonism is false.

We have already argued in Sect. 8.5 that works of art may be regarded as permutations or ordered arrangements of elements. Artistic platonists are likely to deny that the argument from creatability is sound. They could deny P3: works of art, in virtue of their existing independently of art-makers as

[3] It should be noted that the selective aspect of art being described here is entirely consistent with our account: we have characterized the creative artistic process as a selective process in which the artist chooses between alternative outcomes.

abstract and mind-independent entities, have been discovered rather than created. Nonetheless, fashioning or constructing a candidate work of art (artifact), though not creation in the strict sense, could still be a creative activity. The discovery or selection of specific permutations, patterns, or structures of sound, line, colour, and so on might still be creative and should not be equated with some unimaginative or rote-based tracing of patterns or structures.[4] Our computationalist approach to art-making would concur with this point, since what is intrinsic to the central artistic task is creativity (including creative discovery and the reliance on heuristic search to make creative discoveries) rather than creatability as such.

Kivy (1987) asks us to imagine three scenarios: Pythagoras taking a stroll when the Pythagorean theorem pops into his head, Mozart at a game of billiards with Salieri when the theme and counterpoint of *Don Giovanni* pop into his head, and Edison having his customary lunch when the idea of putting a tungsten filament in a vacuum or airtight container pops into his head.[5] These are all creative achievements and we need simply to avoid the mistake of equating the creative with creation, at the expense of discovery. It may be countered: do we not traditionally describe Edison as having invented the light bulb? Without doing violence to common sense or ordinary language, we could as easily say that Edison discovered a practical way of getting light from electricity. This way of getting light from electricity is an abstract platonic entity, its existence timeless, although it was eventually ferreted out by Edison (Kivy 1987).

Artistic platonism, it may be further objected, appears to imply that two art-makers who fashion or construct the same pattern or structure of sound, line, colour, and so on necessarily fashion or construct the same work of art. However, as we intuitively regard these works as numerically distinct, artistic platonism must be false and works of art cannot therefore simply be equated with these patterns or structures. Artistic platonists may point out that two works w_1 and w_2, though indiscernible in their abstract properties (structure, pattern), may differ widely in other properties or relations. If w_1 has at least one property or relation that w_2 lacks or vice

[4] Analogously, if we take thoughts to be abstract entities, then we must concede that thinkers do not create thoughts but must instead take them as they are (Salmon and Soames 1988). At the same time, nothing prevents these thinkers from thinking creatively.

[5] According to the Pythagorean theorem, $a^2 + b^2 = c^2$, where c denotes the length of the hypotenuse of a right-angled triangle and a and b denote the lengths of the other two sides. Recall T3 from Sect. 9.1.

versa, then $w_1 \neq w_2$. An appeal could be made to the historical context of production to distinguish between two works of art that are indiscernible at the abstract level of structure or pattern.[6]

According to Levinson (1980), a work of art w is a compound or conjunction of two structures: an abstract structure (of sound, line, colour, and so on) and a concrete one (of musical instruments, recording halls, orchestras, canvases, pigments, and so on). For convenience, we may denote this compound of two structures as a ψ-structure. A work of art may be defined as the ψ-structure, as indicated by the art-maker A at t_i. By indication is meant the fixing, determination, or selection of a ψ-structure by the art-maker. We may associate the art-maker's indication of a ψ-structure with the art-maker's identification of members of subset S having certain properties or relations, given a set P of elements (Sect. 8.3).

In both instances, the art-maker is navigating a problem space, choosing between alternative outcomes, and tracing solution paths, with a view to accomplishing her artistic goals. The indexing of a work of art to time (t_i) and a person (A) ensures that any two works of art w_1 and w_2 are necessarily distinct if composed either by different people or at different times. Levinson's account yields a sophisticated version of artistic platonism, in which works of art, though existing as abstract entities, have been fashioned or constructed by particular art-makers at particular times in history.

More generally, it is our belief that artistic platonism is highly compatible with an information-theoretic philosophy of art (Chap. 3), the theory of problem-solving (Chap. 5), and the computational account of creativity (Chap. 10). These three accounts are deeply concerned with an abstract and immaterial space of information, concepts, and ideas. In addition, the latter two accounts inform us that this space can be navigated, searched through the use of heuristics, explored through the plotting of solution paths, and even radically transformed. The action type hypothesis, a corollary of the abstract entity hypothesis, anticipates our computationalist approach to art-making. This hypothesis asserts that works of art are structures of sounds, colours, and so on, discovered through specific heuristic paths first used by art-makers and then retraced subsequently by the human audience in reception (Currie 1989).

[6] This move is likely to please the historicist (Sect. 7.9).

11.4 Works of Art as Abstract Particulars

Since the nineteenth century, artistic interest in works of art as the sorts of objects that can afford various aesthetic experiences has been predominant. Interest in works of art for their own sake has even overtake practical or utilitarian interests in these works as objects capable of satisfying social, religious, or other non-artistic functions (De Clercq 2020).[7] It is tempting to describe works of art as abstract particulars rather than abstract universals, since this interest in works of art is highly individualizing: it tends to attach itself to objects in their particularity. In our experience of art, only this object in this particular condition will do, and no other object in any other condition will be able to satisfy certain aesthetic functions. We could even be more specific about the kinds of abstract particulars that works of art comprise: they are specific permutations or ordered arrangements of elements (Sect. 8.5). Works of art may be characterized as objects whose parts are arranged or configured in a certain way, all the while preserving a certain appearance (Levinson 1996).

This idea of the work of art as a specific permutation whose parts are arranged in a certain way is a metaphysical idea. Consistently maintained, this metaphysical idea could give rise to certain assumptions about part replacement and approaches to art restoration (De Clercq 2020). For a long time, works of art were restored in the same way that ordinary concrete artifacts such as tables, chairs, clothes, and cars have been repaired. Once this metaphysical idea of a work of art as a specific permutation of elements is taken seriously, however, part replacement becomes metaphysically impossible: we cannot have parts of an artwork arranged if at least one of these parts is missing or lacking. Part replacement for works of art, considered as unproblematic before the nineteenth century, has become highly problematic ever since. In particular, purist approaches to art restoration emphasize the irreplaceability of original parts.[8]

[7] Not all philosophers of art agree with this divorce of works of art from their practical basis or intellectual function (Santayana 1904). At least some philosophers of art have pointed to the double character of art (its being both autonomous and socially embedded) and the ideological forces behind the idea of art's autonomy (Adorno 1997).

[8] For instance, Ruskin (1880/1989) asserts the impossibility of replacing a missing part by a new part in a building if the original builders are no longer around.

11.5 The Benacerraf-Field Challenge

If proofs, theorems, and works of art are abstract entities and abstract entities, by definition, are causally inert and non-efficacious, then how do mathematicians and artists causally interact with these abstract entities? Furthermore, how do we explain mathematical and artistic discovery, mathematical and artistic knowledge, or the acceptance of mathematical and artistic truths?

This challenge was first posed in the form of the Benacerraf-Field challenge to mathematical platonists (Field 1988, 1989; Benacerraf 1973). Here is Liggins's (2010, p. 68) argumentative reconstruction of Benacerraf's (1973) version of the challenge: P1: If mathematical platonism is true, then we have knowledge of abstract mathematical entities.
P2: If we have knowledge of abstract mathematical entities, then we are causally related to them.
P3: We are not causally related to abstract mathematical entities.
C: ∴ Mathematical platonism is false.

Mathematical platonists typically accept P1 and P3. P3 follows from our definition of abstract entities as entities that lie outside space, time, and the causal nexus. However, P2 is controversial. It is thought to follow from a more general constraint on knowledge (Nutting 2020):
(Universal causal constraint) Causal interaction with an object is required for knowledge of it.

Benacerraf's (1973) support for the universal causal constraint may be inferred from his remarks favouring a causal theory of knowledge. Benacerraf cites works from contemporaries such as Goldman (1967), Harman (2015), and Skyrms (1967) and agrees with the core intuition of this theory. According to the causal theory of knowledge, *S* cannot know that *p* without there being a causal connection between *S* and the grounds of *p*'s truth.[9] The causal theory of knowledge, though in vogue at the time of Benacerraf's writing, is subject to famous objections: it seems to rule out justified beliefs about future entities, since backward causation is impossible and effects (such as justified beliefs in future entities) cannot temporally precede their cause (the future entities that these justified beliefs

[9] Benacerraf puts it this way: for *S* to know that *p* is true, there must be some causal relation that obtains between *S* and the referents of the names, predicates, and quantifiers of *p*.

are about); fails to solve the Gettier problem that motivated it in the first instance; and has trouble accounting for our knowledge of general facts.[10]

The general philosophical consensus is that Benacerraf's version of the challenge founders on the basis of its reliance on the flawed causal theory of knowledge. In addition, Field's (1988, 1989) version of the challenge is superior, because it avoids any appeal to a theory of knowledge (causal or non-causal) (Burgess and Rosen 1997; Linnebo 2006; Liggins 2010).[11] How does Field's version of the challenge to mathematical platonism work? Whereas Benacerraf's version focuses on knowledge, Field's version focuses on accepting truths. It is taken for granted that many mathematicians' mathematical beliefs are non-accidentally true: for a vast majority of mathematical sentences (p), if mathematicians accept that p, then p is true.[12] We may call this fact MMA or mathematicians' mathematical accuracy. According to Field, MMA is so striking as to demand an explanation.

A mathematical platonist might appeal to proofs and their truth-preserving nature: most sentences that mathematicians accept are sentences that they prove from other sentences they accept (theorems that have already been proven, axioms, and so on). What needs explaining on this view, then, is the strong and reliable correlation between mathematicians accepting certain axioms and their being true (as opposed to false). Field's version of the challenge takes the following argumentative form (Liggins 2010, p. 74):

P1: If mathematical platonism is true, then there is an explanation of MMA.
P2: Any such explanation must be either causal or non-causal.
P3: If mathematical platonism is true, then there is no causal explanation of MMA.

[10] A Gettier problem refers to a problem in which S can have a justified true belief that p and still fail to know that p (Gettier 1963). See also our discussion of Gettier cases in the context of Dretske's information-theoretic analysis of knowledge (Sect. 3.3). Not all the objections against the causal theory of knowledge, however, are knockdown objections. Some of our beliefs about future entities could count as knowledge, because these beliefs share a common cause with future entities (Goldman 1967). Nevertheless, for a detailed account of the fall from grace of the causal theory of knowledge, see Shope (1983).

[11] For dissent, see Nutting (2020) and Kasa (2010).

[12] In other words, there is a strong and reliable correlation between mathematicians accepting certain sentences and their being true (as opposed to false). Field takes this to be the explanandum or phenomenon that has to be explained.

P4: If mathematical platonism is true, then there is no non-causal explanation of MMA.
C: ∴ Mathematical platonism is false.

As mathematical platonists are unlikely to impute the reliability of mathematicians to a matter of sheer coincidence, they will probably accept P1. They will also accept P2 and P3. According to Field, P4 seems to be true, since it is hard to see what the non-causal explanation would look like. As no argument or justification is offered for P4, mathematical platonists might deny P4 and reject the argumentative form of Field's version of the challenge as unsound. Nonetheless, the Benacerraf–Field challenge is a challenge to mathematical platonists to provide an account of MMA.

By analogy, artistic platonists will have to confront the challenge of explaining the widespread agreement about certain artistic claims in the artworld: the *Iliad* being a great epic, Sophocles being a great tragedian, the *Divine Comedy* being a masterpiece, Shakespeare being better than Beaumont and Fletcher, and so on. We may term the strong and systematically reliable correlation between art professionals accepting certain claims and their being true AAA or art professionals' artistic accuracy. Mathematicians rely epistemically on testimony and inference from other mathematical claims (including proof) to accept certain mathematical claims. There are however at least some claims that mathematicians accept on the basis of neither testimony nor inference (Nutting 2020). By analogy, professionals in the artworld (art-makers, art critics, art historians, art curators, and so on) accept certain artistic claims on the basis of testimony and inference. However, there are at least some claims that are accepted on the basis of neither testimony nor inference. The challenge is to explain why these claims are accepted. Artistic platonists cannot appeal to a causal explanation for AAA, since they hold that works of art and their properties are abstract, non-spatiotemporal, and causally inert. If artistic platonists cannot explain AAA, then worries will arise about the epistemological foundations on which the practice of art rests.

Generally construed, the Benacerraf-Field challenge is a challenge to platonists to account for the epistemological implications of their ontological commitments. Applied to abstract artistic entities, it is a challenge to artistic platonists to provide an explanation of the strong and reliable correlation in the artworld between certain artistic claims being accepted as true and their being true. If artistic platonists maintain that there can be some perception-like cognition and therefore perception-like and non-inferential knowledge of abstract artistic entities, then this perceptual or perception-like account of knowledge or accepting truths would have to admit a perceptual or perception-like mechanism that is causal in nature.[13]

We would still have to explain how this mechanism could causally interact with causally inert abstract entities. The only other remaining option, a non-causal account of AAA, is equally unpalatable. As aforementioned, artistic platonism is highly compatible with our computationalist approach to art-making (Sect. 11.3). At the same time, we need secure epistemological foundations for the practice of art, especially as art-makers navigate the problem space, choose between alternative outcomes, and generate candidate works of art (artifacts). Therefore, we must carefully consider the epistemological implications of our ontological commitments and whether or how we might provide an explanation (causal or non-causal) of AAA.

11.6 Maps of the Artistic Problem Space

Here is our attempt to explain AAA. We may think of our artistic knowledge or store of artistic claims, accepted as true, as a map of the problem space of art or, in the platonist's terms, the realm of abstract, non-spatiotemporal, and acausal entities. There are many possible ways in which a space can be mapped out. Each ordinary map of the world is a response to the challenge of representing the three-dimensional and curved surface of the Earth and its features adequately and accurately on a two-dimensional map plane. Certain cartographic assumptions may be made, involving the use of map projections such as the Mercator projection, the use of symbols to represent certain features, the simplification of certain complex features, the omission of other unnecessary ones, and so on. These observations will hold by analogy for maps of the problem space of art.

The success conditions of maps are tied to their use and ability to pass the test of experience and time. We test the degree of effectiveness of each map by using it: a good map helps us navigate successfully through a space and toward our destination or goal (something's qualifying as a work of

[13] Gödelian mathematical platonists believe that at least some mathematical beliefs are formed on the basis of a perception-like faculty of mathematical intuition. Additional knowledge may be inferred from and tested against this perception-like cognition of mathematical objects (Benacerraf (1973), cited in Nutting (2020)).

art, for instance). We count as knowledge or accept as true whatever helps us to find our way about or navigate around a space.[14] Maps that, more often than not, lead us away from our destination rather than toward it, despite having been correctly interpreted, will likely be discarded as bad or inaccurate.

Our state-of-the-art artistic knowledge or store of artistic claims, accepted as true, is a map by which we steer, for it has repeatedly stood the test of experience and time. This map is recorded in the cultural memory (artistic canon), which in turn is part of the shared background of cultural information between the art-maker (source) and her intended audience (destination) (Sect. 3.6). Future expeditions may confirm the value of this map or suggest that at least some of its assumptions might stand in need of correction.[15] We must therefore understand AAA in the context of an artistic tradition, a history of navigation of the problem space of art, trial and error with respect to the construction of maps and their rigorous testing through use, and the cultural memory as a recording device.

The explanandum is AAA or widespread agreement about certain artistic claims in the artworld. The explanans should be located, not at the level of individual art professionals, but rather at the level of the socio-historical. There is a strong and reliable correlation between art professionals accepting certain claims and their being true (as opposed to false) because these claims are disseminated, tested, and evaluated within groups, institutions, and communities and have stood the test of experience and time. Our explanation of AAA does not require us to determine whether *p* has for its epistemic basis perception, perception-like cognition, inference, testimony, and so on. To focus on the cognitive faculties of individuals rather than the social context in which knowledge and related epistemic claims arise is to reduce social epistemology to mere analytic epistemology.

Abortive mathematical proofs help to illuminate the socio-historical nature of knowing or accepting as true that *p*. Following Kempe's (1879)

[14] The idea of belief, knowledge, and other related epistemic states as maps by which we steer is not new. It may be traced to Ramsey (1929) and Armstrong (1973). The cartographic metaphor has also been applied to philosophical problems. According to Wittgenstein (1953/2009), a philosophical problem has the form 'I don't know my way about' and the aim of philosophy is to show the fly the way out of the fly-bottle.

[15] In the latter instance, it will be sufficient to reflect on the implications of Cubism and Schoenberg's atonal music on map-making in a world confined to representationalist or realist art and music whose foundational structures are either the major or minor scales (Sect. 10.3).

submission of a candidate proof of the four-colour theorem, errors in the proof were identified by Heawood (1890/1949), and a valid proof of the four-colour theorem was not forthcoming until the second half of the twentieth century (Appel and Haken 1977a,b; Appel et al. 1977).[16] Let *p* denote the statement 'The four-colour conjecture has a proof and must therefore be reclassified as a theorem'. We cannot say that mathematicians knew or accepted as true that *p* as early as 1879, because of the flaws subsequently discovered in Kempe's proof in 1890. Nor can we say that mathematicians knew or accepted as true that *p* upon the computer-aided proof being furnished in 1977, because this proof still had to undergo checking and verification. Only after the computer-aided proof had been extensively peer-reviewed and proven its worth as a map by which we might reliably steer can it be said that *p* is known or accepted as true by mathematicians.

The epistemic move of accepting a claim as true must be understood in terms of a function of time and rigorous testing. Proofs are accepted as valid, as a result of their having undergone the peer-review process of checking and verification to ensure the rigour of mathematical knowledge. There is an analogy between abortive mathematical proofs and abortive artistic judgments. Consider Louis Leroy's (1874) scathing review of the Impressionists, comparing Monet's paintings to sketches or impressions rather than finished paintings. Following the inclusion of works of Impressionist art—including Monet's (1872) *Impression, Sunrise*—in the Western artistic canon, we cannot say that Leroy's claims have been accepted as true.[17] Again, the epistemic move of accepting a claim as true must be understood in terms of a function of time and rigorous testing.

Our account of knowing or accepting as true that *p* in terms of maps by which we steer does not imply a constructivism in which knowledge is constituted by a community of knowers. Maps are maps of an external reality and platonists will add that this reality includes a platonic realm of abstract, mind-independent, non-spatiotemporal, and causally inert enti-

[16] The four-colour theorem states that any planar map Γ can be coloured by no more than four colours, such that no two adjacent regions of Γ share the same colour. By a map is meant a division of a plane into any number of regions. See also our discussion of Nelson's abortive proof of the inconsistency of Peano arithmetic toward the end of this section.

[17] There are similarities between the mathematical process of proof-checking and verification and the artistic process of determining whether to include or exclude certain works in an artistic canon. Both processes help to maintain the rigour and reliability of knowledge (mathematical or artistic) at the frontlines.

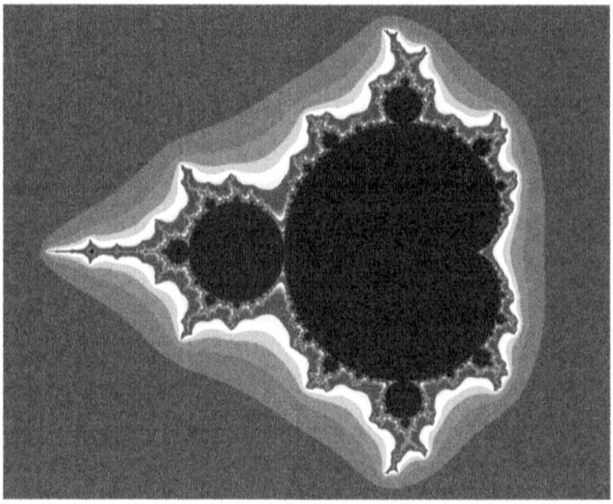

Fig. 11.2 A Mandelbrot set with well-defined colour stripes. Reproduced under the Creative Commons Attribution-Share Alike 2.0 Generic license via Wikimedia Commons

ties (mathematical, artistic, and so on). Notwithstanding the mathematical aspiration toward simplicity and elegance (Sects. 9.1 and 10.4), artistic and mathematical reality remains complex, in part precisely because its entities lie outside space, time, and the causal nexus. It is far easier to determine that Brâncuşi's *Bird in Space* is a piece of metal (concrete) than it is to determine that it qualifies as a work of art (abstract), hence the whole court case in the first instance (Sect. 11.2).

A similar point may be made about the complexity of abstract mathematical reality. A Mandelbrot set is defined within a complex plane through an iterative operation on complex numbers (Fig. 11.2).[18]

The Mandelbrot set has been identified as the most complex object in all of mathematics. It has been argued that mathematical reality is even more complex than the Mandelbrot set (Boolos 1990). '$0 \neq 1$' is typically held to be known or accepted as true by mathematicians. Relative to the system of Peano arithmetic, 0 cannot be equal to 1, because 1 has been defined as the successor of zero or $S(0)$. In September 2011, Edward Nelson (Princeton), after having devoted 25 years to constructing the proof, announced that he

[18] A complex number z is expressed as $z = x + yi$, where $\{x, y\} \in \mathbb{R}$ and i is an imaginary number ($i^2 = -1$). z will be represented on a complex plane as the point (x, y), where x and y are the real and imaginary parts of the complex number z.

had proof of the inconsistency of Peano arithmetic.[19] Shortly after Nelson's announcement, Terence Tao (UCLA) and Daniel Tausk (University of São Paulo) identified errors in the proof. By 1 October 2011, Nelson had withdrawn his claim and retracted his proof.

Despite Nelson's abortive proof of the inconsistency of Peano arithmetic, it by no means follows that a proof of the inconsistency of Peano arithmetic will be impossible in the future.[20] In a related vein, we cannot rule out that '0 = 1' may be derived from a million-page proof 200 years from now, involving concepts and arguments of which we are currently unaware (Boolos 1990). The maps by which we steer in mathematics and art are maps of an abstract, mind-independent reality that have stood the test of experience and time. Future discoveries (new concepts, theories, arguments, works of art, and so on) may, however, compel us to question what we currently think we know or accept as true.

[19] If the system of Peano arithmetic (PA) is inconsistent, then a contradiction ($\bot$) may be derived from it. We may use $0 = 1$ as a shorthand for $\bot$. Therefore, $\vdash_{PA} 0 = 1$ can be used to represent the inconsistency of Peano arithmetic. See Nelson (2015).

[20] Furthermore, even if Peano arithmetic is consistent, consistency, combined with other properties such as sufficient power and axiomatizability, will ensure that Peano arithmetic becomes a clear target of Gödel's (1931) incompleteness theorems. We will have more to say about these theorems in Sect. 13.1.

CHAPTER 12

Symbol Systems

12.1 Computer Science as Empirical Inquiry

Rembrandt's dramatic painting ***Belshazzar's Feast*** depicts a moment of divine judgment upon the titular Babylonian king, conveyed through a glowing Hebrew inscription at the upper right corner of the painting (Fig. 12.1). This enigmatic string of symbols places cognitive demands on both the figures within the painting and its viewers, inviting interpretation and reminding us that artworks can function as complex symbolic structures. In this chapter, we will trace certain continuities between the theory of problem-solving and Newell and Simon's (1976) theory of computer science as empirical inquiry under the Newell-Simon research paradigm. The highly symbolic nature of information processes undergirding problem-solving and intelligent behaviour will be foregrounded and we will identify (with caveats) another philosophical tool that may be used to our advantage: Goodman's (1968) theory of symbol systems. Goodman's philosophy is wide-ranging and contains many strands: nominalism, irrealism, aesthetic cognitivism, and so on. We will argue that with the appropriate care, certain parts of Goodman's philosophy (aesthetic cognitivism, the theory of symbol systems) could be used for the benefit of our computationalist approach to art-making, while others must be discarded (nominalism, irrealism) because they may result in inconsistencies in our theoretical and ontological commitments.

M. Chen, *Art-Making as Problem-Solving*,
https://doi.org/10.1007/978-3-031-90639-8_12

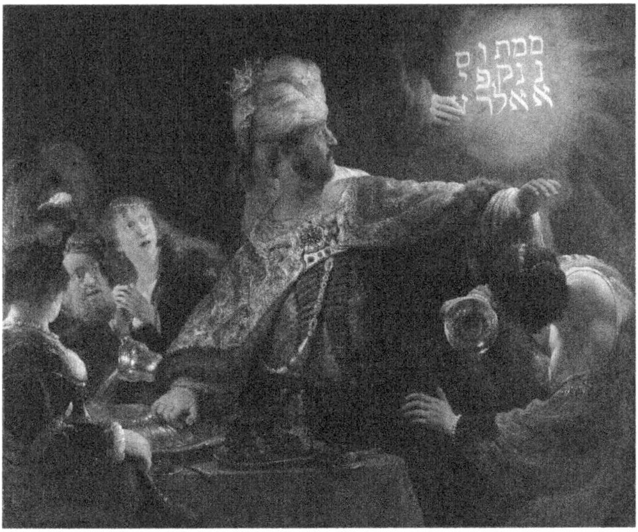

Fig. 12.1 Rembrandt's (c. 1635–1638) *Belshazzar's Feast*. Oil on canvas. Bought with a contribution from the Art Fund, 1964. © The National Gallery, London

The selection of some parts of Goodman's position and not others is neither accidental nor arbitrary. Instead, we have been guided throughout by the goal of theoretical coherence. Goodman's aesthetic cognitivism and theory of symbol systems provide a structured way of interpreting works of art in terms of rule-governed symbol manipulation, aligning well with our computationalist approach. By contrast, nominalism and irrealism must be set aside, because they are bound to give rise to potential conflicts in our theoretical and ontological commitments. Furthermore, Goodman's position is rarely used in the contemporary philosophy of art, not least because it is often perceived as overly rigid or formalist. However, Goodman's framework, through its foregrounding of the structured, symbol-based, and cognitive nature of art and artistic problem-solving, offers certain straightforward theoretical virtues and can serve as a useful tool in our approach. Accepting this framework or a modified version of it becomes more than just a preference: it may even be regarded as a theoretical necessity.

Nevertheless, before we delve into Goodman's theory of symbol systems, we must first understand the AI research tradition within which

Table 12.1 The standard ontology of approaches to AI research (Russell and Norvig 2010; Bringsjord and Govindarajulu 2020)

	Human-based or bounded rationality	*Ideal rationality*
Reasoning-based	Thinking humanly	Thinking rationally
Behaviour-based	Acting humanly	Acting rationally

Newell and Simon's (1976) theory of computer science as empirical inquiry is situated. According to the standard ontology of approaches to AI research (Table 12.1), we have at least four possible approaches: the thinking rationally approach, the thinking humanly approach, the acting humanly approach, and the acting rationally approach (Russell and Norvig 2010; Bringsjord and Govindarajulu 2020). For the purposes of our discussion, the Newell-Simon research paradigm is associated with the thinking rationally approach (reasoning-based, ideal rationality) to AI research.[1]

The thinking rationally approach is best regarded as a family of approaches to understanding and building intelligent entities that rely on high-level symbolic representations. Members of this family include symbolic AI, classical AI, logic-based AI, knowledge-based AI, and what Haugeland (1985) terms 'GOFAI' (or Good Old-Fashioned Artificial Intelligence). Furthermore, the thinking rationally approach is associated with a philosophical view about personhood known as logicism (Bringsjord 2008). Logicism is an view of personhood according to which a person is the bearer of propositional attitudes. The basic units of logicism are propositions. Propositions convey propositional content and they are denoted by propositional variables such as p, q, r, s, and so on. In addition, they can be assigned values such as true, false, unknown, probable, and so on. Knowing that p, believing that p, and suspending judgment that p are examples of propositional attitudes. p is a propositional variable and it may denote any of the following utterances (S1–S2):

[1] The thinking humanly approach is associated with the artificial neural networks (ANN) or cognitive modelling approach, the acting humanly approach is associated with the Turing test approach, and the acting rationally approach is associated with reinforcement learning-based approaches. Hybrid approaches to AI research (for instance, neurosymbolic AI, combining the thinking humanly and thinking rationally approaches) are also permitted.

S1: The Mona Lisa is smiling.
S2: John Milton is a better writer than John Ogilby.[2]

According to Newell and Simon's (1976) theory of computer science as empirical inquiry, computer science is an empirical discipline. It consists of the study of phenomena surrounding computers. Machines are the organisms being studied and machines and programs (hardware and software) are artifacts that have been designed and we can open them up and look inside. Furthermore, laws of qualitative structure are found everywhere in science and may equally be discerned in computer science.[3] There exist two laws of qualitative structure governing computer science: the physical symbol system hypothesis (hereafter: PSSH) and the heuristic search hypothesis (hereafter: HSH). Both hypotheses, in turn, provide theoretical support for the logicist view about personhood.

What do these two laws of qualitative structure assert? PSSH tells us that a physical symbol system has the necessary and sufficient means for intelligent action. PSSH is an empirical hypothesis and the relevant empirical evidence starts with human beings, the class of intelligent systems best known to us. HSH tells us that physical symbol systems solve problems using the processes of heuristic search. As PSSH does not tell us how physical symbol systems accomplish intelligent action, HSH is required.

According to HSH, solutions to a problem are represented as symbol structures. A physical symbol system exercises its intelligence by searching (generating and modifying symbol structures) until the symbol structures of solutions are produced. It should be relatively straightforward for us to recognize HSH as the theory of problem-solving under a slightly different guise. Continuities therefore exist between the theory of problem-solving and Newell and Simon's (1976) theory of computer science as empirical inquiry and will inform our computationalist approach to art-making accordingly.

[2] S2 references the Ogilby-Milton phenomenon, addressed in Hume (1757). Hume famously claims that no one would think that Ogilby and Milton have no difference in their qualities as writers.

[3] Examples of these laws of qualitative structure include the cell doctrine in biology, the theory of plate tectonics in geology, and the germ theory of disease in medicine and biology.

12.2 Cryptarithmetic

Just as creativity is a special class of problem-solving behaviour (Sect. 10.2), problem-solving behaviour is a special class of intelligent behaviour. In addition, the theory of computer science as empirical inquiry allows us to equate entities capable of intelligent behaviour with physical symbol systems capable of manipulating symbols. Equally, we may construe intelligent behaviour in terms of computations over symbols. We have already agreed on the ontological implications of the theory of problem-solving when it is applied to works of art: artworks should be recognized as abstract entities after the manner of logical proofs (Chap. 11). We can now identify the sort of abstraction involved with works of art: the abstraction is symbolic in nature.

We have already pointed out how the theory of problem-solving, more than a mere ivory-tower view, has been followed through with the conscientious programming of computer systems capable of solving various problems (Sect. 9.3). We may now add that the problems solved by these computer systems, designed under the Newell-Simon research paradigm, are highly symbolic in nature (theorem-proving in symbolic logic, in the case of LT). Here is another example of a problem of a highly symbolic nature:

$$\begin{array}{r} \text{DONALD} \\ +\text{GERALD} \\ \hline \text{ROBERT} \end{array}$$

This is a widely studied cryptarithmetic task or problem (Newell 1967; Bartlett 1958). Usually, the sole hint for this cryptarithmetic task is that D = 5. Relative to a uniform assignment of nine digits to the nine remaining letters (A, B, E, G, L, N, O, R, T), we should be able to produce the correct arithmetic sum by substituting numbers for letters in these three names.[4] There are 9! or 362,880 ways to assign nine digits to nine letters, and you may recognize this number as the generous upper bound for the size of the complete game tree of tic-tac-toe (Sect. 5.5).

[4] For anyone who might be interested, the solution to this cryptarithmetic problem is A = 4, B = 3, E = 9, G = 1, L = 8, N = 6, O = 2, R = 7, and T = 0.

The structure of the problem permits a heuristic that involves prioritizing the processing of those columns that are the most constrained. If two digits in a column are already known, then the value of the third digit (unknown) can be computed using the ordinary rules of arithmetic. In the final column, for instance, we have D + D = T. From D = 5 (our sole hint), we can derive T = 0. The computer systems designed under the Newell-Simon research paradigm typically focus on problems whose solution requires the use of highly symbolic processes. If we apply the both the theory of problem-solving and the theory of computer science as empirical inquiry to art-making and works of art, are there any philosophical theories that could help us to characterize art-making in terms of symbol manipulation?

12.3 Goodman's Nominalism

The answer, happily, is yes. Goodman's (1968) cognitivism and theory of symbol systems could help us to characterize art-making in terms of symbol manipulation. The caveat is that Goodman's nominalism, a central part of his philosophy, may jar with our computationalist approach to art-making. Recall the contrast between platonists and nominalists in Sect. 11.3: the former assert that at least some abstract entities exist, whereas the latter flatly deny the existence of abstract entities across the board. We have already argued in favour of the compatibility between artistic platonism and our computationalist approach to art-making (Chap. 11). We must therefore exercise caution in how we accept certain parts of Goodman's framework (cognitivism, the theory of symbol systems), without accepting others (nominalism, irrealism) that may result in inconsistencies in our philosophical commitments.

Goodman's nominalist agenda is laid out clearly in terms of a series of renunciations in Goodman and Quine's (1947) 'Steps toward a constructive nominalism'. First, abstract entities (classes, relations, properties, and so on) are renounced, as are variables that call for abstract objects as values (for instance, '*x* is a zoological species').[5] Nominalism has no space for works of art as abstract particulars whose parts are arranged or configured

[5] See the Benacerraf-Field challenge for worries about the epistemological implications of admitting non-spatiotemporal and causally inert abstract entities into our ontology (Sect. 11.5).

in a certain way (Sect. 11.4). Infinity is also renounced, since there is no general principle supported by physicists that there are more than finitely many physical objects in space-time. If the concrete world is finite, then acceptance of any theory that presupposes infinity would require us to assume at least some abstract entities alongside concrete ones (finite in number). Nominalism strives after clarity and an avoidance of commitment to abstract entities.

Broadly construed, nominalism consists of a refusal to recognize abstract entities such as classes and a requirement that whatever is admitted as an entity be construed as an individual (Goodman 1972, pp. 156–157). The nominalist agenda, involving a renunciation of abstract universals in favour of concrete individuals, is pursued as a logical program in the calculus of individuals (Leonard and Goodman 1940). This calculus of individuals is essentially an axiomatization of a theory of parthood, based on the single primitive for the discreteness of two individuals (Cohnitz and Rossberg 2022). The calculus of individuals is formally indistinguishable from a system developed by the father of mereology, Stanisław Leniewski (1916, 1927, 1929).[6]

The only primitive idea in the calculus of individuals may be formally represented as $x \urcorner y$: the individuals x and y are discrete and have no part in common. On the basis of this primitive idea, other concepts such as proper parthood, overlap, fusion, nucleus, the universe, and so on may be defined (Leonard and Goodman 1940, pp. 47–48):[7]

[6] Indeed, given some straightforward assumptions, Leśniewski's system, its axiomatization under Leśniewski's student Alfred Tarski (1929/1983), and Leonard and Goodman's calculus of individuals are equivalent. See Ridder (2002) for more details.

[7] The original enumeration has been preserved. I.01 is the definition for parthood: x is a part of y if whatever is discrete from y is also discrete from x. I.011 is the definition for proper parthood: x is a proper part of y if x is a part of y and x is not equal to y. I.02 is the definition for overlap: x and y overlap if they have a part z in common. I1.03 is the definition for fusion: x is the fusion of class α if and only if everything that is discrete from x is discrete from every member of α and everything discrete from every member of α is discrete from it. I.04 is the definition for nucleus: x is the nucleus of class α if and only if everything that is a part of x is a part of α and everything that is a part of α is a part of x. I.05 is the definition of the universe U in terms of the fusion of the set of all individuals. $x\mathrm{Fu}\alpha$ means 'x fuses the members of α', whereas $\mathrm{Fu}'\alpha$ means 'the fusion of the members of α. I.06 is the definition of the mereological sum of x and y in terms of the fusion of the set containing only x and y. I.07 is the definition of the mereological product of x and y in terms of the nucleus of the set containing only x and y.

(I.01 or parthood) $x < y \overset{\text{def}}{=} \forall z(z \lfloor y \rightarrow z \lfloor x)$
(I.011 or proper parthood) $x \ll y \overset{\text{def}}{=} (x < y) \wedge (x \neq y)$
(I.02 or overlap) $x \circ y \overset{\text{def}}{=} \exists z((z < x) \wedge (z < y))$
(I.03 of fusion) $x\text{Fu}\alpha \overset{\text{def}}{=} \forall z((z \lfloor x) \leftrightarrow \forall y(y \in \alpha \rightarrow z \lfloor y))$
(I.04 or nucleus) $x\text{Nu}\alpha \overset{\text{def}}{=} \forall z(z < x \leftrightarrow \forall y(y \in \alpha \rightarrow z < y))$
(I.05 or the universe) $U \overset{\text{def}}{=} \text{Fu}'V$
(I.06 or mereological sum) $x + y \overset{\text{def}}{=} \text{Fu}'(\{x\} \cup \{y\})$
(I.07 or mereological product) $xy \overset{\text{def}}{=} \text{Nu}'(\{x\} \cup \{y\})$

In addition, the calculus of individuals has three axioms or postulates (Leonard and Goodman 1940, pp. 48–49):[8]

(I.1) $\exists x(x \in \alpha) \rightarrow \exists y(y\text{Fu}\alpha)$
(I.2) $((x < y) \wedge (y < x)) \rightarrow (x = y)$
(I.3) $(x \circ y) \leftrightarrow \neg(x \lfloor y)$

Theorems in the calculus of individuals include the following (Leonard and Goodman 1940, p. 49):

(I.3) $((x < y) \wedge (y < z)) \rightarrow (x < z)$
(I.31) $x < x$
(I.325) $\neg(x \ll x)$
(I.326) $(x \ll y) \rightarrow \neg(y \ll x)$
(I.328) $((x \ll y) \wedge (y \ll z)) \rightarrow (x \ll z)$

Theorems I.3–I.31 tell us that the part-whole relation ($<$) is transitive and reflexive. Theorems I.325–I.328 tell us that the proper part relation ($\ll$) is irreflexive, asymmetrical, though transitive. The calculus of individuals has been described at this level of detail (primitive idea, concepts I.01–I.07, axioms I.1–I.3, theorems I.3–I.328) to provide a clear sense that Goodman's nominalism is not merely stated as an ontological commitment: it is backed up by a rigorous logical program. Abstract entities do not exist,

[8] According to I.1, if set α is not empty, then α has a fusion. According to I.2, if x is a part of y and y is a part of x, then x and y are identical. According to I.3, x overlaps with y if and only if x is not discrete from y.

platonism is false, and the only entities in the world are concrete particulars and individuals.[9]

12.4 Cognitivism About Art

According to Plato (360 B.C.E.), successful theories should carve nature at its joints. If nature is thought of as having joints, then we may have to admit the existence of natural kinds or groupings that reflect the structure of the natural world rather than the interests of human beings. Given their renunciation of abstract entities, we have good reason to expect nominalists to be averse to natural kinds too (Sect. 12.3). Indeed, Goodman denies that nature can dictate its own proper description. Rather, any order is an order that we impose on the world: there is no unique way the world is and we create worlds through scientific theories or works of art.[10] There is no world beyond scientific theories and works of art and the world is only present in these theories and works and accessible to us through them. Here is where Goodman's nominalism joins forces with two other aspects of his philosophy: his irrealism and his cognitivism about art. According to Goodman's irrealism, the world dissolves into versions. According to his cognitivism about art, the languages of art must be recognized as cognitively valuable representational systems alongside science.

Goodman's nominalism has additional implications on the kinds of terms and concepts available to him in his philosophy of art (Shottenkirk 2009). As we have already discovered, Goodman's nominalism involves a rejection of abstract entities (classes, relations, properties, and so on). The basic units in Goodman's (1951) philosophy of art are phenomenal qualia (phenomenal colours, phenomenal sounds, and so on), as they exist

[9] The calculus of individuals also has logical applications: it can be used to solve logical problems such as the difficulty of imperfect community (Carnap 1928). A class can be a community (every two members share some property) or a non-community (not every two members share some property). A community, in turn, can be either perfect (some property is common to all members) or imperfect (no property is common to all members). The difficulty of imperfect community refers to the problem of finding necessary and sufficient conditions for distinguishing between perfect and imperfect communities in terms of resemblances (Rodriguez-Pereyra 1999). Leonard and Goodman (1940) solve the difficulty of imperfect community by replacing a calculus of classes with a calculus of individuals.

[10] Robinson (2000) once heard Goodman say that Derrida deconstructs worlds, whereas he constructs them.

in space and time.[11] Furthermore, Goodman's nominalism compels him to reject meaning in favour of reference. Theories of meaning typically rest on a distinction between sense (meaning) and reference.[12] 'Phosphorus' and 'Hesperus' have the same referent: the planet Venus. However, they do not have the same meaning: 'Phosphorus' has for its sense the morning star, whereas 'Hesperus' has for its sense the evening star. Goodman is interested in the extensions of terms (reference) in the form of concrete individuals, rather than the intensions of terms (meaning or sense). The demand for concrete and extensional individuals negates any consideration of intensional objects.

Goodman's cognitivism about art provides the essential context for his theory of symbol systems. The debate between cognitivism and non-cognitivism about art may be framed in the form of the following two questions (Gaut 2003):

Q1 (epistemic): Can art confer knowledge on its audience?
Q2 (axiological): If art has the capacity to confer knowledge, then does this knowledge-conferring capacity enhance its artistic value?

This debate is at least as old as Plato and Aristotle. According to Plato (360 B.C.E./1953), poetry does not give us knowledge but rather the mere appearance of it. By contrast, Aristotle (350 B.C.E.) believes that poetry can give its audience knowledge of the abstract universals loathed by nominalists.[13] More generally, cognitivists about art answer in the affirmative to both Q1 and Q2 (Goodman 1968; Walsh 1969; Nussbaum 1985, 1990; Kivy 1997). Cognivitists about art may be contrasted with non-cognivists, who answer in the negative to at least one of Q1 and Q2 (Lamarque and Olsen 1994). According to Goodman's version of cognitivism about art (inflected with nominalism and irrealism), we use symbols to perceive, understand, and construct the worlds of our experience. These symbols may be found in chemistry (H for hydrogen, He for helium, Li for lithium, and so on), physics (*G* for the gravitational constant, *c* for the physical

[11] It has been suggested that qualia are the only abstract entities that Goodman admits in his ontology (Cohnitz and Rossberg 2022).

[12] For instance, see the distinction between sense (*sinn*) and reference (*bedeutung*) in Frege (1960).

[13] According to Gaut (2003), both Plato and Aristotle would have answered in the affirmative to Q2.

constant of the speed of light in the vacuum, and so on), art, and a variety of other domains.

Goodman regards the philosophy of art as a branch of epistemology, with understanding rather than knowledge as the focus of its concern. To understand a work of art is not to appreciate it, consider its beauty, and so on, but rather to recognize what it represents or symbolizes and how it fits with or reacts against other versions of the world. Understanding works of art is a matter of active intellectual engagement with symbols (Elgin 1993). All things considered, artistic activity is similar to scientific activity, since it consists to a large extent of symbol processing: inventing, applying, interpreting, transforming, and manipulating symbols and symbol systems.

Both Goodman's cognitivism about art and the theory of symbol systems (which we shall discuss in the next section) provide theoretical support for the view that art-making can be characterized in terms of symbol manipulation. This will be relevant to our computationalist approach to art-making, since its associated Newell-Simon research paradigm (the theory of problem-solving and the theory of computer science as empirical inquiry) supports the view that intelligent entities are physical symbol systems capable of symbol manipulation, intelligent behaviour may be construed as computations over symbols, and the sort of abstraction associated with artistic problem-solving will be symbolic in nature (Sects. 12.1–12.2).

12.5 The Theory of Symbol Systems

Goodman's philosophy is characterized by its breadth: it ranges over logic, epistemology, philosophy of science, philosophy of psychology, aesthetics, and other domains (Abel 1991). Certain aspects of Goodman's philosophy will be difficult or impossible to accommodate under our computationalist approach to art-making: nominalism (Sect. 12.3) and irrealism (Sect. 12.4), for instance. Other aspects of his philosophy, including cognitivism about art (Sect. 12.4) and the theory of symbol systems, will be useful in informing any discussion about the symbolic nature of art-making and artistic problem-solving.

We are now ready to engage with the theory of symbol systems. A symbol scheme is a set of characters employed in a system, together with principles by which they are combined into complex characters (Goodman 1968, p. 131). This symbol scheme is the pure syntactic level of a system, detached from reference. A symbol system is a symbol scheme correlated with a field of reference: it is a set of characters correlated with a set of extensions (Goodman 1968, p. 143).[14] Propositional logic, Arabic numerals, and natural languages all constitute distinct symbol systems. The extension of the character or symbol 'T' is truth, the extension of the character or numeral '1' is the number 1, and the extension of the string of characters 'cat' is a specific carnivorous mammal (*Felis catus*).[15]

A symbol system is syntactically dense if and only if it has an infinite number of characters so ordered that between each two there is a third character (Goodman 1968, p. 136).[16] Otherwise, it is syntactically articulate or differentiated. The distinction between syntactic density and syntactic articulateness is equivalent to the distinction between analog (continuous) and digital (discrete) systems. An analog clock is syntactically dense: each position of its minute hand is a character of the clock's symbol system and between two positions of the hand (say at 45° and 46°) there is a third intermediate position (45.5°). A painting is syntactically dense, since it is either difficult or impossible to assign line and colour in an unambiguous fashion to definite characters in an articulate schema (for instance, an alphabet).[17] By contrast, the musical notation on which works of music rely is syntactically articulate: there is no third intermediate character between C♯ from C.[18] The first necessary condition for a symbol system to be depictive is syntactic density. A symbol system is semantically dense if and only if it has an infinite number of extensions so ordered that between each two there is a third extension. The symbol system of an analog clock is semantically dense: between every pair of times (say four o'clock and half past four), there is a third intermediate time (a quarter past four). The second necessary condition for depiction is semantic density.

Relative repleteness is the third necessary condition for a symbol system to be depictive. One symbol system is less replete relative to another if

[14] See our discussion of the referential nature of Goodman's aesthetics in Sect. 12.4.

[15] Furthermore, a string of characters may have multiple extensions. While the string of characters 'bank' in the English language is syntactically unique, it has multiple extensions: an establishment for the custody, loan, exchange, or issue of money, the extension of credit, etc; the land alongside or sloping down to a river or lake; and so on.

[16] In the first edition of *Languages of Art*, Goodman fails to specify the ordering in question, although this omission is rectified in the second edition.

[17] Matters may of course be quite different with *n*-dot dot matrix pictures, as discussed in Sect. 8.4.

[18] See our discussion of the Western chromatic scale in Sects. 8.4 and 10.3.

and only if the character-constitutive aspects under the first system are properly included among the character-constustive aspects of the second system. To illustrate relative repleteness, consider the contrast between an electrocardiogram (ECG) and Hokusai's (1831) *The Great Wave off Kanagawa* woodblock drawing. Both the ECG and the Hokusai drawing rely on the use of lines. However, only the relative distances from the originating point of the line are relevant in the ECG. By contrast, the colour, thickness, intensity, and contrast of the line are relevant in the Hokusai drawing. Therefore, the Hokusai drawing is more relatively replete than the ECG diagram.[19]

12.6 The Symptoms of Art

Density (syntactic and semantic) and repleteness allow us to depict (show) rather than describe (tell) and are characteristic symptoms of the artistic. According to Goodman, syntactic density, semantic density, and repleteness are necessary and jointly sufficient for a symbol system to be depictive. Paintings are typically syntactically dense, semantically dense, and more relatively replete than diagrammatic symbol systems. Songs with lyrics, though syntactically articulate and semantically articulate, are more relatively replete than the lyrics when they are merely spoken.

Furthermore, there are two forms of reference: denotation and exemplification (literal and metaphorical). Denotation involves a relationship between symbols and the concrete individuals that they pick out or refer to. 'I. M. Pei' denotes a historical individual, the Chinese-American architect Ieoh Ming Pei (1917–2019). If a painting represents an object *o* and *o* exists, then we say that the painting denotes *o*. However, if *o* does not exist, then we say that the painting is a painting of a certain kind: it is an *o*-representing painting. Paintings are filled with fictional persons, places, and things. The man in Rembrandt's etching *Landscape with a Huntsman* is not an actual person but rather a man in Rembrandt's etching. Given Goodman's nominalist agenda, he must say that Rembrandt's etching

[19] Certain diagrams (for instance, diagrams capable of illustrating both the overlap and size of sets) are more relatively replete than other diagrams (for instance, diagrams capable of illustrating only the overlap of sets). Similar distinctions can be made between drawings and photographs: a black-and-white photograph is replete relative to a line drawing, whereas a colour photograph is replete relative to a black-and-white photograph (Blumson 2011).

does not represent a man (an abstract entity) but rather the-man-in-Rembrandt's-*Landscape-with-a-Huntsman*-picture (a concrete individual) (Goodman 1976, p. 26).

Exemplification involves a relationship between symbols and concrete individuals sharing a certain property: we say that these symbols exemplify some shared characteristic.[20] More generally, *x* expresses *F*-ness if *x* refers to *F*-ness and *x* is metaphorically *F* (Goodman 1968). A painting may express sadness, although a painting cannot literally be sad. We say that the feature of sadness is metaphorically exemplified or expressed. A building may express movement, dynamism, and jazziness, although it cannot, being immobile and inert, have any of those properties (Goodman 1988). We say that the building expresses these characteristics of being jazzy, soaring, and singing, in spite of the fact that the building cannot literally have any of these properties. I. M. Pei's glass-and-steel Louvre Pyramid both is a pyramid and literally exemplifies its shape. Works of art can both denote and exemplify: Whistler's (1871) *Arrangement in Grey & Black No. 1* both denotes Whistler's mother (a concrete individual) and literally exemplifies shades of grey (Elgin 1993). Certain works of art may appear to exemplify, despite not literally possessing, certain characteristics.

Denotation, exemplification, and expression can all contribute to the construction of a world. According to Goodman, we use symbols to discover and build the worlds in which we live. Art and science contribute equally to our understanding of the world. Scientific symbols such as the ECG (Sect. 12.5) are articulate and attenuated, because science values reproducibility and intersubjective agreement. Density and repleteness, by contrast, are symptomatic of artistic symbols such as Hokusai's woodblock drawing (Sect. 12.5 and Fig. 12.2), because art values sensitivity more highly than intersubjective agreement and aspires to results that cannot be reproduced.[21] According to Goodman, both art and science are part of a general project of advancing and deepening understanding. This recognition of the continuities between art and science and their cognitive value is consonant with our computationalist approach to art-making. According to PSSH, a physical symbol system has the necessary and sufficient means for intelligent action (Sect. 12.1). We can now recognize

[20] Goodman (1968) describes exemplification as possession plus reference.

[21] This distinction between art and science is drawn from Elgin (1993), who further identifies ambiguity, vagueness, and equivocality as both scientific vices and artistic virtues.

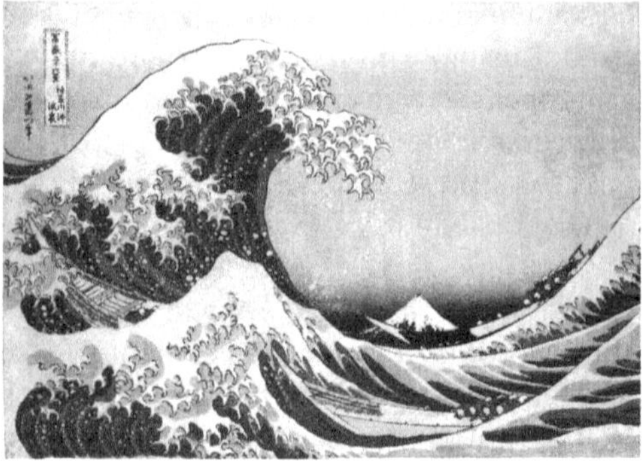

Fig. 12.2 Katsushika Hokusai's (1831) *The Great Wave off Kanagawa*. Woodblock print; ink and color on paper. H. O. Havemeyer Collection, Bequest of Mrs. H. O. Havemeyer, 1929. Reproduced under a Creative Commons Zero (CC0) license

that intelligent action may consist of computation over scientific symbols (articulate and attenuated) or artistic symbols (whose symptoms are density and repleteness). Both sets of symbols (scientific and artistic) are cognitively valuable and contribute to physical symbol systems understanding the world in which they live and solve problems.

Under Goodman's theory of symbol systems, works of art are meaningful entities, possess cognitive value, and are capable of rewarding effortful interpretation. They are not merely objects for passive aesthetic appreciation. At the same time, Goodman denies a theoretical unity across the various arts. Works of music are referents of sequences of characters in one notational system (a score). Works of literature are referents of sequences of characters in another notational system (a script). Each notational system, in turn, is syntactically and semantically disjoint and differentiated. By contrast, paintings, sculpture, etchings, woodcuts, and lithographs belong to syntactically dense and undifferentiated symbol systems. Works of music and literature are allographic arts: two sequences of tones (music) or words (literature) are instances of the same work if there is a sameness of spelling.[22] Paintings, sculpture, etchings, woodcuts, and lithographs are autographic arts, identifiable solely in terms of their history of production.

Goodman's cognitivism about art (Sect. 12.4) and theory of symbol systems (Sect. 12.5) help us to extend the theory of problem-solving and the theory of computer science as empirical inquiry in an artistically

[22] Goodman's theory of symbol systems notoriously implies that a performance with one wrong note is no longer a performance of that work in a strict sense.

relevant manner, especially when intelligence is understood in terms of symbol manipulation and computation over symbols. Further theoretical gains include a deeper appreciation of the continuities and similarities between scientific theories and works of art as distinct though cognitively valuable representational systems, implicated in either denotation or the richer possibilities of exemplification and expression (in the case of art). At the same time, our general theoretical commitment remains firmly rooted to the theory of problem-solving (both the philosophical position and its proofs of concept in computer systems capable of solving various problems), its theoretical milieu (including the theory of computer science as empirical inquiry), and their application to concerns in the philosophy of art.

Goodman's theory of symbol systems allows us to characterize art in terms of symbol systems and their features.[23] This makes it easier for us to apply the theory of problem-solving to art, since the Newell-Simon research paradigm characterizes human beings as physical symbol systems and typically focuses on problems whose solution require the use of highly symbolic processes. The theory of symbol systems allows us to understand art-making in terms of symbol manipulation. At the same time, our computationalist approach is a platonist rather than a nominalist position: works of art exist as abstract and mind-independent entities to be creatively discovered, alongside other abstract entities such as logical proofs. Our computationalist approach is also a cognitivist one: there is cognitive value in works of art. This platonist and cognitivist account of art is supported by the theory of problem-solving, the theory of computer science as empirical inquiry, Goodman's cognitivism about art, and the theory of symbol systems. It foregrounds the symbolic nature of art and artistic problem-solving in a manner that is both coherent and internally consistent. In the next chapter, we will discover how our computationalist approach to art-making can be applied to machine art.

[23] At the pedagogical level, Goodman's account has provided the inspiration for Harvard Project Zero. The principal research tasks of Harvard Project Zero include the following: analyzing and classifying different types of symbol systems characteristic of different art forms, identifying and studying the skills and abilities required for understanding and manipulating art symbols, and investigating the methods of nurturing and training those abilities generally and as they bear upon particular art forms. For further information about Harvard Project Zero, see Howard (1971).

CHAPTER 13

Machine Art

The research in this chapter is part of the programme DesCartes and is supported by the National Research Foundation, Prime Minister's Office, Singapore under its Campus for Research Excellence and Technological Enterprise (CREATE) programme.

13.1 The Mathematical Objection to Machine Intelligence

We have already defined works of art as various ways in which art-makers solve problems and overcome obstacles (Chap. 5) and exhibit creativity (Chap. 10), relative to certain goals the accomplishment of which ensures that artifacts will come to be regarded as works of art (Chap. 7). We have also encountered LT, a proof of concept for the theory of problem-solving that is capable of constructing logical proofs while exhibiting at least some degree of creativity (Sect. 9.6). The protagonists of our computationalist approach to art-making are intelligent, symbol-manipulating physical symbol systems, capable of navigating a problem space, solving problems using heuristic search, and fashioning or constructing works of art. Jason M. Allen & Midjourney's *Théâtre D'opéra Spatial* is an AI-generated, award-winning digital artwork that exemplifies the core features of our computationalist approach to art-making: intelligent problem-solving, symbolic manipulation, and the exhibition of creative behaviour within a structured problem space. Like LT's logical proofs, this artwork reflects goal-directed activity under constraints (Fig. 13.1).

M. Chen, *Art-Making as Problem-Solving*,
https://doi.org/10.1007/978-3-031-90639-8_13

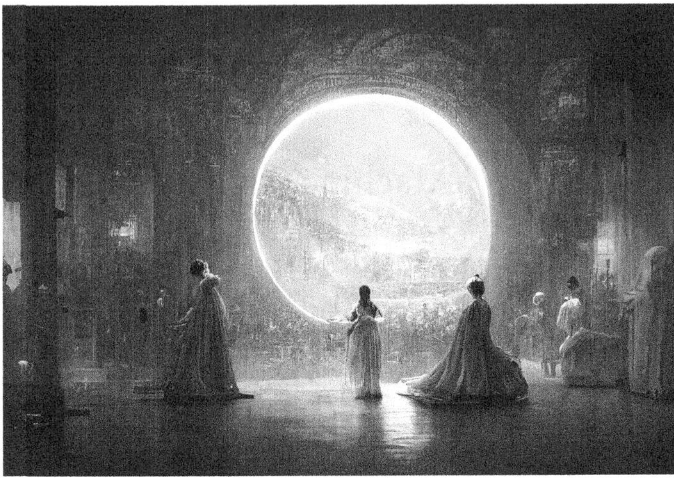

Fig. 13.1 Jason M. Allen & Midjourney's (2022) *Théâtre D'opéra Spatial*. Digital image. © 2022 Jason M. Allen (https://www.jasonmallen.com/)

Before we discuss the possibility of machine art, it will be useful for us to determine whether machines can be classified as intelligent. Gödel's (1931) incompleteness theorems identify certain limits in formal systems possessing a certain set of properties. The target of these theorems are formal systems that are consistent, axiomatizable, and sufficiently powerful to perform basic arithmetic.[1] According to the first incompleteness theorem, if a formal system L is sufficiently powerful, axiomatizable, and consistent, then it is incomplete. In other words, there will be at least some mathematical statements that are true though unprovable relative to L.

According to the second incompleteness theorem (a corollary of the first theorem), it is impossible for a consistent system to prove its own consistency.[2] Here is another way of stating the incompleteness theorems:

[1] Formal systems possessing these three properties include Peano arithmetic without multiplication, Peano arithmetic with subtraction and division, ZFC set theory (or Zermelo-Fraenkel set theory with the axiom of choice included), and several other formal systems besides.

[2] The first theorem applies to consistent systems, while the second theorem tells us that formal systems, even if they are consistent, cannot prove their own consistency. These true-though-unprovable mathematical statements are known as Gödel sentences. For an excellent and accessible survey of the incompleteness theorems, see Smith (2007).

in a sufficiently powerful and axiomatizable formal system, statements can be formulated that can neither be proven nor disproven relative to that system, unless the system itself is inconsistent. Furthermore, formal systems cannot prove their own consistency. To apply these theorems to a discussion about machine intelligence, we would need in addition some means of describing formal systems in terms of machines and machines in terms of logical systems (Turing 1950).

The halting problem is a decision problem that is related to Gödel's incompleteness theorems.[3] A decision problem is a problem that has only two possible outputs relative to a given input: 'yes' or 'no'. Here is an example of a decision problem: given a list of numbers (a, b, c, d), is there at least one pair of numbers in this list that sum to a given target value x? While the output of a decision problem is relatively straightforward, the output of a function problem, by contrast, is far more complex. Here is an example of a function problem: given a list of numbers (a, b, c, d), how many pairs of numbers in this list sum to a given target value x? The halting problem refers to the problem of determining whether a computer program, given a certain input, will eventually halt or run indefinitely.

A proof exists for the theorem that the halting problem is undecidable. As this proof relies on the use of Gödel numbers to refer to computer programs, it may be helpful for us to understand how Gödel numbers work. Gödel numbers were first assigned to statements in Gödel's proof of his incompleteness theorems. Suppose that our task is to determine the Gödel number $\ulcorner\phi\urcorner$ of a string of symbols 'ϕ'. The first step involves assigning a Gödel number to each symbol in the alphabet of the formal system (for instance, Peano arithmetic) under consideration. The first step is illustrated in Table 13.1.

Next, prime numbers p_i shall be assigned as the base of each slot in a string of symbols 'ϕ'.[4] Thereafter, the Gödel number g_i shall be assigned to each corresponding symbol in that slot and it will function as the exponent. Where p_i denotes the ith prime number and g_i denotes the Gödel number for the ith symbol in the string, the Gödel number $\ulcorner\phi\urcorner$ for a string 'ϕ' of

[3] The German term for a decision problem, '*Entscheidungsproblem*', features in the title of Turing's (1936) article.

[4] A prime number is a natural number greater than 1 that has only two factors, 1 and itself. In addition, prime factorization with exponents is a technique that allows us to express a composite number as a product of its prime factors raised to various powers. The idea of prime factorization was first introduced in our discussion of Proof 2 of T2 in Sect. 9.1.

Table 13.1
Assignment of Gödel numbers to symbols in Peano arithmetic

Symbol	*Gödel number*
$\forall$	1
$\exists$	2
$\neg$	3
$\vee$	4
$\wedge$	5
$\rightarrow$	6
$\leftrightarrow$	7
S	8
$+$	9
$\times$	10
$=$	11
0	12
(	13
)	14
x	15
y	16
$\vdots$	$\vdots$

Table 13.2
Assignment of Gödel numbers to the string '0 = 0'

Symbol in string	*0*	*=*	*0*
Gödel number (g_i)	12	11	12
Prime number (p_i)	2	3	5

length m can be computed in accordance with the following equation:

$$\overline{\ulcorner\phi\urcorner} = \prod_{i=1}^{m} p_i^{g_i}$$
$$= p_1^{g_1} \times p_2^{g_2} \times \cdots \times p_m^{g_m}$$

Consider the string '0 = 0'. Table 13.2 contains the values that may be used for computing the Gödel number $\overline{\ulcorner 0 = 0 \urcorner}$ of the string '0 = 0':

The Gödel number for the string '0 = 0' will be equal to $2^{12} \times 3^{11} \times 5^{12} \approx 1.77 \times 10^{17}$ (or 1.77E17). Therefore, given 1.77×10^{17} (or 1.77E17) as the Gödel number encoding information about a string, we can derive via prime factorization with exponents the following: $2^{12} \times 3^{11} \times 5^{12}$. Relative to our enumeration scheme in Table 13.1, we should be able to decode the string as '0 = 0'. The Gödel enumeration scheme may be applied to computer programs. Let H denote a halting oracle that can decide whether other computer programs halt or not. If H exists, then the halting problem is decidable. H takes as its input $(\ulcorner A \urcorner, x)$, where $\ulcorner A \urcorner$ denotes the Gödel number of program A and x denotes an arbitrary string. Since H is a halting oracle, H should be able to answer 'yes' if A halts given input x and 'no' otherwise.

The theorem about the undecidability of the halting problem tells us that this halting oracle H does not exist (viz. $\neg\exists H$) (Turing 1936). Its proof may be stated in the following manner:

1. ass.: $\exists H$ (i.e. H exists)
2. Let computer program A be a program that either halts or does not halt when given its own Gödel number $\ulcorner A \urcorner$ as input.
3. If H is run on input $(\ulcorner A \urcorner, \ulcorner A \urcorner)$, then H returns 'no' if A does not halt when given its own Gödel number $\ulcorner A \urcorner$ as input or 'yes' if A halts.
4. Let G denote a program that runs H on input $(\ulcorner A \urcorner, \ulcorner A \urcorner)$, such that G halts when H returns 'no' or G is forced into an infinite loop (does not halt) when H returns 'yes'.
5. $\therefore$ If H is run on input $(\ulcorner G \urcorner, \ulcorner G \urcorner)$, then H returns 'no' if G does not halt when given its own Gödel number $\ulcorner G \urcorner$ as input or 'yes' if G halts. (from 3; uniformly substitute G for A)
6. $\therefore$ If program G runs H on input $(\ulcorner G \urcorner, \ulcorner G \urcorner)$, then G halts when H returns 'no' or G is forced into an infinite loop (does not halt) when H returns 'yes'. (from 4; uniformly substitute G for A)
7. $\therefore$ G halts when G does not halt or G does not halt when G halts (from 5 and 6, contradiction)
8. $\therefore \neg\exists H$ (from 1 and 7) (QED)

Any intelligent mathematician should be able to follow the proof and understand its implications: there are limits to what can be computed by computer programs, Turing machines, and other kinds of effective procedures in the real world.[5] This is analogous to the limits to what can be recognized as true by formal systems that are sufficiently powerful, axiom-

[5] Penrose (1994, 1989) further insists that human insight must be algorithmic in nature and human consciousness must arise through quantum processes. Given the interdisciplinary nature of our undertaking, however, it will not be unreasonable to expect that at least some of our readers might not have a background in maths or logic and may struggle to unpick what is going on in this proof. It will be sufficient for them to note that an explanation (or proof)

atizable, and consistent under Gödel's incompleteness theorems. Gödel's incompleteness theorems and the theorem about the undecidability of the halting problem may be wielded as objections to the claim that machines are intelligent and can think.

Human mathematicians are able to recognize that there are true-though-unprovable Gödel sentences in certain types of formal systems, even though the formal systems themselves cannot. Machines cannot be designed to tell us whether a computer program, given a certain input, will halt or run indefinitely. These objections are known more generally as the mathematical objection to machine intelligence. If the mathematical objection holds, then our account of machine art founders at the first step: unintelligent machines will be unable to don the mantle of the intelligent protagonists at the centre of our computationalist approach to art-making.

The mathematical objection may be stated in terms of the following argument:

P1: If machines are intelligent, then they must be infallible.
P2: If Gödel's incompleteness theorems and the theorem about the undecidability of the halting problem are true, then machines are not infallible.
P3: Gödel's incompleteness theorems and the theorem about the undecidability of the halting problem are true.
C1: ∴ Machines are not infallible.
C2: ∴ Machines cannot be intelligent.

We may however deny P1, since it is false that only infallible machines are candidates for intelligence. Machines need not be infallible and even intelligent human beings can still make mistakes. In response to the mathematical objection, Turing cites Gödel's incompleteness theorems in his 1951 BBC radio address, providing motivation for allowing intelligent machines to make mistakes (Abramson 2008, p. 160). We have already identified human-level intelligence as a necessary (though insufficient) condition for art-making and the production of works of art (Sect. 4.2). There is no requirement for superhuman-level intelligence or infallibility.

can be furnished, relative to a formal system, demonstrating that the statement (or theorem) in question is true.

13.2 The Lovelace Objection to Machine Intelligence

The Lovelace objection, like the mathematical objection, is an objection to machine intelligence: It runs as follows:

> The Analytical Engine has no pretensions whatever to originate anything. It can do [only] whatever we know how to order it to perform
> — Lovelace (1953, p. 398)

It has been speculated that we could be tempted to define thinking as consisting of those mental processes that we do not understand (Newman et al. 1952/2004). On this construal, making a machine capable of thinking would involve making one that does interesting things without our really understanding how these things are done. This has been described as the epistemic-limitation condition on intelligence and Turing's argument in favour of the epistemic-limitation condition on intelligence may be constructed in the following manner (Abramson 2008, p. 161):

P1: Creativity involves the ability to originate at least something.
P2: Following a set of rules intended by the human architect to bring about a particular behaviour does not involve originating anything.
P3/C1: ∴ Machines that are programmed to have intended behaviour are not creative.
P4: Creativity is essential for intelligence.
C2: ∴ Intelligent machines must have behaviours not intended by their human architects.

According to the Lovelace objection, machines are incapable of satisfying this epistemic-limitation condition on intelligence. Variations of the Lovelace objection might assert that machines can never really do anything new or that machines can never take us by surprise. Rather, machines merely do what we order them, via programs, to do. Creativity is often taken to imply novelty: improbabilist creativity involves novel combinations of familiar ideas, while impossibilist creativity involves the generation of novel ideas (Sect. 10.3). If machines are incapable of coming up with anything new, then they cannot be creative. If they cannot be creative and the construction of works of art typically involves the exhibition of creativity, then machines cannot be capable of constructing works of art either. Neither will the architects of these machines be taken by surprise, if machines can only do what their programs enable them to do.

A possible response to the Lovelace objection might involve identifying examples that could serve as proofs of concept for a machine-art-friendly approach to art. Perhaps the data available to Lady Lovelace at the time of her writing convinced her that machines could neither originate anything nor satisfy the epistemic-limitation condition. This may, in turn, have led to her being skeptical about the prospects of machine intelligence, machine creativity, and machine art. However, once we look beyond Babbage's Analytical Engine and Lovelace's limited sample size, a larger body of data may lead us to conclude that machines can in fact do something novel, originate at least something, take us by surprise, and even fashion or construct works of art. While it is important to respond to the various objections to machine intelligence (the mathematical objection in Sect. 13.1 and the Lovelace objection in Sect. 13.2), a positive argument or criterion for machine intelligence may be needed to press home the case. The epistemic-limitation condition on intelligence could function as this criterion for machine intelligence, especially in the context of machine art.

13.3 Proofs of Concept

LT functions as a proof of concept for the theory of problem-solving (Sect. 9.3). Are similar proofs of concept available for a machine-art-friendly, computationalist approach to art-making? AARON is a machine that is capable of computer-generated visual art (Cohen 1988). EMI or Emmy (Experiments in Musical Intelligence) is a machine that is capable of composing music in the style of Bach, Bartok, Brahms, Chopin, Gershwin, Mozart and even its own human architect David Cope (1996). The human architects of AARON and EMI are Harold Cohen, a visual artist, and David Cope, a musical composer. If works of art are construed as various ways in which artists solve problems and overcome obstacles, then Cohen and Cope may be regarded as professional problem-solvers who, through introspection on the creative thinking process, managed to invent artificial counterparts capable of solving problems in the same artistic medium.

Just as LT can generate solutions possessing certain aesthetic qualities (elegance) in the mathematical realm, AARON, EMI, and related machines can generate solutions that have a good claim to being regarded as works of art. The art of AARON has been exhibited at galleries such as the Tate

Modern Gallery (London), the Stedelijk Museum (Amsterdam), and the San Francisco Museum of Modern Art. EMI was used by Cope to help break his writer's block and assist in the composition of an opera. Some of EMI's works have been recorded and produced by record labels. Emily Howell, a computer program that may be regarded as the successor of EMI, has composed music that is available on Spotify and Apple Music (Paul and Stokes 2023).

Besides AARON and EMI, several other machines could function as proofs of concept in the categories of painting and music. The Painting Fool is a sophisticated painting program: whereas AARON specializes in figurative scenes and is programmed or trained only by Cohen, the Painting Fool can depict a wider variety of scenes and be trained by artists, designers, and virtually anyone else to produce more varied works (Colton 2012). Furthermore, the emotion detection software of Valstar and Pantic (2006) can be used to identify the emotion of the portrait sitter, before this information is translated into the selection of a painting style from the Painting Fool's database for painting the portrait. An artificial neural network by researchers from the University of Tübingen is able to construct, on the basis of a source image, works in the styles of famous artists from different periods of art (Fig. 13.2). More recently, large language model-based programs have been developed to generate images from text prompts in natural language, including DALL-E (OpenAI) and VQGAN-CLIP.

Shimon is a four-armed marimba-playing robot that is able to jam with musicians, improvise in real time, and adapt its choreography, while listening to and building on a human pianist's performance (Hoffman and Weinberg 2011). Researchers from Waseda University and Toyota have developed WAS-2 (Waseda Saxophonist Robot No. 2), a humanoid alto saxophone-playing robot that operates on the basis of the mechanical simulation of the lips, fingers, tongue, oral cavity, and lungs (Solis et al. 2010). HARMI (Human and Robotic Musical Improvisation), yet another example of a creative musical machine, is a software and hardware system that enables robots to improvise with human performers and facilitates the exploration of novel kinds of musical expression (Barton 2013). Given our proofs of concept in AARON, EMI, the Painting Fool, DALL-E, VQGAN-CLIP, Shimon, WAS-2, and HARMI, a machine's ability to originate at least something in the artistic realm is getting exhibited with increasing frequency. Any account of art (computationalist or otherwise), if it wishes to remain futureproof, must find a way to accommodate the possibility of machines creating works of art.

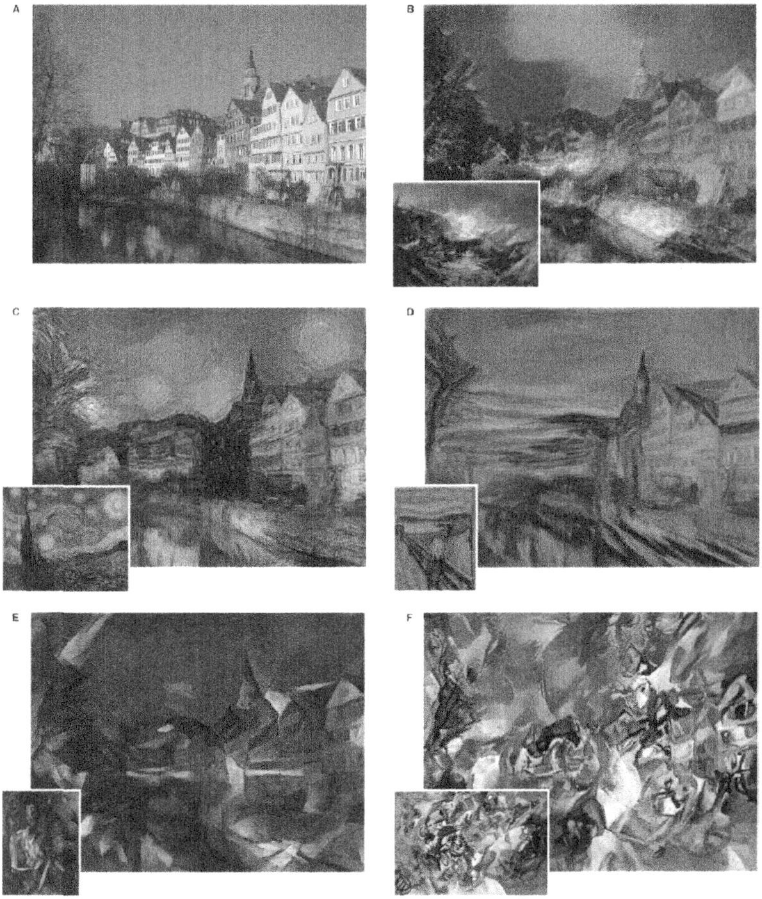

Fig. 13.2 Relative to a photo depicting a part of Tubingen (Germany) by Andreas Praefcke (**a**), several images have been generated in the style of Turner's (c. 1810) *The Shipwreck of the Minotaur* (**b**), Vincent van Gogh's (1889) *The Starry Night* (**c**), Edvard Munch's (1893) *The Scream* (**d**), Picasso's (1910) *Seated Nude* (**e**), and Kandinsky's (1913) *Composition VII* (**f**) (Gatys et al. 2015, p. 5)

13.4 The Possibility of Machine Art

We must remember three things. Firstly, machines such as AARON and EMI resemble the works they create in the sense that both machines and their works are artifacts. Secondly, technical artifacts besides machines have regularly been employed in artistic practice. The difference between machines and these other technical artifacts is often merely a difference in their degree of autonomy. Thirdly, these machines typically embody a lot of the knowledge, experience, understanding, and theory of artistic practice that have gone into the making of these machines.

Artifacts are distinguished from natural objects by being intended products of our activities, produced with a certain purpose in mind (Baker 2004; Hilpinen 1992). Machines are technical artifacts and technical artifacts such as machines, knives, keys, and can openers are a subclass of artifacts: they are created intentionally for a specific function (Houkes and Vermaas 2009). Works of art are yet another subclass of artifacts, produced with the intention of being regarded or treated as works of art (Levinson 2007).[6] The maker of an artifact (a knife, a machine, or a work of art) is someone to whose intention we can track back the process of fashioning or constructing the artifact in question (Thomasson 2007). Indeed, it may not matter that human beings do not directly interfere in, control, or monitor the process when machines autonomously generate certain works. All that matters is that these machines produce artifacts in virtue of human intentions to which we can track back (Steinert 2017).

In addition, writers use pens or laptops, sculptors use a chisel or 3D digital sculpting software, and composers use keyboards or computer programs to compose. The use of technical artifacts should not count against something qualifying as a work of art. A key difference between AARON and EMI and pens, chisels, laptops, or standard software is the autonomous functioning of AARON and EMI. Given their autonomous nature, these machines may engage in behaviours that are both unintended by their human architects and artistically valuable (for instance, the use of a novel palette, the unexpected exploration of certain chord progressions, and so

[6] For an excellent account of the artifactual nature of both machines and works of art, see Steinert (2017). Not all philosophers of art, however, regard works of art as artifacts. Pragmatic aesthetics, for instance, regards works of art not as artifacts but rather as experiences.

on).[7] When this happens, these machines will have a good claim to having satisfied the epistemic-limitation condition on intelligence (Sect. 13.2).

We should not rule out the possibility that the epistemic-limitation condition on intelligence may be satisfied on at least certain occasions. A lot of knowledge, experience, understanding, and theory of artistic practice have typically gone into the making of these machines, and it will be fair to say that these machines will embody much art-relevant knowledge, experience, understanding, and theory. In several instances, the human architects of these machines are themselves practising artists, deeply invested in the traditions and trends of their respective artistic fields: Cohen in the case of AARON, Cope in the case of EMI. The designers of Shimon and HARMI have incorporated ideas from music theory and compositional practice, while the Painting Fool embodies the behavioral and cognitive components of a human painter (Steinert 2017, p. 282).

13.5 The Possibility of Machine Artists

Machines can create works of art. Any robust account of art must be future-proof and able to take into proper consideration the steady stream of proofs of concept of machine art (Sect. 13.3). Machines function as technical artifacts and differ from other technical artifacts that have been used in the history of artistic practice by their autonomous nature. As a lot of art-relevant knowledge, experience, understanding, and theory is embodied in machines, we should not rule out the possibility that machines may behave in ways that are both unintended and artistically valuable. If the epistemic-limitation condition is satisfied, then the case for machine intelligence and machine creativity will only grow stronger. The questions 'Can machines create works of art?' and 'Can machines be regarded as artists?' are however distinct and must be addressed separately. We have already answered the first question in the affirmative (Sect. 13.4). Responding to the second question, however, requires more care, sensitivity, and nuance.

Suppose that an ant crawling over a patch of sand traces a line in the sand. By pure coincidence, this line curves and recrosses itself such that it resembles a portrait of Winston Churchill (Putnam 1981). Next, suppose that a parrot has been trained to reproduce phonologically some utterance in the natural language of English (Bender and Koller 2020). We would

[7] Compare with the semantic bug phenomenon in Sect. 9.6.

no more say that the ant has traced a line drawing depicting Churchill than we would say that the parrot has produced a meaningful utterance in the natural language of English. Had the ant seen either Churchill or an image of Churchill at least once in the past, possessed the intelligence and skill to depict Churchill, and produced the portrait intentionally, we would have stronger grounds to conclude that the lines in the sand represents Churchill. We have already argued that art-making is a goal-directed activity, whose characteristic artifacts are communication channels through which art-makers share semantic information with their intended audience (H1 and H2). The lines in the sand are not directed by the artistic goal of representation, nor does the ant intend these lines to represent anyone (let alone Churchill). Last but not least, the ant does not have any intended audience. In a similar vein, since the parrot lacks the relevant natural language understanding, it cannot possibly intend that its utterance express specific mental states or communicative intentions. Therefore, the parrot's utterance is meaningless, just as the ant's 'line drawing' is non-art.

The mere reproduction (however perfect) of patterns or structures of sound, line, colour, and so on is insufficient for an artifact to count as a work of art. The art-maker must in addition possess intentionality (aboutness and directedness). Some might argue that it is only a matter of time before we recognize machine-generated works as works of art. This argument may be termed the argument from historical inevitability and could even appeal, as Elgammal (2018) has done, to related watersheds in the history of technology and art. After all, photography was not considered art when it was first invented, owing to its heavily mechanized nature. However, just as photography has since become established as a fine art genre, we have good reason to believe that AI-generated works will one day be accepted by the art world too. As Anscomb (2022) has observed, what allowed photography to gain artistic credibility was a far greater awareness of how human agency and intentionality permeate the photographic process. By analogy, once we stop downplaying the role of human authorship in the information-processing procedures of autonomous AI systems and recognize the human-machine interface in the production of even the most advanced machine-generated works, we will be better able to identify the artistic intent in the generative process and rely on this intent to ground the artistic significance of machine-generated works.

Neither the ant nor the parrot can participate in art, language, and culture in the way that ordinary human beings can. The same unfortunately applies to state-of-the-art machines. Machines and ants do not understand artistic conventions any more than parrots understand linguistic conventions. In addition, we have argued that candidate works of art (artifacts) are produced relative to certain artistic goals. Is it even possible for machines to share some of these goals? Representationalists are interested in the representation of objects in the world, including society and human action. Can machines be described as understanding the artistic brief, if they lack the relevant experience in a human society in which actions are meaningful and can be praise- or blameworthy? Expressivists are interested in the communication of moods, emotions, or attitudes. Can machines achieve expressivist goals if they lack the relevant ability to feel moods and emotions? Certain historicists are interested in the historical relation between an artist's intentions and earlier artworks. Can machines possess the relevant intentionality to ensure that their works have a shot at becoming part of the historical narrative of art? More generally, if a work of art must be an artifact produced with the intention of being regarded as a work of art, can a machine be said to possess the relevant intentionality?

In these instances, an understanding of human society and human action, an ability to feel the emotions and moods that human beings do, and intentionality appear to be presupposed as part of the prerequisites for the central artistic task. More generally, the humanity of the art-maker as an information-processing or physical symbol system appears to be presupposed. Human beings will still have to be in the loop, since certain anthropocentric presuppositions are active and we must be able to track back the process of production to some human being's intentions. At the same time, other artistic goals may be identified that are less anthropocentric and more machine-friendly. Formalists are interested in the properties that are accessible by direct sensation (typically sight or hearing). As long as these formal properties are instantiated in certain works, formalists might have no qualms about recognizing machines as artists.

Even more tantalizingly, anti-essentialists urge that the conditions of application for the concept of art remain open and emendable (Sect. 7.8). The open-textured and open-ended nature of the concept of art suggests a possibility that the concept of the artist may be extended to include machine artists, especially as machines become more sophisticated and their human architects become more adept at understanding and mechanizing the art-relevant information processes and schemes of heuristic search. Better yet, perhaps machines will learn what these information processes and heuristic search schemes are through regular interaction with artists and figure out how best to employ these processes and schemes in the production of art. It is possible that machines will satisfy the epistemic-limitation condition on intelligence through unintended though artistically valuable behaviours. In doing so, they will have a good claim to intelligence and creativity in art. However, as machines still lack the relevant intentionality, human perspective, and art-historical awareness, we shall refrain from conferring on them the laurels of the artist for the foreseeable future.

13.6 Concerns and Worries About Machine Art

As machines get better at creating works, the probability of encountering machine-produced works that are indistinguishable from works produced by human artists will only increase over time. The ability to deceive and provide an output that is Turing-indistinguishable is precisely what is being tested for in the Turing (1950) test for conversational intelligence. In this test, a judge is given the task of determining, on the basis of text-based interaction with two test candidates (one human and the other a computer), which is the human being and which is the computer. A computer passes this test, just in the case the judge can successfully distinguish between the human and the computer no more than 50% of the time. Should we be disturbed or worried, if we become increasingly unable to distinguish between works of art produced by human artists and machine-produced works?

In 2022, Jason Allen, a video game designer, submitted the digital image *Théâtre D'opéra Spatial* to the Colorado State Fair's fine arts competition. This digital image beat 20 other artists in the digitally manipulated photography category to win the first-place blue ribbon and USD 300 prize.[8] The digital image was AI-generated and it was one of the first AI-generated pieces to win a prize at a fine arts competition. Nevertheless, Allen claimed that he did not break any rules and had already made it clear that his digital image had been created using AI. As machine art increasingly becomes a live option, we seem to be an inflection point. This inflection point is

[8] Since no traditional painterly media or techniques were involved in the production of *Théâtre D'opéra Spatial*, we must guard against the tendency to describe this printed digital image as a 'painting'. For recent work in the philosophy of art on the concept of the medium, see Davies (2003) and Gaut (2010). For even more recent work in the philosophy of art concerning how digital technology might change our understanding of and engagement with the visual arts, see Thomson-Jones (2021).

comparable to the one described by Benjamin (1935/1987), when he pondered over the fate of aesthetic experience in the age of mechanical reproduction (marked by the invention and proliferation of photography and film).

Another concern involves the black-box nature of machines. Human beings are capable of introspection and several self-reports of creative artistic processes have made their way to public consciousness through compilations of testimonies in the aggregative version of introspectionism. Is it possible to make the internal processes and mechanisms of machines more transparent? We could subject machines and their human architects to the criterion of reproducibility and request details about how certain things can be done and reproduced, as these machines solve artistic problems and overcome artistic challenges.[9] These details, in turn, should not decrease our wonder at the machines through demystification. Rather, they should enhance our appreciation of the simplicity of information processes underlying complex, creative, and artistic problem-solving behaviour (compare with Sect. 10.4).

Human architects might consider the details of their computer programs to be part of art and therefore not subject to detailed and public scrutiny. Neither Harold Cohen nor David Cope have supplied sufficient information about their machines (AARON and EMI) to ensure that the criterion of reproducibility will be satisfied. More generally, the problem of reproducibility is faced by artists who wish to refrain from sharing at least some computer-scientific aspects of their work.[10] Was there this level of scrutiny when Vermeer, as has generally been held, used camera obscura technology to attain perfect perspective?[11] Was Andy Warhol not permitted the use of silkscreen printing technology to produce multiple identical copies of his works of art? Has Brian Eno not used tape loops, synthesizers, and computer algorithms to generate music and is he not exempt from this criterion of reproducibility? While possible objections to machine art

[9] Reproducibility is a basic criterion for publishability in a strictly scientific context. At the same time, if art, unlike science, aspires to results that cannot be reproduced, then the demand for reproducibility with respect to machine art may be ill-advised. See our discussion of the contrast between art and science in Sect. 12.6.

[10] For a more detailed account of the criterion of reproducibility in the context of AARON and EMI, see Wiggins (2008).

[11] While there is a general consensus that Vermeer used this technology for his artistic purposes, it must be conceded that there is no definitive proof that this was, in fact, the case.

should be raised and considered, we must ensure that these objections are not the mere expression of luddism or an aversion to new technology.

13.7 Penrose Art Problems

The Penrose chess problem is a chess problem originally devised by Sir Roger Penrose, an English mathematician, physicist, and philosopher of science. The Penrose chess problem is designed to show that human intuition is still superior to the computational powers of AI.

Supercomputers are capable of challenging human world chess champions: Deep Blue famously defeated Garry Kasparov in a chess match in 1997. At the same time, supercomputers are likely to be flummoxed by the Penrose chess problem (Fig. 13.3): they will predict a victory for black because of the material advantage of an extra queen, two extra rooks, an extra pawn, and three extra bishops enjoyed by black. According to the setup proposed by Penrose, black has three dark-squared bishops. This implies that two pawns have already reached the promotion rank and been promoted to dark-squared bishops. It is intuitive to most human chess players that white can force a draw in 50 moves, without a pawn being moved. All white needs to do is move the king on the light squares, while black (most of whose pieces are blocked) can only move the dark-squared bishops

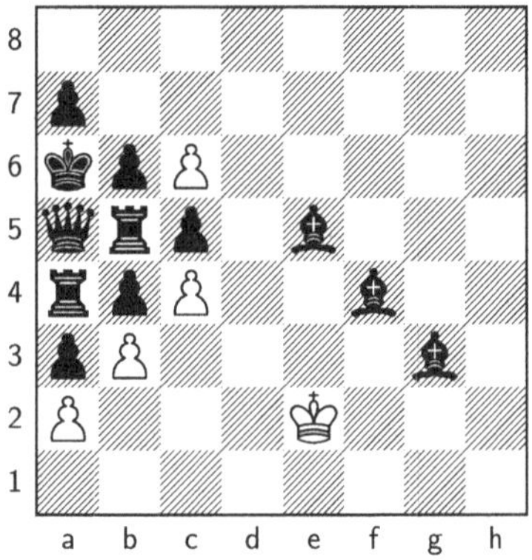

Fig. 13.3 The Penrose chess problem

along the diagonals.[12] The Penrose chess problem is hard for computers to solve. This chess problem is part of Penrose's broader position that human understanding and human creativity are non-computational and cannot be replicated by a sufficiently complex computer (Penrose 1989, 1994).[13] Indeed, at least some mathematical understanding is non-computational in nature: this includes our mathematical understanding of Gödel's (1931) incompleteness theorems (Sect. 13.1).

The Penrose chess problem is a member of what has been described as a Penrose set of challenging chess problems (Zahavy et al. 2023). Can similarly challenging problems be posed in the artistic domain that are easy for human beings but difficult for computers to solve? These problems may be termed Penrose art problems, in honour of the Penrose chess problem and the Penrose set. O*NET (https://www.onetonline.org/), an online service developed for the U.S. Department of Labor, has identified creative intelligence as a specific engineering bottleneck to computerization (Frey and Osborne 2017). It is difficult to design machines with the ability to either come up with unusual or clever ideas about a given topic or situation or develop creative ways to solve a problem. It is equally difficult to design machines with the knowledge of theory and techniques required to compose, produce, and perform works of music, dance, visual arts, drama, and sculpture. Another engineering bottleneck concerns manual and finger dexterity: it is difficult to design machines that can mimic the precisely coordinated movements of fingers, hands, and arms to grasp, manipulate, or assemble objects.

Originality-based Penrose art problems may test the ability of machines to develop creative ways to solve a problem. Given an incomplete line drawing, can a few lines be added to ensure the symmetry of the image? Knowledge-based Penrose art problems may require machines to demonstrate their art-relevant knowledge. Can a machine distinguish between a generic empty canvas and Robert Rauschenberg's (1953) *Erased de Kooning Drawing*? Dexterity-based Penrose art problems may require machines to demonstrate their manual dexterity and haptic sensitivity

[12] It is also theoretically possible for white to win, if black somehow erroneously moves all three dark-squared bishops away from the diagonal attacking the c7 square. Such a grievous oversight will allow white to advance the c6 pawn to the promotion rank, promote it to become a queen, and checkmate the black king.

[13] The Penrose chess problem has been proposed as a way to learn more about the uniqueness of the human mind (Doggers 2018).

in tasks commonly found in sculpting, pottery, and traditional painting. Can a paintbrush and a numbered palette be used to colour a paint-by-numbers landscape? As expressivists claim a central role for the emotions in the artistic domain, sentiment-analysis-based Penrose art problems may require machines to demonstrate their ability to associate works of art with the appropriate emotions. Is Pablo Picasso's (1903–1904) *The Old Guitarist* associated with happiness, anger, or sadness? Is Gustav Holst's (1914–1917) *Mars, the Bringer of War*, from his seven-movement orchestral suite *The Planets*, associated with happiness, anger, or sadness?

A team at Google DeepMind has demonstrated that a team of diverse AI systems can outperform a single AI system or a more homogeneous team when tackling chess problems in the Penrose set: more ideas are first generated as a group, before the best ones get selected (Zahavy et al. 2023). Perhaps similar computational advances might be made when these hypothetical Penrose art problems (originality-based, knowledge-based, dexterity-based, sentiment-analysis-based, and so on) are more carefully formulated and addressed by researchers. Penrose art problems will provide us with an opportunity to understand how the human brain works in the artistic domain. The gap to machine artisthood could even be narrowed through an engagement with these Penrose art problems, as we attain a better grasp of the nature of human intuition, understanding, and creativity in the artistic domain and how best to model them computationally.

In conclusion, the mathematical objection and the Lovelace objection to machine intelligence are not knockdown objections. In the case of the former objection, we can allow for intelligent machines to make mistakes. In the case of the latter objection, we may introduce an epistemic-limitation condition on intelligence. The case for machine intelligence and machine creativity in art is invariably strengthened when an appeal is made to such proofs of concept as AARON, EMI, the Painting Fool, and so on. At least some machines can create works of art, because they may have been designed intentionally for the purpose of creating works of art, typically embody a lot of art-relevant knowledge, experience, understanding, and theory, and may behave in ways that are both unintended by their human architects and artistically valuable.

Although there is a case for both machine intelligence and the ability of machines to create works of art, machines lack the intelligence that we characteristically attribute to artists, as they lack certain characteristics (intentionality, art-historical awareness, and so on). Therefore, we hesitate to designate machines as artists. As the probability of machines producing works that are indistinguishable from the works of human artists increases over time, we may worry about getting deceived by machines. We may also wish to consider introducing the criterion of reproducibility in the case of machine art. Our worries or concerns should not, however, be the mere reflection of a luddite attitude. Last but not least, Penrose art problems (easy for human beings and difficult for computers to solve) may be introduced to help us to develop a keener awareness of the nature of human intuition, understanding, and creativity in the artistic domain. The computational advances that an engagement with Penrose art problems may inspire could help us to narrow the gap to machine artisthood.

CHAPTER 14

Conclusion

Paolo Uccello, an Italian Renaissance painter and mathematician, was famously obsessed with linear perspective and often approached spatial representation as a visual puzzle, searching for geometrical solutions within a constrained problem space. His mosaic in Fig. 14.1, demonstrating a mastery of space, geometry, and form, aligns beautifully with our account of how artistic innovation emerges from structured computational processes. Creativity is a special class of problem-solving activities, just as problem-solving behaviour is a special class of intelligent behaviour. Intelligent behaviour is associated with computations over symbols and intelligent, symbol-manipulating physical symbol systems such as human beings exercise their intelligence by searching a problem space until the symbol structures of solutions are produced. This is the account of creativity, intelligence, and problem-solving under the Newell-Simon research paradigm. Its two central planks are the theory of problem-solving and the theory of computer science as empirical inquiry.

Our computationalist approach to art-making and the production of works of art has been formulated with the theory of problem-solving and the computational theory of mind as its central theoretical loci. This approach has also been formulated against the backdrop of an information-theoretic philosophy of art. Three hypotheses have been identified as central to an information-theoretic philosophy of art: art-making is a goal-directed activity whose characteristic artifacts are works of art (H1); artifacts are communication channels through which art-makers (source)

M. Chen, *Art-Making as Problem-Solving*,
https://doi.org/10.1007/978-3-031-90639-8_14

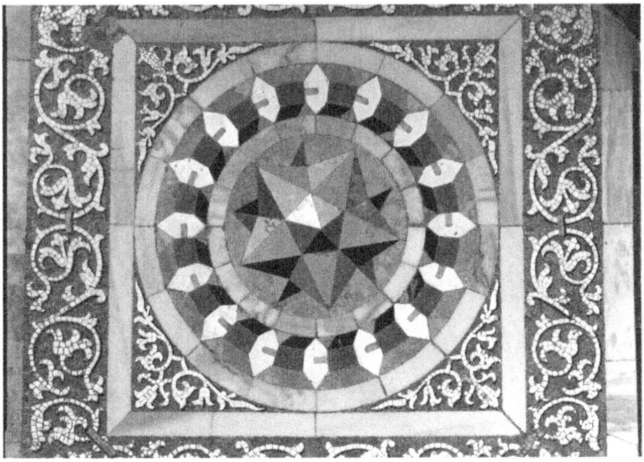

Fig. 14.1 Paolo Uccello's (1425–1430) untitled mosaic in St. Mark's Basilica, Venice. Marble mosaic

share semantic information with their intended audience (destination) (H2); and the generation of artifacts and their possible inclusion (as 'hits') in the artistic canon depend, in the final analysis, on answers to yes-no questions ('bits' or binary choices) (H3). According to our computationalist approach, the central artistic problem or task consists of an art-specific challenge to be overcome or a problem to be solved, the overcoming or solving of which is conditional on the available materials at the disposal of each artist. Our protagonists are intelligent, symbol-manipulating physical symbol systems, capable of navigating a problem space, solving problems using heuristic search, and fashioning or constructing works of art. We have accepted an ontological commitment to artistic platonism: at least some works of art may be identified as abstract entities that exist in a non-spatiotemporal, mind-independent, acausal manner.

Given this ontological commitment, we may ultimately be better off speaking in terms of creative discovery rather than creation. Creative discovery may be characterized in terms of the mapping, exploration, and transformation of the conceptual space and our artistic knowledge or store of artistic claims, accepted as true, would constitute a map of the problem space by which we steer. This account of art has an epistemological commitment to Goodman's cognitivism about art and theory of symbol systems. Intelligent behaviour may consist of computation over scientific symbols (articulate and attenuated) or artistic symbols (whose symptoms are density and repleteness) and both sets of symbols (scientific and artistic) are cognitively valuable and contribute to our understanding of the world. Machines embody a lot of art-relevant knowledge, experience, understanding, and theory and may sometimes exhibit unintended and artistically valuable behaviours, lending credence to the claim that machines can construct or fashion works of art. However, the intelligence of machines is insufficient for them to count as artists: they still lack the relevant intentionality, human perspective, and art-historical awareness.

Our computationalist approach is interdisciplinary, grounded in theories and approaches from big history, physics, mathematics, computer science, artificial intelligence research, psychology, and cognitive science. By bridging art with these and other related disciplines and defending important continuities in problem-solving behaviour across the artistic and scientific domains, our approach fosters a more integrated understanding of art-making and its underlying creative processes. True to the spirit of philosophy, it allows us to better understand how things in the broadest possible sense of the term hang together in the broadest possible sense of the term (Sellars, 1963). At the same time, our approach is not only broad and systematic: it is present-oriented. Although contemporary art practices are pluralistic, multidisciplinary, and conceptually fluid, our approach can explain how human minds continue to cope, function as the loci of intentionality, and make art-making-relevant decisions in the face of fluidity, dynamism, complexity, volatility, uncertainty, grey areas, and edge cases. It is also future-proof. As more machine-generated works will get produced in the future and at greater levels of sophistication, they will be ripe for conceiving of in computationalist terms. In addition, our approach will provide theoretical support for the development and incorporation of computational models (for instance, artificial neural networks) into creative and art-making processes and even art education.

Our approach is philosophically robust, undergirded by rigorous argumentation and support from various philosophical theories, concepts, and tools. Our account is determinate: it is a computationalist, platonist, and cognitivist account of art. Our account is futureproof: it can explain both the possibility of machine art and the need to withhold assent from the claim that machines should be regarded as artists. We hope that it may in time become a map by which to steer the wonderful and exciting problem space of art. Our approach is philosophically robust, undergirded by rigorous argumentation and support from various philosophical theories, concepts, and tools. Our account is determinate: it is a computationalist, platonist, and cognitivist account of art. Our account is futureproof: it can explain both the possibility of machine art and the need to withhold assent from the claim that machines should be regarded as artists. We hope that it may in time become a map by which to steer the wonderful and exciting problem space of art.

Bibliography

Šalda, F. X. (1969). The violent dreamer: Some remarks on the work of Edvard Munch. *Journal of Aesthetics & Art Criticism, 28*(2), 149–153. https://doi.org/10.2307/428564
Abel, G. (1991). Logic, art, and understanding in the philosophy of Nelson Goodman. *Inquiry: An Interdisciplinary Journal of Philosophy, 34*(3–4), 311–321. https://doi.org/10.1080/00201749108602259
Abramson, D. (2008). Turing's responses to two objections. *Minds & Machines, 18*(2), 147–167. https://doi.org/10.1007/s11023-008-9094-6
Adajian, T. (2022). The definition of art. In E. N. Zalta (Ed.), *The Stanford encyclopedia of philosophy* (Spring 2022). Metaphysics Research Lab, Stanford University.
Adams, F. (2003). The informational turn in philosophy. *Minds & Machines, 13*(4), 471–501. https://doi.org/10.1023/a:1026244616112
Adorno, T. W. (1997). *Aesthetic theory.* In G. Adorno, R. Tiedemann, & R. Hullot-Kentor (Eds.). Continuum.
Adorno, T. W. (2006). *Philosophy of new music.* University of Minnesota Press.
Alperson, P., & Carroll, N. (2008). Music, mind, & morality: Arousing the body politic. *Journal of Aesthetic Education, 42*(1), 1–15. https://doi.org/10.1353/jae.2008.0001
Anscomb, C. (2022). Creating art with AI. In C. Moruzzi, M. Verdicchio, & F. Fossa, (Eds.). *Odradek, 8*(1), 14–51.
Appel, K., & Haken, W. (1977a). Every planar map is four colorable. Part I: Discharging. *Illinois Journal of Mathematics, 21*(3), 429–490. https://doi.org/10.1215/ijm/1256049011

M. Chen, *Art-Making as Problem-Solving*,
https://doi.org/10.1007/978-3-031-90639-8

Appel, K., & Haken, W. (1977b). The solution of the four-color-map problem. *Scientific American, 237*(4), 108–121.
Appel, K., Haken, W., & Koch, J. (1977). Every planar map is four colorable. Part II: Reducibility. *Illinois Journal of Mathematics, 21*(3), 491–567.
Aristotle. (350 B.C.E.). Poetics (S. H. Butcher, Trans.). In *The Internet classics archive*.
Armstrong, D. M. (1973). *Belief, truth & knowledge*. Cambridge University Press.
Ayer, A. J. (1946). *Language, truth and logic*. Dover.
Azevedo, F. A., Carvalho, L. R., Grinberg, L. T., Farfel, J. M., Ferretti, R. E., Leite, R. E., Filho, W. J., Lent, R., & Herculano-Houzel, S. (2009). Equal numbers of neuronal & nonneuronal cells make the human brain an isometrically scaled-up primate brain. *Journal of Comparative Neurology, 513*(5), 532–541.
Baker, L. R. (2004). The ontology of artifacts. *Philosophical Explorations, 7*(2), 99–111. https://doi.org/10.1080/13869790410001694462
Bar-Hillel, Y. (1955). An examination of information theory. *Philosophy of Science, 22*(2), 86–105. https://doi.org/10.1086/287407
Barrière, L. (2017). Combinatorics in the art of the twentieth century. In *Proceedings of Bridges 2017: Mathematics, Art, Music, Architecture, Education, Culture* (pp. 321–328).
Barrow, J. D. (2003). Art & science les liaisons dangereuses? In *Art & complexity* (pp. 1–20). Elsevier.
Bartlett, F. C. (1958). *Thinking*. Basic Books.
Barton, S. (2013). The human, the mechanical, & the spaces in between: Explorations in human-robotic musical improvisation. In *Proceedings of the AAAI Conference on Artificial Intelligence and Interactive Digital Entertainment* (Vol. 9(5), pp. 9–13).
Bateson, G. (2000). *Steps to an ecology of mind: Collected essays in anthropology, psychiatry, evolution, & epistemology*. University of Chicago Press.
Battersby, C. (1989). *Gender & genius: Towards a feminist aesthetics*. Indiana University Press.
Batteux, C. (1746). *Les beaux-arts réduits à un seul principe*. Durand.
Baumgarten, A. G. (1735). *Reflections on Poetry*. University of California Press.
Baumgarten, A. G. (1750). *Aesthetica*. G. Olms.
Baxandall, M. (1985). *Patterns of intention: On the historical explanation of pictures*. Yale University Press.
Beardsley, M. C. (1958). *Aesthetics*. Harcourt Brace.
Beardsley, M. C. (1965). On the creation of art. *Journal of Aesthetics & Art Criticism, 23*(3), 291–304. https://doi.org/10.2307/428176
Beebe-Center, J. G., & Pratt, C. C. (1937). A test of Birkhoff's aesthetic measure. *The Journal of General Psychology, 17*(2), 339–353.
Bell, C. (1914). *Art*. Chatto & Windus.

Benacerraf, P. (1973). Mathematical truth. *The Journal of Philosophy, 70*(19), 661–679.

Bender, E. M., & Koller, A. (2020). Climbing towards NLU: On meaning, form, & understanding in the age of data. In *Proceedings of the 58th Annual Meeting of the Association for Computational Linguistics* (pp. 5185–5198).

Benjamin, W. (1935/1987). *The Work of Art in the Age of its Technological Reproducibility, & Other Writings on Media*. In M. W. Jennings, B. Doherty, T. Y. Levin, & E. F. N. Jephcott (Eds.). Belknap Press of Harvard University Press.

Bennett, C. H., & Landauer, R. (1985). The fundamental physical limits of computation. *Scientific American, 253*(1), 48–57.

Bense, M. (1969). Einführung in die informationstheoretische ästhetik grundlegung und anwendung in der texttheorie.

Berkeley, G. (1710). *A treatise concerning the principles of human knowledge*. In (T. J. McCormack (Ed.). Dover Publications.

Berlyne, D. E. (1976). Similarity & preference judgments of Indian & Canadian subjects exposed to western paintings. *International Journal of Psychology, 11*(1), 43–55.

Binkley, T. (1977). Piece: Contra aesthetics. *Journal of Aesthetics & Art Criticism, 35*(3), 265–277. https://doi.org/10.2307/430287

Birkhoff, G. D. (1933). *Aesthetic measure*. Harvard University Press.

Birkhoff, G. D. (1938). The present status of esthetic measure. *The Scientific Monthly, 46*(4), 351–357.

Blackburn, S. (1984). *Spreading the word: Groundings in the philosophy of language*. Oxford University Press.

Blumson, B. (2011). Depictive structure? *Philosophical Papers, 40*(1), 1–25. https://doi.org/10.1080/05568641.2011.560026

Boden, M. A. (1994). Creativity: A framework for research. *Behavioral & Brain Sciences, 17*(3), 558–570. https://doi.org/10.1017/s0140525x00035986

Boden, M. A. (2004). *The creative mind: Myths & mechanisms*. Routledge.

Boden, M. A. (2010). The Turing test & artistic creativity. *Kybernetes, 39*(3), 409–413.

Boolos, G. (1990). On “seeing” the truth of the Gödel sentence. *Behavioral & Brain Sciences, 13*(4), 655–656. https://doi.org/10.1017/s0140525x00080687

Bouleau, C. (2014). *The Painter's secret geometry: A study of composition in art*. Courier Corporation.

Bringsjord, S. (2008). The logicist manifesto: At long last let logic-based artificial intelligence become a field unto itself. *Journal of Applied Logic, 6*(4), 502–525. https://doi.org/10.1016/j.jal.2008.09.001

Bringsjord, S., & Govindarajulu, N. S. (2020). Artificial intelligence. In E. N. Zalta (Ed.), *The Stanford encyclopedia of philosophy* (Summer 2020). Metaphysics Research Lab, Stanford University.

Bringsjord, S., Bello, P., & Ferrucci, D. (2001). Creativity, the Turing test, & the (better) Lovelace test. *Minds & Machines, 11*, 3–27.

Bruineberg, J., & Rietveld, E. (2014). Self-organization, free energy minimization, & optimal grip on a field of affordances. *Frontiers in Human Neuroscience, 8*, 599.

Bruineberg, J., Seifert, L., Rietveld, E., & Kiverstein, J. (2021). Metastable attunement & real-life skilled behavior. *Synthese, 199*(5–6), 12819–12842.

Brunet, J. (1703). *Projet d'une nouvelle métaphysique*. Publisher Unknown.

Bryson, N. (1983). *Vision & painting: The logic of the gaze*. Yale University Press.

Burgess, J. P., & Rosen, G. (1997). *A subject with no object: Strategies for nominalistic interpretation of mathematics* G. A. Rosen (Ed.). Oxford University Press.

Cardoso, A., & Wiggins, G. A. (Eds.) (2007). In *Proceedings of the 4th International Joint Workshop on Computational Creativity*. Goldsmiths, University of London.

Carey, J. (1985). *Communication as culture: Essays on media & society*. Unwin Hyman.

Carnap, R. (1928). *Der Logische Aufbau der Welt*. Meiner Verlag.

Carney, J. D. (1991). The style theory of art. *Pacific Philosophical Quarterly, 72*(4), 272–289. https://doi.org/10.1111/j.1468-0114.1991.tb00321.x

Carroll, N. (1994). Identifying art. In R. J. Yanal (Ed.), *Institutions of art* (pp. 3–38). Pennsylvania State University Press.

Carroll, N. (1999). *Philosophy of art: A contemporary introduction*. Routledge.

Carroll, N. (2000). Formalism. In B. N. Gaut & D. Lopes (Eds.), *The Routledge companion to aesthetics*. Routledge.

Carroll, N. (2001). *Beyond aesthetics: Philosophical essays*. Cambridge University Press.

Carroll, N. (2002). Aesthetic experience revisited. *British Journal of Aesthetics, 42*(2), 145–168. https://doi.org/10.1093/bjaesthetics/42.2.145

Carroll, N. (2012a). Essence, expression, & history. In E. Lepore & M. Rollins (Eds.), *Danto & his critics* (pp. 118–145). Wiley-Blackwell.

Carroll, N. (2012b). Art in an expanded field: Wittgenstein & aesthetics. *Nordic Journal of Aesthetics, 23*(42), 14–31. https://doi.org/10.7146/nja.v23i42.5873

Cassirer, E. (1953). *The philosophy of symbolic forms*. Yale University Press.

Chaitin, G. J. (1977). Algorithmic information theory. *IBM Journal of Research & Development, 21*(4), 350–359.

Chanan, M. (1972). Art as experiment. *British Journal of Aesthetics, 12*(2), 133–147. https://doi.org/10.1093/bjaesthetics/12.2.133

Checkland, P., & Scholes, J. (1999). *Soft systems methodology in action*. John Wiley & Sons.
Chen, M. (2018). Criterial problems in creative cognition research. *Philosophical Psychology, 31*(3), 368–382.
Chen, M. (2023). Take a chance on me: Aleatory poetry, generative AI, & the external demarcation problem. *The Journal of Aesthetics & Art Criticism, 81*(4), 508–524. https://doi.org/10.1093/jaac/kpad042
Chen, M. (forthcoming). *The immortal game: A guide to chess*. Thinkers Publishing.
Chesterton, G. K. (1953). *The everlasting man*. Hodder & Stoughton.
Christian, D. (2004). *Maps of time: An introduction to big history* (Vol. 2). University of California Press.
Coeckelbergh, M. (2016). Can machines create art? *Philosophy & Technology, 30*(3), 285–303. https://doi.org/10.1007/s13347-016-0231-5
Cohen, H. (1988). How to draw three people in a botanical garden. *AAAI, 89*, 846–855.
Cohnitz, D., & Rossberg, M. (2022). Nelson Goodman. In E. N. Zalta (Ed.), *The Stanford encyclopedia of philosophy* (Summer 2022). Metaphysics Research Lab, Stanford University.
Collier, M. (2014). Toward a Science of Criticism: Aesthetic Values, Human Nature, & the Standard of Taste. In *Cognition, literature, & history* (pp. 229–242). Routledge.
Collingwood, R. G. (1958). *The principles of art*. Oxford University Press.
Colton, S. (2012). The Painting Fool: Stories from building an automated painter. In *Computers & creativity* (pp. 3–38). Springer.
Colton, S., & Wiggins, G. A. (2012). Computational creativity: The final frontier? In *ECAI 2012: 20th European Conference on Artificial Intelligence* (Vol. 12, pp. 21–26).
Cope, D. (1996). *Experiments in musical intelligence*. A-R Editions.
Costello, D. (2007). Kant after Lewitt: Towards an aesthetics of conceptual art. In P. Goldie & E. Schellekens (Eds.), *Philosophy & conceptual art* (p. 92). Oxford University Press.
Croce, B. (1909/1922). *Aesthetic: As science of expression & general linguistic* (D. Ainslie, Trans.). Noonday.
Csikszentmihalyi, M. (1997). *Creativity: Flow & the psychology of discovery & invention*. HarperCollins Publishers.
Currie, G. (1989). *An ontology of art*. St. Martin's Press.
Danto, A. (1964). The artworld. *The Journal of Philosophy, 61*(19), 571–584.
Danto, A. C. (1981). *The transfiguration of the commonplace: A philosophy of art*. Harvard University Press.
Davies, S. (1998). Artistic expression. In *The Routledge encyclopedia of philosophy*. Taylor & Francis.

Davies, D. (2003). Medium in art. In J. Levinson (Ed.), *The Oxford handbook of aesthetics* (p. 181). Oxford University Press.
Davies, S. (2004). The cluster theory of art. *British Journal of Aesthetics, 44*(3), 297–300. https://doi.org/10.1093/aesthj/44.3.297
Davis, R. C. (1936). An evaluation & test of Birkhoff's aesthetic measure formula. *The Journal of General Psychology, 15*(2), 231–240.
Davis, G. B., & Olson, M. H. (1984). *Management information systems: Conceptual foundations, structure, & development.* McGraw-Hill, Inc.
Davis, P. J., Hersh, R., & Marchisotto, E. A. (2012). *The mathematical experience, study edition.* Springer.
Dawkins, R. (2000). *Unweaving the rainbow: Science, delusion & the appetite for wonder.* HMH.
De Clercq, R. (2020). The historical ontology of art. *The Philosophical Quarterly, 70*(279), 268–281.
de Groot, A. D. (1978). *Thought & choice in chess.* De Gruyter Mouton. https://doi.org/doi:10.1515/9783110800647
Devlin, K. J. (1995). *Logic & information.* Cambridge University Press.
Dewey, J. (1934). *Art as experience.* Perigee Books.
Dicke, U., & Roth, G. (2016). Neuronal factors determining high intelligence. *Philosophical Transactions of the Royal Society B: Biological Sciences, 371*(1685), 20150180.
Dickie, G. (1964). The myth of the aesthetic attitude. *American Philosophical Quarterly, 1*(1), 56–65.
Dickie, G. (1974). *Art & the aesthetic: An institutional analysis.* Cornell University Press.
Dirac, P. A. M. (1963). The evolution of the physicist's picture of nature. *Scientific American, 208*(5), 45–53.
Dodd, J. (2000). Musical works as eternal types. *British Journal of Aesthetics, 40*(4), 424–440. https://doi.org/10.1093/bjaesthetics/40.4.424
Doggers, P. (2018). *Will this position help understand human consciousness?* Retrieved February 10, 2021, from https://www.chess.com/news/view/will-this-position-help-to-understandhuman-consciousness-4298
Douchová, V. (2015). Birkhoffs aesthetic measure. *Acta Universitatis Carolinae Philosophica et Historica, 21*(1), 39–53.
Doyle, B. (2016). *Great problems in philosophy & physics solved?* I-Phi Press.
Dretske, F. I. (1981). *Knowledge & the flow of information.* MIT Press.
Drucker, T. (2009). *Perspectives on the history of mathematical logic.* Springer.
Dutton, D. (1979). Artistic crimes: The problem of forgery in the arts. *British Journal of Aesthetics, 19*(4), 302–314. https://doi.org/10.1093/bjaesthetics/19.4.302
Eaton, A. W. (2012). Robust immoralism. *Journal of Aesthetics & Art Criticism, 70*(3), 281–292. https://doi.org/10.1111/jaac.2012.70.issue-3

Ecker, D. W. (1963). The artistic process as qualitative problem solving. *Journal of Aesthetics & Art Criticism, 21*(3), 283–290. https://doi.org/10.2307/427437

Einstein, A. (1935/2011). *The world as i see it.* Open Road Media.

Elgammal, A. (2018). Meet AICAN, a machine that operates as an autonomous artist. *The Conversation, 17.*

Elgin, C. Z. (1993). Relocating aesthetics: Goodman's epistemic turn. *Revue Internationale de Philosophie, 46*(185), 171–186.

Engler, G. (1990). Aesthetics in science & in art. *British Journal of Aesthetics, 30*(1), 24–34. https://doi.org/10.1093/bjaesthetics/30.1.24

Fechner, G. T. (1860). *Elemente der psychophysik* (Vol. 2). Breitkopf u. Härtel.

Fechner, G. T. (1876). *Vorschule der Aesthetik* (Vol. 1). Breitkopf & Härtel.

Fechner, G. T. (1897). Kollektivmasslehre, ed.

Field, H. (1988). Realism, mathematics & modality. *Philosophical Topics, 16*(1), 57–107. https://doi.org/10.5840/philtopics19881613

Field, H. (1989). *Realism, mathematics, & modality.* Basil Blackwell.

Fincham, D. (2015). How law defines art. *John Marshall Review of Intellectual Property Law, 14*(3), 314–325.

Fine, R. (1949). *The ideas behind the chess openings.* McKay.

Fine, R. (1952). *The middle game in chess.* McKay.

Fine, R. (1941/1974). *Basic chess endings.* McKay.

Fisher, R. A. (1922). On the mathematical foundations of theoretical statistics. *Philosophical Transactions of the Royal Society of London. Series A, Containing Papers of a Mathematical or Physical Character, 222*(594–604), 309–368.

Floridi, L. (2007). Is semantic information meaningful data? *Philosophy & Phenomenological Research, 70*(2), 351–370. https://doi.org/10.1111/j.1933-1592.2005.tb00531.x

Floridi, L. (2009). Philosophical conceptions of information. In *Formal theories of information: From shannon to semantic information theory & general concepts of information* (pp. 13–53). Springer.

Fodor, J. A. (1975). *The language of thought.* Harvard University Press.

Fodor, J. A. (1981). *Representations: Philosophical essays on the foundations of cognitive science.* MIT Press.

Fodor, J. A. (2008). *LOT 2: The language of thought revisited.* Oxford University Press.

Frege, G. (1960). On sense & reference. In D. Byrne & M. Kölbel (Eds.), *Arguing about language* (pp. 36–56). Routledge.

Frey, C. B., & Osborne, M. A. (2017). The future of employment: How susceptible are jobs to computerisation? *Technological Forecasting & Social Change, 114,* 254–280.

Frieden, B. R. (1998). *Physics from fisher information: A unification.* Cambridge University Press.

Fry, R. (1920). *Vision & design*. Chatto & Windus.
Fuller, S. (2017). The demarcation of science: A problem whose demise has been greatly exaggerated. *Pacific Philosophical Quarterly, 66*(3–4), 329–341. https://doi.org/10.1111/j.1468-0114.1985.tb00257.x
Gödel, K. (1931). Über formal unentscheidbare sätze der principia mathematica und verwandter systeme I. *Monatshefte für Mathematik und Physik, 38*, 173–198.
Gassendi, P. (1644/1964). *Disquisitio metaphysica* (B. Rochot, Ed.). J. Vrin.
Gassendi, P. (1644/1986). *Disquisitio metaphysica seu dubitationes et instantiae adversus renati cartesii metaphysicam et responsa*. Librarie Philosophique J. Vrin.
Gatys, L. A., Ecker, A. S., & Bethge, M. (2015). A neural algorithm of artistic style. arXiv preprint arXiv:1508.06576.
Gaut, B. (2000). "art" as a cluster concept. In N. Carroll (Ed.), *Theories of art today* (pp. 25–44). University of Wisconsin Press.
Gaut, B. (2003). Art & knowledge. In J. Levinson (Ed.), *The Oxford handbook of aesthetics* (pp. 439–441). Oxford University Press.
Gaut, B. (2005). The cluster account of art defended. *British Journal of Aesthetics, 45*(3), 273–288. https://doi.org/10.1093/aesthj/ayi032
Gaut, B. (2010). The role of the medium. In *A philosophy of cinematic art* (pp. 282–307). Cambridge University Press.
Gaut, B., & Kieran, M. (Eds.). (2018). *Creativity & philosophy*. Routledge.
Gaut, B., & Livingston, P. (2003). The creation of art: Issues & perspectives. In *The creation of art: New essays in philosophical aesthetics* (pp. 1–32). Cambridge University Press.
Gell-Mann, M. (1964). A schematic model of Baryons & Mesons. *Physics Letters, 8*, 214–215. https://doi.org/10.1016/S0031-9163(64)92001-3
Gettier, E. L. (1963). Is justified true belief knowledge? *Analysis, 23*(6), 121–123. https://doi.org/10.1093/analys/23.6.121
Ghiselin, B. (1952). *The creative process: A symposium*. New American Library.
Gibbard, A. (1992). *Wise choices, apt feelings: A theory of normative judgement*.
Gibbard, A. (2002). The reasons of a living being. *Proceedings & Addresses of the American Philosophical Association, 76*(2), 49–60. https://doi.org/10.2307/3218628
Gibbard, A. (2003). *Thinking how to live*. Harvard University Press.
Gligoric, S. (2003). *Shall we play fischerandom chess?* Sterling Publishing Company.
Glynn, I. (2013). *Elegance in science: The beauty of simplicity*. Oxford University Press.
Goldman, A. I. (1967). A causal theory of knowing. *Journal of Philosophy, 64*(12), 357–372. https://doi.org/10.2307/2024268
Gollon, J. (1974). *Chess variations: Ancient, regional, & modern*. Tuttle Publishing.
Gombrich, E. (1951). *The story of art*. Phaidon Publishers.
Goodman, N. (1951). *The structure of appearance*. Harvard University Press.

Goodman, N. (1968). *Languages of art: An approach to a theory of symbols*. Bobbs-Merrill.
Goodman, N. (1972). *Problems & projects*. Bobbs-Merrill.
Goodman, N. (1976). *Languages of art*. Hackett.
Goodman, N. (1988). *Reconceptions in philosophy & other arts and sciences*. In C. Z. Elgin, (Ed.). Routledge.
Goodman, N., & Quine, W. v. O. (1947). Steps toward a constructive nominalism. *Journal of Symbolic Logic, 12*(4), 105–122. https://doi.org/10.2307/2266485
Gould, C. S. (1994). Clive Bell on aesthetic experience & aesthetic truth. *British Journal of Aesthetics, 34*(2), 124–133. https://doi.org/10.1093/bjaesthetics/34.2.124
Gowers, T. (2002). *Mathematics: A very short introduction* (Vol. 66). Oxford University Press.
Greenberg, C. (1986). University of Chicago Press.
Grene, M., & Ravetz, J. R. (1962). Leibniz's cosmic equation: A reconstruction. *Journal of Philosophy, 59*(6), 141–146. https://doi.org/10.2307/2022829
Grice, H. P. (1989). *Studies in the way of words*. Harvard University Press.
Guilford, J. P. (1950). Creativity. *American Psychologist, 5*(9), 444–454.
Hübner, R., & Ufken, E. S. (2023). On the beauty of vases: Birkhoff's aesthetic measure versus Hogarth's line of beauty. *Frontiers in Psychology, 14*, 1114793.
Hadamard, J. (1954). *An essay on the psychology of invention in the mathematical field*. Courier Corporation.
Hardy, G. H. (1999). *Ramanujan: Twelve lectures on subjects suggested by his life & work* (Vol. 136). American Mathematical Society.
Hare, R. M. (1952). *The language of morals*. Oxford University Press.
Harman, G. (1973). *Thought*. Princeton University Press.
Haugeland, J. (1985). *Artificial intelligence: The very idea*. MIT Press.
Heawood, P. J. (1890/1949). Map-colour theorem. *Proceedings of the London Mathematical Society, 2*(1), 161–175.
Helliwell, A. C. (2023). *Artificial: The philosophy of AI art*. Doctoral dissertation, University of Kent.
Hilpinen, R. (1992). On artifacts & works of art. *Theoria, 58*(1), 58–82. https://doi.org/10.1111/j.1755-2567.1992.tb01155.x
Hobbes, T. (1651). *Leviathan*.OIn C. B. Macpherson, (Ed.). Penguin Books.
Hoffman, G., & Weinberg, G. (2011). Interactive improvisation with a robotic marimba player. *Autonomous Robots, 31*, 133–153.
Houkes, W., & Vermaas, P. E. (2009). Produced to use. *Techné: Research in Philosophy and Technology, 13*(2), 123–136. https://doi.org/10.5840/techne200913211
Howard, V. (1971). *Harvard Project Zero: A Fresh Look at Art Education. Technical Report No. 1.* (tech. rep.). ERIC.

Hume, D. (1757). Of the standard of taste. In D. Hume (Ed.), *Essays moral, political, & literary* (pp. 226–249). Libertyclassics.

Hutcheson, F. (1726). *An inquiry into the original of our ideas of beauty & virtue.* In W. Leidhold (Ed.). Garland.

Israel, D., & Perry, J. (2012). What is information? In *Machine intelligence* (pp. 221–239). Routledge.

Kant, I. (1790/2000). *Critique of the power of judgment.* In P. Guyer, (Ed.). Cambridge University Press.

Kao, J., & Jurafsky, D. (2012). A computational analysis of style, affect, & imagery in contemporary poetry. In *Proceedings of the NAACL-HLT 2012 Workshop on Computational Linguistics for Literature* (pp. 8–17).

Kasa, I. (2010). On Field's epistemological argument against platonism. *Studia Logica, 96*(2), 141–147. https://doi.org/10.1007/s11225-010-9278-y

Kaufman, J. C., & Sternberg, R. J. (2010). *The Cambridge handbook of creativity.* Cambridge University Press.

Kelso, J. S. (2012). Multistability & metastability: Understanding dynamic coordination in the brain. *Philosophical Transactions of the Royal Society B: Biological Sciences, 367*(1591), 906–918.

Kempe, A. B. (1879). On the geographical problem of the four colours. *American Journal of Mathematics, 2*(3), 193–200.

Kennick, W. E. (1958). Does traditional aesthetics rest on a mistake? *Mind, 67*, 317.

Kieran, M. (2004). *Revealing art.* Routledge.

Kind, A., & Langkau, J. (Eds.). (forthcoming). *Oxford handbook of philosophy of imagination & creativity.* Oxford University Press.

Kivy, P. (1987). Platonism in music: Another kind of defense. *American Philosophical Quarterly, 24*(3), 245–252.

Kivy, P. (1993). Differences. *Journal of Aesthetics & Art Criticism, 51*(2), 123–132. https://doi.org/10.2307/431377

Kivy, P. (1997). *Philosophies of arts: An essay in differences.* Cambridge University Press.

Kline, M. (1953). *Mathematics in Western Culture.* Oxford University Press.

Koestler, A. (1964). *The act of creation: A study of the conscious & unconscious processes of humor, scientific discovery & art.* Macmillan.

Kolmogorov, A. N. (1965). Three approaches to the quantitative definition of information. *Problems of Information Transmission, 1*(1), 1–7.

Kosso, P. (2002). The omniscienter: Beauty & scientific understanding. *International Studies in the Philosophy of Science, 16*(1), 39–48.

Kristeller, P. O. (1951). The modern system of the arts: A study in the history of aesthetics part I. *Journal of the History of Ideas, 12*(4), 496–527.

Kristeller, P. O. (1952). The modern system of the arts: A study in the history of aesthetics part II. *Journal of the History of Ideas, 13*(1), 17–46.

Lamarque, P., & Olsen, S. H. (1994). *Truth, fiction, & literature: A philosophical perspective* . In S. H. Olsen, (Ed.). Oxford University Press.
Landauer, R. (1991). Information is physical. *Physics Today, 44*(5), 23–29.
Landauer, R. (1996). The physical nature of information. *Physics Letters A, 217*(4–5), 188–193.
Lasker, E. (1950). *The adventure of chess.* Doubleday.
Latto, R., Brain, D., & Kelly, B. (2000). An oblique effect in aesthetics: Homage to Mondrian (1872–1944). *Perception, 29*(8), 981–987.
Laudan, L. (1983). The demise of the demarcation problem. In R. S. Cohen & L. Laudan (Eds.), *Physics, philosophy & psychoanalysis: Essays in honor of adolf grünbaum* (pp. 111–127). D. Reidel.
Laurence, S., & Margolis, E. (1999). Concepts & cognitive science. In E. Margolis & S. Laurence (Eds.), *Concepts: Core readings* (pp. 3–81). MIT Press.
Leniewski, S. (1916). Podstawy ogólnej teoryi mnogoci. i. *Prace Polskiego Koa Naukowego w Moskwie, 2*, 129–173.
Leniewski, S. (1927). O podstawach matematyki. *Przeglad Filozoficzny, 30*, 164–206.
Leniewski, S. (1929). Grundzüge eines neuen systems der grundlagen der mathematik. *Fundamenta Mathematicae, 14*(1), 1–81.
Leonard, H. S., & Goodman, N. (1940). The calculus of individuals & its uses. *Journal of Symbolic Logic, 5*(2), 45–55. https://doi.org/10.2307/2266169
Leroy, L. (1874). The exhibition of the impressionists. *Le Charivari.*
Levinson, J. (1979). Defining art historically. *British Journal of Aesthetics, 19*(3), 21–33. https://doi.org/10.1093/bjaesthetics/19.3.232
Levinson, J. (1980). What a musical work is. *Journal of Philosophy, 77*(1), 5–28. https://doi.org/10.2307/2025596
Levinson, J. (1996). *The pleasures of aesthetics: Philosophical essays.* Cornell University Press.
Levinson, J. (2006). *Contemplating art: Essays in aesthetics.* Oxford University Press.
Levinson, J. (2007). Artworks as artifacts. In E. Margolis & S. Laurence (Eds.), *Creations of the mind: theories of artifacts & their representation* (pp. 74–82). Oxford University Press.
Levinson, J. (2011). *Music, art, & metaphysics.* Oxford University Press.
Liggins, D. (2010). Epistemological objections to Platonism. *Philosophy Compass, 5*(1), 67–77. https://doi.org/10.1111/j.1747-9991.2009.00259.x
Linnebo, ‰. (2006). Epistemological challenges to mathematical platonism. *Philosophical Studies, 129*(3), 545–574. https://doi.org/10.1007/s11098-004-3388-1
Linnebo, ‰. (2023). Platonism in the Philosophy of Mathematics. In E. N. Zalta & U. Nodelman (Eds.), *The Stanford encyclopedia of philosophy* (Summer 2023). Metaphysics Research Lab, Stanford University.

Livio, M. (2008). *The golden ratio: The story of Phi, the world's most astonishing number*. Crown.

Longworth, F., & Scarantino, A. (2010). The disjunctive theory of art: The cluster account reformulated. *British Journal of Aesthetics, 50*(2), 151–167. https://doi.org/10.1093/aesthj/ayq001

Lovelace, A. (1953). Notes on Menabrea's sketch of the analytical engine invented by Charles Babbage. In B. V. Bowden (Ed.), *Faster than thought*. Pitman.

Mackay, D. M. (1951). Mindlike behaviour in artefacts. *British Journal for the Philosophy of Science, 2*(6), 105–121. https://doi.org/10.1093/bjps/ii.6.105

Mackay, D. M. (1956). Towards an information-flow model of human behavior. *British Journal of Psychology, 47*, 30–43.

MacKay, D. M. (1969). *Information, mechanism & meaning* (Vol. 134). MIT Press.

Mandelbaum, M. (1965). Family resemblances & generalization concerning the arts. *American Philosophical Quarterly, 2*(3), 219–228.

Maor, E. (2018). *Music by the numbers: From pythagoras to Schoenberg*. Princeton University Press.

Margolis, J. (1965). *The language of art & art criticism*. Wayne State University Press.

McCarthy, J. (2008). The philosophy of AI & the AI of philosophy. In *Philosophy of information* (pp. 711–740). Elsevier.

McCulloch, W. S., & Pitts, W. (1943). A logical calculus of the ideas immanent in nervous activity. *The Bulletin of Mathematical Biophysics, 5*, 115–133.

McManus, I. C., Cheema, B., & Stoker, J. (1993). The aesthetics of composition: A study of Mondrian. *Empirical Studies of the Arts, 11*(2), 83–94.

McWhinnie, H. J. (1968). A review of research on aesthetic measure. *Acta Psychologica, 28*, 363–375.

Mendelssohn, M. (1757). Betrachtungen über die quellen und die verbindungen der schönen künste und wissenschaften. *Bibliothek der schönen Wissenschaften und der freyen Künste, 1*(1757), 231–68.

Moles, A. A. (1966). *Information theory & esthetic perception*. University of Illinois Press.

Moore, G. E. (1953). *Some main problems of philosophy*. Routledge.

Murdoch, I. (1977). *The fire & the sun: Why Plato banished the artists*. Viking Press.

Murray, B. (2007). Kant on genius & art. *British Journal of Aesthetics, 47*(2), 199–214. https://doi.org/10.1093/aesthj/ayl056

Nanay, B. (2018). The aesthetic experience of artworks & everyday scenes. *The Monist, 101*(1), 71–82. https://doi.org/10.1093/monist/onx037

Nanay, B. (2023). Aesthetic experience as interaction. *Journal of the American Philosophical Association*, 1–13. https://doi.org/10.1017/apa.2023.21

Nelson, E. (2015). Elements. arXiv preprint arXiv:1510.00369.

Newell, A. (1967). Studies in problem solving; subject 3 on the crypt-arithmetic task Donald + Gerald = Robert.

Newell, A., & Simon, H. A. (1972). *Human problem solving*. Prentice-Hall.

Newell, A., & Simon, H. A. (1976). Computer science as empirical inquiry: Symbols & search. *Communications of the ACM, 19*(3), 113–126.

Newell, A., Shaw, J. C., & Simon, H. A. (1957). Empirical explorations of the logic theory machine: A case study in heuristic. *Papers Presented at the February 26–28, 1957, Western Joint Computer Conference: Techniques for Reliability* (pp. 218–230). https://doi.org/10.1145/1455567.1455605

Newell, A., Shaw, J. C., & Simon, H. A. (1958). Elements of a theory of human problem solving. *Psychological Review, 65*(3), 151–166.

Newell, A., Shaw, J. C., & Simon, H. A. (1959). *The processes of creative thinking*. Rand Corporation.

Newman, J. R. (1956). *The world of mathematics* (Vol. 1). George Allen & Unwin.

Newman, M. H. A., Turing, A. M., Jefferson, G., Braithwaite, R. B., & Shieber, S. (1952/2004). Can automatic calculating machines be said to think? In S. M. Shieber (Ed.), *The Turing test: Verbal behavior as the hallmark of intelligence*. MIT Press.

Nussbaum, M. (1985). Finely aware & richly responsible. *Journal of Philosophy, 82*(10), 516–529. https://doi.org/10.2307/2026358

Nussbaum, M. (1990). *Love's knowledge: Essays on philosophy & literature*. Oxford University Press.

Nutting, E. S. (2020). Benacerraf, Field, & the agreement of mathematicians. *Synthese, 197*(5), 2095–2110. https://doi.org/10.1007/s11229-018-1785-9

Nwodo, C. S. (1984). Philosophy of art versus aesthetics. *British Journal of Aesthetics, 24*(3), 195–205. https://doi.org/10.1093/bjaesthetics/24.3.195

O'Leary-Hawthorne, J. (1995). Towards ontological nihilism. *Philosophical Studies: An International Journal for Philosophy in the Analytic Tradition, 79*(2), 143–165.

Ocvirk, O., Stinson, R., Wigg, P., Bone, R., & Cayton, D. (1968/2012). *Art fundamentals: Theory & practice*. McGraw-Hill.

Ohlsson, S. (2012). The problems with problem solving: Reflections on the rise, current status, & possible future of a cognitive research paradigm. *The Journal of Problem Solving, 5*(1), 7.

Osborne, H. (1984). Mathematical beauty & physical science. *British Journal of Aesthetics, 24*(4), 291–300. https://doi.org/10.1093/bjaesthetics/24.4.291

Ottman, R. W., & Mainous, F. D. (1995). *Rudiments of music*. Prentice Hall.

Paley, W. (1802). *Natural theology: Or, evidences of the existence & attributes of the deity*. J. Faulder.

Paul, E. S., & Kaufman, S. B. (2014). Introducing the philosophy of creativity. In E. S. Paul & S. B. Kaufman (Eds.), *The philosophy of creativity: New essays* (pp. 3–14).

Paul, E. S., & Stokes, D. (2023). Creativity. In E. N. Zalta & U. Nodelman (Eds.), *The Stanford encyclopedia of philosophy* (Spring 2023). Metaphysics Research Lab, Stanford University.

Penrose, R. (1989). *The emperor's new mind*. Oxford University Press.

Penrose, R. (1994). *Shadows of the mind: A search for the missing science of consciousness*. Oxford University Press.

Perrault, C. (1690). *Le cabinet des beaux arts*. Edelinck.

Plato. (1997). *Plato: Complete works*. In J. M. Cooper (Ed.). Hackett.

Plato. (360 B.C.E.). Phaedrus (B. Jowett, Trans.). In *The Internet classics archive*.

Plato. (360 B.C.E./1953). The Republic (B. Jowett, Trans.). In *The dialogues of plato* (pp. 1–452). Charles Scribner's Sons.

Pliny. (1938–1962). *Natural history* (H. Rackham, W. H. S. Jones, & D. E. Eichholz, Trans.). Classical Library.

Plotinus. (c. 270 C.E./2017). *Plotinus: The enneads*. In L. P. Gerson (Ed.). Cambridge University Press.

Poincaré, H. (1910). Mathematical creation (G. B. Halsted, Trans.). *The Monist* (pp. 321–335).

Poincaré, H. (1914). *Science & method*. In F. Maitland (Ed.). Dover Publications.

Porter, J. I. (2009). Is art modern? kristeller's 'modern system of the arts' reconsidered. *British Journal of Aesthetics, 49*(1), 1–24. https://doi.org/10.1093/aesthj/ayn054

Pratt, C. C. (1938). Structural vs. expressive form in music. *The Journal of Psychology, 5*(1), 149–156.

Putnam, H. (1967). Psychological predicates. In W. H. Capitan & D. D. Merrill (Eds.), *Art, mind, & religion* (pp. 37–48). University of Pittsburgh Press.

Putnam, H. (1981). *Reason, truth & history*. Cambridge University Press.

Ramsey, F. P. (1929). General propositions & causality. In F. P. Ramsey (Ed.), *The foundations of mathematics & other logical essays* (pp. 237–255). Kegan Paul, Trench, Trübner.

Ratzsch, D., & Koperski, J. (2023). Teleological arguments for gods existence. In E. N. Zalta & U. Nodelman (Eds.), *The Stanford encyclopedia of philosophy* (Summer 2023). Metaphysics Research Lab, Stanford University.

Rhodes, M. (1961). An analysis of creativity. *The Phi Delta Kappan, 42*(7), 305–310.

Ridder, L. (2002). *Mereologie*. Klostermann.

Robinson, J. (2000). Languages of art at the turn of the century. *Journal of Aesthetics & Art Criticism, 58*(3), 213–218. https://doi.org/10.2307/432102

Rodriguez-Pereyra, G. (1999). Resemblance nominalism & the imperfect community. *Philosophy & Phenomenological Research, 59*(4), 965–982. https://doi.org/10.2307/2653564

Rohrbaugh, G. (2013). The ontology of art. In B. Gaut & D. Lopes (Eds.), *Routledge companion to aesthetics* (pp. 235–45). Routledge.

Rosch, E., & Mervis, C. B. (1975). Family resemblances: Studies in the internal structure of categories. *Cognitive Psychology, 7*(4), 573–605.

Rosen, G. (2012). Abstract objects. In E. N. Zalta (Ed.), *The Stanford encyclopedia of philosophy*. The Metaphysics Research Lab, Center for the Study of Language; Information, Stanford University.

Rosenblueth, A., Wiener, N., & Bigelow, J. (1943). Behavior, purpose & teleology. *Philosophy of Science, 10*(1), 18–24. https://doi.org/10.1086/286788

Ruskin, J. (1880/1989). *The seven lamps of architecture*. Dover.

Russell, B. (1912). *The problems of philosophy*. William & Norgate.

Russell, B. (1921). *The analysis of mind*. Allen & Unwin.

Russell, S., & Norvig, P. (2010). *Artificial intelligence: A modern approach*. Prentice Hall.

Søe, S. O. (2019). A unified account of information, misinformation, & disinformation. *Synthese, 198*(6), 5929–5949. https://doi.org/10.1007/s11229-019-02444-x

Salmon, N. U., & Soames, S. (Eds.). (1988). *Propositions & attitudes*. Oxford University Press.

Santayana, G. (1904). What is aesthetics? *Philosophical Review, 13*(3), 320–327. https://doi.org/10.2307/2176284

Sartre, J.-P. (1966). *The psychology of imagination* (B. Frechtman, Trans.). Washington Square Press.

Scarantino, A., & Piccinini, G. (2010). Information without truth. *Metaphilosophy, 41*(3), 313–330. https://doi.org/10.1111/j.1467-9973.2010.01632.x

Schwartz, L. (2003/2006). Six words. In *How to eat a poem* (pp. 8–9). Oxford University Press.

Sellars, W. (1963). Philosophy & the scientific image of man. In W. Sellars (Ed.), *Science, perception & reality*. Humanities Press.

Shannon, C. (1950). Programming a computer for playing chess. *Philosophical Magazine, 41*, 256–275.

Shannon, C. E., & Weaver, W. (1949). *The mathematical theory of communication*. University of Illinois Press.

Sharpe, R. A. (1978). A transformation of a structuralist theme. *British Journal of Aesthetics, 18*(2), 155–171. https://doi.org/10.1093/bjaesthetics/18.2.155

Sheets-Johnstone, M. (2011). *The primacy of movement*. John Benjamins Publishing.

Shelley, J. (2022). The concept of the aesthetic. In E. N. Zalta (Ed.), *The Stanford encyclopedia of philosophy* (Spring 2022). Metaphysics Research Lab, Stanford University.

Shiner, L. E. (2001). *The invention of art: A cultural history*. University of Chicago Press.

Shope, R. K. (1983). *The analysis of knowing: A decade of research*. Princeton University Press.

Shottenkirk, D. (2009). *Nominalism & its Aftermath: The Philosophy of Nelson Goodman*. Springer.
Shusterman, R. (1980). The logic of evaluation. *Philosophical Quarterly, 30*(121), 327–341. https://doi.org/10.2307/2219526
Silver, G. A., & Silver, M. L. (1990). *Systems analysis & design*. Addison Wesley Longman Publishing.
Simon, H. A., & Newell, A. (1971). Human problem solving: The state of the theory in 1970. *American Psychologist, 26*(2), 145.
Skyrms, B. (1967). The explication of "x knows that p". *Journal of Philosophy, 64*(12), 373–389. https://doi.org/10.2307/2024269
Smith, P. (2007). *An introduction to Gödel's theorems*. Cambridge University Press.
Solis, J., Takanishi, A., & Hashimoto, K. (2010). Development of an anthropomorphic saxophone-playing robot. In *Brain, Body & Machine: Proceedings of an International Symposium on the Occasion of the 25th Anniversary of the McGill University Centre for Intelligent Machines* (pp. 175–186).
Solomonoff, R. J. (1964). A formal theory of inductive inference. *Information & Control, 7*(2), 224–254.
Sommerhoff, G. (1974). *Logic of the living brain*.
Soueif, M. I., & Eysenck, H. J. (1972). Factors in the determination of preference judgments for polygonal figures: A comparative study. *International Journal of Psychology, 7*(3), 145–153.
Staszkow, R., & Bradshaw, R. (2004). *The mathematical palette*. Cengage Learning.
Stecker, R. (1996). *Artworks: Meaning, definition, value*. Pennsylvania State University Press.
Stecker, R. (2003). Definition of art. In J. Levinson (Ed.), *The Oxford handbook of aesthetics* (pp. 136–154). Oxford University Press.
Steinert, S. (2017). Art: Brought to you by creative machines. *Philosophy & Technology, 30*(3), 267–284. https://doi.org/10.1007/s13347-016-0230-6
Stevenson, C. L. (1957). On "what is a poem?" *Philosophical Review, 66*(3), 329–362. https://doi.org/10.2307/2182438
Stokes, P. D. (2006). *Creativity from constraints: The psychology of breakthrough*. Springer Publishing.
Stokes, D. (2014). The role of imagination in creativity. In E. S. Paul & S. B. Kaufman (Eds.), *The philosophy of creativity: New essays* (pp. 157–184).
Sulzer, J. G. (1778). *Allgemeine theorie der schönen künste*. In der Weidmannschen Buchhandlung.
Swoyer, C. (2008). Abstract entities. In T. Sider, J. Hawthorne, & D. W. Zimmerman (Eds.), *Contemporary debates in metaphysics* (pp. 1–31). Blackwell.
Tarski, A. (1929/1983). Foundation of the geometry of solids (J. H. Woodger, Trans.). In J. Corcoran (Ed.), *Logic, semantics,metamathematics* (pp. 24–29). Hackett.

Terzidis, K. (2014). *Permutation design: Buildings, texts, & contexts*. Routledge.
Thomasson, A. (2005). The ontology of art & knowledge in aesthetics. *Journal of Aesthetics & Art Criticism, 63*(3), 221–229. https://doi.org/10.1111/j.0021-8529.2005.00202.x
Thomasson, A. (2006). Debates about the ontology of art: What are we doing here? *Philosophy Compass, 1*(3), 245–255. https://doi.org/10.1111/j.1747-9991.2006.00021.x
Thomasson, A. (2007). Artifacts & human concepts. In E. Margolis & S. Laurence (Eds.), *Creations of the mind: Theories of artifacts & their representaion* (pp. 52–73). Oxford University Press.
Thompson, K. (1986). Retrograde analysis of certain endgames. *Journal of the International Computer Games Association, 9*(3), 131–139.
Thompson, K. (1996). 6-piece endgames. *ICGA Journal, 19*(4), 215–226.
Thomson-Jones, K. (2021). *Image in the making: Digital innovation & the visual arts*. Oxford University Press.
Todd, C. (2018). Fitting feelings & elegant proofs: On the psychology of aesthetic evaluation in mathematics. *Philosophia Mathematica, 26*(2), 211–233. https://doi.org/10.1093/philmat/nkx007
Turing, A. (1936). On computable numbers, with an application to the *entscheidungsproblem*. *Proceedings of the London Mathematical Society, 42*(1), 230–265. https://doi.org/10.2307/2268810
Turing, A. M. (1950). Computing machinery & intelligence. *Mind, 59*(October), 433–60. https://doi.org/10.1093/mind/lix.236.433
Turing, A. M. (1953). Chess. In B. V. Bowden (Ed.), *Faster than thought* (pp. 286–295). Pitman.
Tzara, T. (1920/2013). To make a Dadaist poem (B. Wright, Trans.). In, *Seven dada manifestos & lampisteries* (p. 39). Alma Classics.
Valstar, M. F., & Pantic, M. (2006). Biologically vs. logic inspired encoding of facial actions & emotions in video. In *2006 IEEE International Conference on Multimedia & Expo* (pp. 325–328).
Van de Water, M. (1934). Mathematical measure for art. In *The science news-letter* (pp. 170–172).
Van Den Herik, H. J., Uiterwijk, J. W., & Van Rijswijck, J. (2002). Games solved: Now & in the future. *Artificial Intelligence, 134*(1–2), 277–311.
van Gogh, V. (1936). *Letters to an artist: Vincent van Gogh to Anton Ridder van Rappard* (R. van Messel, Trans.). Viking Press.
van Gogh, V. (1889/2000). *The complete letters of vincent van gogh: With reproductions of all the drawings in the correspondence*. Little, Brown.
Walsh, D. (1969). *Literature & knowledge*. Wesleyan University Press.
Walton, K. (1990). *Mimesis as make-believe: On the foundations of the representational arts*. Harvard University Press.

Walton, K. (2007). Aesthetics - what? why? & wherefore? *The Journal of Aesthetics & Art Criticism, 65*(2), 147–161.
Weaver, W. (1953). Recent contributions to the mathematical theory of communication. In *ETC: A Review of General Semantics* (pp. 261–281).
Weisberg, R. W. (2006). *Creativity: Understanding innovation in problem solving, science, invention, & the arts.* John Wiley & Sons.
Weitz, M. (1956). The role of theory in aesthetics. *Journal of Aesthetics & Art Criticism, 15*(1), 27–35. https://doi.org/10.2307/427491
Wheeler, J. A. (1989/2002). Information, physics, quantum: The search for links. In *Feynman & computation* (pp. 309–336).
Whitehead, A. N., & Russell, B. (1910, 1912, 1913/1956). *Principia mathematica, to *56.* In B. Russell & A. N. Whitehead (Eds.). Cambridge University Press.
Wiener, N. (1948). *Cybernetics or control & communication in the animal & the machine.* MIT Press.
Wiener, N. (1948/2019). *Cybernetics or control & communication in the animal & the machine.* MIT Press.
Wiggins, G. A. (2008). Computer models of musical creativity: A review of computer models of musical creativity by David cope. *Literary & Linguistic Computing, 23*(1), 109–116.
Wilson, M. (2001). How should we speak about art & technology? *Crossings: Electronic Journal of Art & Technology, 1*(1), 1–6.
Wimsatt, W. K., & Beardsley, M. C. (1946). The intentional fallacy. *The Sewanee Review, 54*(3), 468–488.
Wimsatt, W. K., & Beardsley, M. C. (1949). The affective fallacy. *The Sewanee Review, 57*(1), 31–55.
Wittgenstein, L. (1953/2009). *Philosophical investigations.* Wiley-Blackwell.
Wollheim, R. (1968). *Art & its objects.* In R. T. Eldridge (Ed.). Cambridge University Press.
Wolterstorff, N. (1980). *Works & worlds of art.* Oxford University Press.
Zahavy, T., Veeriah, V., Hou, S., Waugh, K., Lai, M., Leurent, E., Tomasev, N., Schut, L., Hassabis, D., & Singh, S. (2023). Diversifying AI: Towards creative chess with AlphaZero. arXiv preprint arXiv:2308.09175.
Ziff, P. (1953). The task of defining a work of art. *Philosophical Review, 62*(1), 58–78. https://doi.org/10.2307/2182722
Zweig, G. (1964). *An SU 3 model for strong interaction symmetry & its breaking* (tech. rep.). CM-P00042884.

Index

Page numbers followed by 'n' refer to notes.

M. Chen, *Art-Making as Problem-Solving*,
https://doi.org/10.1007/978-3-031-90639-8

The manufacturer's authorised representative in the EU is Springer Nature Customer Service Centre GmbH, Europaplatz 3, 69115 Heidelberg, Germany. If you have any concerns regarding our products, please contact ProductSafety@springernature.com

Printed and bound by CPI Group (UK) Ltd, Croydon, CR0 4YY
30/09/2026
02225565-0003